UNDERSTANDING LOHAS* MARKET SEGMENTATION

*(Lifestyles of Health & Sustainability)

LOHAS
18% 43,000,000

- Trend predictors and influencers • Dedicated to personal & planetary health • Values driven (Less price sensitive) • Most prolific green buyers • Information junkies • Eco-lifestyle • Environmental stewards • CSR seekers (and boycotters)

NATURALITES
12% 27,000,000

- Driven by personal health and wellness • Avoid artificial ingredients • Buy natural products for health and wellness reasons • Pure nutrition (e.g., low cholesterol) influences food/beverage purchases • Income dictates green behaviour and purchases, creating attitudinal vs behavioral disconnects • More likely to use LOHAS consumables than durables

DRIFTERS
26% 60,000,000

- Newer green consumers • Image-conscious and trendy • Practicing "easy" green • Need education on benefits and relevance to them • Knowledge and understanding limit purchases, especially of durables • Currently driving growth of green products

CONVENTIONALS
27% 63,000,000

- Rooted in practicality • Waste reducers and heavy recyclers • Driven more by cost than environment • Sustainability benefits are secondary to personal benefits • Well-educated and rational; case must be made for sustainable products

UNCONCERNED
17% 40,000,000

- Not "against" the environment, but not actively engaged in protecting it, buying green products, or CSR

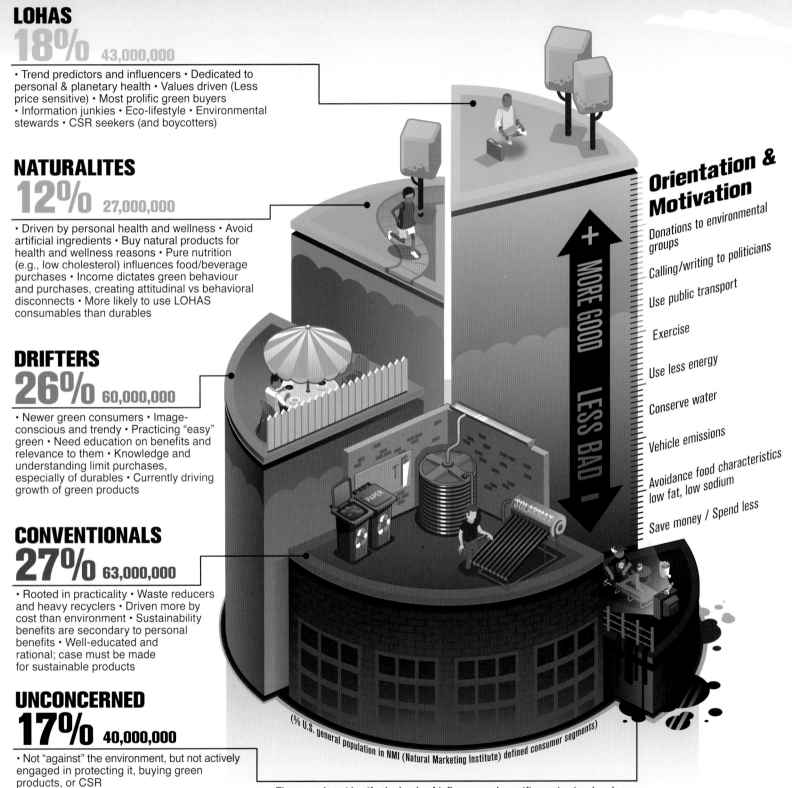

Orientation & Motivation

MORE GOOD + / LESS BAD -

- Donations to environmental groups
- Calling/writing to politicians
- Use public transport
- Exercise
- Use less energy
- Conserve water
- Vehicle emissions
- Avoidance food characteristics low fat, low sodium
- Save money / Spend less

(% U.S. general population in NMI (Natural Marketing Institute) defined consumer segments)

These markets identify the levels of influence and specific motivational and behavioral drivers in each consumer segment across a multitude of factors.

Information provided by Natural Marketing Institute Source: NMI's LOHAS Consumer Trends Database®

GOODVERTISING
CREATIVE ADVERTISING THAT CARES

THOMAS KOLSTER

Thames & Hudson

Let us work together for greater good

If you want to get hold of me and have a chat about the possibilities and pitfalls in the responsible revolution and how to take the three steps 'Get naked, get together and get out there', then visit me at thomaskolster.com or on Twitter @thomaskolster. I have more than 12 years' experience in the communications industry and have worked with a diverse range of clients from McDonalds to Amnesty International. I'm also an experienced speaker on various topics and lead workshops. I look forward to hearing from you.

thomaskolster.com
@thomaskolster

First published in 2012 in hardcover in the United States of America by Thames & Hudson Inc., 500 Fifth Avenue, New York, New York 10110

thamesandhudsonusa.com

Library of Congress Catalog Card Number 2012931634

ISBN 978-0-500-51626-3

Printed and bound in China by 1010 Printing International Ltd

CONTENTS

INTRODUCTION

I don't like most advertising. In fact I hate 99% of it. If somebody is trying to sell me something then why is the communication so pushy? Why is it so disrespectful? Why waste my time forcing me to watch a commercial just so I can see the content I really care about? There is, however, 1% of advertising that really makes a difference, and that is where brands start by showing an interest in me – the consumer. In that sense, this is advertising for good because the premise or licence to operate begins with shared interest. The brand begins a dialogue about something that I happen to care about – and genuinely caring brands take one step further and make a real, tangible difference in my life.

In this way, I do believe that advertising can save the world and itself. Yes, now I've said it – it's out there. You may even chuckle when you read this. I'm not an idealist or a tree-hugger and, yes, ironically, advertising has got us neck deep in today's climate and humanitarian crises, but this just makes me even more confident that advertising can also get us out of it. Nobody knows consumers, brands and the market better than those of us in the advertising industry and we need to take on the challenge.

From a quick laugh to a lasting difference

A responsible advertising industry might sound hypocritical. At least, that's how it used to be. In 2010, when Pepsi turned its back on using celebrities such as Britney Spears and a 23-year-long presence at the Super Bowl, it signalled the end of advertising as we know it. Instead, Pepsi chose to make $20 million available to fund a community project, 'Pepsi Refresh', in the US and subsequently around the world. This shift has shown not only that advertising has moved in a more responsible direction, but also that the mass market has too. Bonin

Bough, Global Director of Digital and Social Media at Pepsi, explains just how far reaching it is becoming: 'More people have voted for projects pitched to "Pepsi Refresh" than voted for the last US president.' We are at the early stages of one of the biggest business transformations in history; and advertising is not exempt. This is a development that no one can afford to ignore because it not only requires new knowledge, but also demands a new approach.

When bad can't hide, good will win

Brands now have nowhere left to hide. A well-connected online community of people is exposing and judging brands' steps and missteps more than ever before. Look at websites such as WikiLeaks or other social networks and see how they have shaken governments and global brands, and helped topple regimes in the Middle East. You and I are just as much a part of that movement when we write an online review criticizing the amount of sugar in a box of our children's cereal or post a Facebook comment about a company's appalling customer service. That tweet or comment can inspire like-minded people and evolve into a screaming kettle of consumer pressure on a brand, with the power to change markets in minutes. As Naomi Klein pinpointed in her book *No Logo*, 'In many ways branding is the Achilles heel of the corporate world'. Here is just one example: in 2012 McDonald's used Twitter to promote their fresh produce along with their farmers, using the hashtags #MeetTheFarmers and #McDStories. One tweet assured, 'When u make something with pride, people can taste it'. Only hours after the campaign was launched, people took over the hashtags and fired some heavy shots at the Golden Arches. One of the worst customer comments came from @Muzzafuzza, who said, 'I haven't been to McDonalds in years, because I'd rather eat my own diarrhoea'. As the example shows, you don't own your story any more: people are telling it for you, so you'd better make sure it's a good one. In fact, a Nielsen Global Online Consumer Survey from 2009 shows that consumers are as likely to trust a complete stranger's opinion online as a brand's website.

Nothing but the whole story

People are no longer only interested in knowing if their new TV is making them look trendy or design oriented, they also want – and sometimes demand – to know its backstory. Where was the TV made? What is its carbon footprint? How were the workers who produced it treated? What materials were used to make it? Were any of these materials toxins? Where did the raw materials used to produce the TV come from, and under what circumstances were they extracted – in a death-trap of a mine? And what happens when you throw it away? What harm to the planet and people will it cause?

When the backstory of products moves to the forefront of the relationship with consumers it imposes a new reality on brands, in which the advertised story no longer stands alone: the market talks. If you fail to understand these issues, the backstories will catch up with you. Whether intentional or not, when your advertised story doesn't match your backstory it is commonly known as greenwashing.

With an increasing demand for companies to be accountable for their environmental impact, both from legislators and consumers, more companies are beginning to change their definitions of costs and revenues to include the costs to the environment and people. Puma is among the big players who have gone the furthest in measuring their impact on the environment. In 2010 the company, together with consultancy firm PwC, found the cost of its impact on the environment in terms of carbon emissions, water, land use, air pollution and waste to be €145 million. These calculated costs can be compared to Puma's net earnings of €202 million for that year. As Jochen Zeitz, CEO of Puma, says, 'The business implications of failing to address nature in decision-making are clear – since ecosystem services are vital to the performance of most companies, integrating the true cost for these services in the future could have significant impacts on corporate bottom lines'.

Another example is the global carbon trading system, which puts a value on pollution. Companies are given fixed quotas of carbon emissions and if a company emits less carbon than the quota and thus pollutes less, it can sell the remainder of the quota to a more heavily polluting company. It's a great way of incentivizing businesses to behave better, and to keep a cap on global carbon emissions.

One of the brands that shares its carbon efforts with consumers is PepsiCo's Tropicana. They have introduced carbon labels on their

'Grrr', Honda, Wieden+Kennedy, London (see pages 126–27)

range of juices and succeeded in turning carbon emissions (a cost for companies) into a communication that connects with shoppers and might even push sales or deliver a premium price. Information like this is most often hidden in a report, but, communicated in this way, it becomes a potential treasure chest for a brand such as Tropicana.

There is no doubt that as soon as the true costs to nature have to be paid by companies – either forced upon them by mindful consumers, by regulators or by inevitable price increases on resources – change will happen and those who are ahead of the curve will be the winners.

It shouldn't come as a surprise to you that our current way of living is at odds with our planet and for the most part also ourselves and our fellow humans. Our capitalist system is built on the idea of growth as the key to delivering higher standards of living. The real paradox is that our growth is dependent on natural resources such as fossil fuels, but these resources are themselves finite. It is simple: endless growth based on limited resources is not possible. I think this old Cree Indian proverb has a cunning foresight to it: 'Only when the last tree has died and the last river been poisoned and the last fish been caught will we realize we cannot eat money'. We already need more resources than we have, somewhere around 1.5 planets, to sustain our current lifestyle. If the world's current population of nearly 7 billion people were to have the same lifestyle as Europeans we would need three planets – or five if they aspire to live like the Americans. And why shouldn't they aspire to the same standard of living?

Why should consumers care about your brand?

Consumers have lost faith in brands. Havas Media undertook a global consumer research study called 'Brand Sustainable Futures', and looked

'Selinah', The Topsy Foundation, Ogilvy,
Johannesburg (see pages 148–49)

'Back to the Start', Chipotle Mexican Grill,
CAA and Chipotle (see pages 26–27)

at over 30,000 people across four continents and nine markets. They found that two-thirds of consumers say that they don't care whether the majority of brands survive or not. In my opinion this is a shocking revelation and shows that there is a lot of work to be done in rebuilding trust. I believe the disconnection has happened because brands didn't seem to care about consumers or what consumers cared about. Why should consumers then care about brands?

Consumers want brands to play a bigger role in their lives. In fact, the same research showed that an estimated 80% of consumers expect corporations not only to take care of shareholders, but also to play a significant part in solving the problems of society – from ensuring good jobs are available, to making donations and going beyond legal requirements in minimizing pollution and other negative effects. Alfonso Rodés Vilà, CEO of Havas Media, adds to these findings: 'Brand Sustainable Futures highlights that sustainability is no longer about responsibility; it's about survival. Companies must embrace sustainability as part of their core business and start developing a fluid dialogue with shared thinking with consumers and other key networks in society so that their brands contribute to a meaningful purpose.'

Unfortunately, research from the Natural Marketing Institute in 2011 showed that brands still have a long way to go: 41% of American consumers state, 'I don't believe what companies are saying about their efforts to protect the environment.' This also hints at the difference between consumer intent and their actual behaviour when it comes to buying sustainable products. Again, there is a lack of trust. Brands are left with the task of rebuilding their relationship with consumers, with regaining trust by making a real difference for people and the planet. It is no longer enough to say that you are doing good; consumers must be able to see it, feel it and believe it.

This introduces a new reality to brands, in which making a difference is not a matter of choice, but a matter of survival. This will force brands to take three important steps from profit to purpose. They will have to:

Get naked
Get together
Get out there

With greater power comes greater responsibility

As consumers expect more from brands, brands must meet those needs. Business has traditionally been about maximizing profits, but today a belief in a more sustainable model is growing not only in small visionary companies, but also in big global conglomerates such as Nike, General Electric and Unilever. This is a consequence of businesses beginning to realize change needs to happen as their income is threatened by a planet in crisis and scarce resources. The average consumer expects brands to provide solutions and behave responsibly. This challenges the old rules of the marketplace. I suggest ten guidelines that can help companies put their best foot forward. In order to stay relevant, a brand should be transparent, connected, simple, collaborative, compassionate, creative, contagious, generous, insightful and positive.

Brands have a large part to play. In the last few decades companies have grown into global conglomerates, and with greater reach their power has become immense, outmuscling that of many governments. Today, 51% of the world's largest economies are corporations, and these corporations are also the world's biggest employers. Added to that, brands touch every aspect of our lives through the products and services we use. Every second of every day 10,450 soft drinks made by Coca-Cola are consumed. Think of the possibility if some of that corporate might were used for good.

Creativity is the single biggest point of difference

In the debate about a new responsible revolution – in the articles, on the blogs and on the bookshelf – a call for creative communication seems to be missing. There should be a firm belief that the advertising industry can make a real, world-changing difference. I think we should push for this again and again. Anyone in the communications industry has a pivotal role to play and, since the industry played a part in building and setting in motion the wagon of consumerism and capitalism that is now driving us towards the edge of the cliff, we should help solve these worldwide problems in a responsible, sustainable and engaging way. Not only do we know the market and the consumers, we also have an abundance of skills. We have built brands stronger than nations. We have built such strong relationships with every little boy and girl from Copenhagen to Cape Town that they can tell you why brand X is better than brand Y. The work we put out there can either help make the world a better place or reinforce ignorance. It's time to stand up as professionals and dare to put your talents to good use.

If it's not good business then it's no good

Unfortunately, our hearts and wallets don't always speak the same language. We might have an idea about what we should do, but our actions are in many cases still driven by price, convenience and habits. People often change their behaviour because of rising fuel prices or other cost incentives. I think this is a consequence of our capitalist-market thinking, in which money is king and time is money. In that sense most people and most companies aren't so different: money rules.

There are people who are still sceptical about companies doing good with their marketing efforts, with their products or just in general. I am often confronted with the question: isn't this simply a very cynical way for companies to sell more? Yes, one hand is helping starving children in Africa, while another is filling the companies' pockets with money. It's up to you to judge, but I am not in doubt. The fact is that doing good is good business – starving children in Africa are being helped continuously as opposed to being offered a philanthropic gesture that ends when the money runs dry or a new cause grabs the attention of the donor.

For the same reason I don't preach about corporate social responsibility – I advocate world-bettering communication and innovation, in which the core idea is sustainable, particularly in an economic sense. It's about sustainable corporate innovation, sustainable corporate communication. If what you do does not convert into more customers, market shares, products sold, relations strengthened or brands built then your efforts will simply not last. It's more than OK that doing good is good business. If it's not then we are never going to reach the mass market with these initiatives. It's about finding the place where your brand or communication can play a vital role for change. It's about how you can align your passion with your compassion and your mission with a vision for a better world. It's about leading people to a new sustainable and responsible reality they might not even know existed. Can you tell that story?

Money stinks – or does it?

Are companies moral and responsible enough to live up to the task of bettering the world? Only time will tell. A company is no better than the sum of its people or the individuals chosen to control its power. Even though the size and strength of multinationals has outmuscled that of governments, it's important to remember that companies do live on the mercy of people and governments. PepsiCo's visionary CEO, Indra Nooyi, acknowledges that obligation in her wise words, 'We believe that every corporation operates with a licence from society and, as a company, we owe society a duty of care.'

Don't be afraid of greenwashing, be afraid of green nothing

I'm going to defend the greenwashers (at least some of them). Personally, I think it's better that a brand adds to the responsible voices in the marketplace rather than continuing to campaign for mindless consumerism – this is why I advise brands to 'get out there' and speak up for change. In the end, it will make more people hear, 'save the world' instead of 'consume the world'. I don't think consumers are dumb. They can easily figure out if the messages are hollow and if promises are not acted on. In that way, they will put pressure on the brand and the brand's greenwashing attempt will turn into real, responsible efforts with tangible results.

As such, I really don't perceive greenwashing as a problem – I see it as potential. It is a brand's first, tentative step in a good direction; it's a brand trying to talk the talk of sustainability. Look at Nike, for example, and how the publicity about bad labour practices in the 1980s and 1990s has turned the company in a responsible direction – and how they are held responsible for that pledge as the latest string of bad labour practice accusations against their Converse brand shows. We're not going to succeed if we have a negative focus, if everybody is talking about what companies and brands are not doing. Let us celebrate what has been done and support those who do something rather than nothing – at least they're trying! Think about that when you fear to take that first cautious step in a better direction or before you join the wolfpack of howling critics of greenwashing. Let's go to work saving our planet and ourselves with a positive mindset.

Today's business is as strange a notion as slavery

When our children look back on the way we did business, our practices will seem as strange a notion as slavery is to us today. How could we be so oblivious to the harm we inflicted on people and the planet? Couldn't we see the icebergs melting or the chemical time bomb ticking away in everything from food to clothing? Weren't we aware that the planet's resources and the ecosystem on which we so depended were being destroyed? We have to move away from self-interest because we are not alone on this planet, either as a people or as a species. I can't help but share this classic joke that adds a little humour to our shortsightedness. Two planets meet each other and Planet 1 says to Planet 2, 'Hey, you look terrible!' Planet 2 answers, 'Yes, I know. I have Homo sapiens.' Planet 1 says, 'Don't worry, I had that too and it will soon disappear.'

For too long our thinking and our capitalist market have been about the needs and, increasingly, the wants of companies, profiting at the expense of others as well as the Earth. We are all equally important global citizens and when it's about getting there together, when it's about benefiting all stakeholders, not just shareholders, we all get richer. A prosperous brand is dependent on a prosperous community. Selling food that is fatty and unhealthy is a short-term profit-making scheme that will result in an unhealthy community who will need more sick leave. This results in fewer people being able to work, which means there is less money to spend – and ultimately less money for you. We need to change our behaviour and thinking to be inclusive, instead of exclusive. I trust the steps and choices of the many will lead to the wider systemic change that is needed: a world in which we don't produce waste and need no new raw materials. We need a more sustainable economic system, we need a more sustainable relationship with our environment and we need a more sustainable relationship with each other. Brands should 'get together' and collaborate with consumers, NGOs, governments, like-minded brands and even competitors to find lasting solutions that will make a difference for you and me and everyone.

Sustainability is mainstream

Thanks to awareness campaigns, public debate and legislation, the majority of people not only remember to turn off their lights when leaving home (95%), but are also switching off electronic devices when not in use (90%) or turning the thermostat down a degree or two. They recycle paper (61%) and think about conserving water (85%). In the supermarket, more people are choosing the most healthy or environmentally friendly products and bringing them home in reusable shopping bags (48%). More people repair, reuse and share products. One example of sharing is car clubs, in which people don't own a car, but share one. Even in the US people are beginning to share rides and use public transport (17%). For some this is driven by higher fuel prices and for others it is driven by conscience – or heart versus wallet, as I like to put it. Over and above this information gathered by the Natural Marketing Institute in 2011, an estimated 83% of US consumers are interested in sustainability in some shape or form. The mainstream market for sustainable products is definitely there, whether your brand provides benefits for health, our society or the planet.

'The Big Knit', Innocent (see page 192)

Anything you can do, I can do greener

We have created extraordinary inventions and advances such as renewable energy that can take us one step towards sustainability. We may be able to be less inefficient – for instance, by using electricity more wisely – but we don't need steps, we need a giant leap, and that is something the market can deliver. The electric vehicle, for instance, is one such invention, but if left in the garage and never adopted by the mass market what use are such inventions? In a fully transparent market consumers reward companies that do good, advancing products that do good. It's a positive circle of reinforcement. I call it the Wheel of Good. As more consumers choose responsible companies, more companies become responsible and launch more responsible products. When more responsible products are launched, more competition arrives which pushes the prices down and paves the way for greater demand – and so the wheel gets bigger and spins faster. Consumers and marketing professionals all have a huge role to play in spinning the wheel. Essentially, I believe if we can get it spinning fast enough and at a large enough size, the market itself can deliver the solutions to creating a sustainable and responsible future empowered by informed consumer choices.

With the Wheel of Good, the consumer demand for products that deliver health, societal or environmental value becomes a mass-market concern. A Sustainable Future report by Havas Media from 2009 supports this change. Over 60% of consumers believe they can influence a company to behave more responsibly not by boycotting or punishing them, but by rewarding them by choosing their products.

The competitors in the old marketing landscape are no longer only competing on what they say, but equally on what they do and what tangible goals they put forward. The backstories are moving to the forefront of their relationship with consumers. Arch rivals Pepsi and Coca-Cola demonstrate this well. In 2009, Coca-Cola launched their PlantBottle made from 30% renewable plant-based material. Just two years later, Pepsi introduced a bottle made from 100% renewable plant-based material. The new responsible competition follows the mantra: anything you can do, I can do greener.

Several companies are launching similar inventions to live up to such values and are helping spin the Wheel of Good faster. Procter & Gamble uses its products to pave the way for its environmental efforts (backed up by advertising campaigns) and has pledged that at least $20 million in sales should come from products that have a smaller environmental footprint than similar products in their respective category, such as Duracell rechargeable batteries, Ariel high efficiency laundry powder and Ariel Coldwater (the 'Turn to 30' campaign). For brands, the sustainability journey begins with the three steps 'get naked, get together, get out there'. It's about leveraging genuine, transparent efforts, collaborating with stakeholders to find solutions, and not being afraid to speak up for change.

The leap of a giant

The ability to use our collective creativity and wisdom has been paramount for our success as a species in the past, and so it is now. This book is about people who believe in challenging our current system and dare to dream of a better world. For every step we take together in the right direction, we make the Wheel of Good spin faster. If we all band together and share the very best solutions for change, we can take these solutions and implement them on a global scale, partly thanks to the internet and mobile solutions. It is no longer the step of a single man, but the soaring leap of a giant. This first step is yours, but be sure to invite someone along. You can begin by telling people about this book.

There is no better time to be generous and share the very best ideas and visions with the world. David Droga, Creative Chairman of Droga5, shared one of his proudest moments at Cannes in 2011 when he saw his agency's Tap Project had been taken on in other countries by other agencies. 'It had nothing to do with me and I was so proud that this idea is far bigger than us, far bigger than this and now it's moved into different countries as this real, genuine, potentially amazing thing.'

This book features many interviews with people who believe change needs to happen. Alex Bogusky left his position as Creative Chairman of the advertising agency Crispin Porter + Bogusky to search for purpose rather than profit in a new set-up he calls FearLess Cottage. In an interview Bogusky shares his fear that one day his kids will ask him a question that will for once leave him speechless: 'The world is just a shit bag, dad, what did you do to try and stop it?' I'm certain the very same question will be posed to brands by customers – and it had better not leave them speechless. Morten Albaek bravely made a similar move from the banking sector to the wind energy company, Vestas, so, in his own words, he could 'positively impact the planet that I was inhabiting and my kids will inherit from me'. You'll also meet many other individuals who have dared to challenge our current paradigm. It's about time we harnessed our collective wisdom and creativity to come up with better solutions for the future. Gandhi once said, 'Be the change you want to see in this world.' I hope that by writing this book I can encourage change and strengthen your belief in the

transformational power of creativity – and hopefully you'll join me in doing so too.

Don't invent a new box, invent a new product

It is now up to brands to prove they deserve to be trusted by consumers – and in doing so answer the 'what's (really) in it for me?' question. Think about how you can add value to people's lives instead of interrupting them while they're watching their favourite movie – and keep an eye on where the target group is on the scale between heart and money or 'less bad' and 'more good'. If you are in the communications industry use it as a tool to evaluate your effort, validating your creative work or steering your concept in a new direction.

Delivering sustainable value makes a major difference: on average, corporate philanthropy accounts for 1% of a company's surplus, whereas a company's use of their products, market offering, innovation and even communication to do good can take advantage of 100% of their efforts. There is a great potential market for social and sustainable innovation and communication: it's up to you to come up with the ideas for an ever expanding creative canvas.

Not only does fierce competition spark a bigger need for great ideas, but so too does the urgent need of people and the planet. There are more opportunities for innovation than ever before, as the stories about brands are not only about what they say, but equally about what they do and the rich soil of their backstories. In this new responsible reality you have to look beyond the traditional media channels and challenge everything from product to brand stories. In other words, don't just invent a new campaign, but reinvent the product, reinvent its lifecycle or reinvent the marketplace.

For the tremendous task ahead a new set of knowledge is needed for anyone involved, from an art director to a marketing director: 'environmental footprint', 'sustainability' and 'cradle to cradle' should be as much part of their vocabulary as 'social media' and 'TRPs'. The future belongs to those who understand the new responsible agenda and dare to experiment and seek new solutions. One rule hasn't changed: creativity is still the single biggest differentiator in the market – and a new market demands new ideas. This responsibility is yours: big hearts and big ideas are needed.

Your creativity is the only limit

There are so many places where you can make a difference. I hope this book will inspire you to see some of the issues facing the world for which brands and communication can step in and find solutions. You can introduce sustainable products to billions of people in the developing world at a price they can afford. You can create awareness around how people can eat more healthily. You can empower women in the developing world to get an education. You can aim high and, like filmmaker and actor Jeremy Gilley, aspire to global peace. He introduced one day a year, 21 September, when everyone around the world is encouraged to put down their arms. There are so many great things we can accomplish together. Again, your creativity is the only limit. Although my views are biased after more than a decade in advertising, I do believe that advertising has a central role to play in making the Wheel of Good get bigger and spin faster. We have the ability to change brands from the inside out – and make them realize that there's no profit without a purpose. We not only have the creative muscle to come up with solutions, but also the power to influence the mind and the behaviour of the future marketplace, as we have done with great success in the past. Together we can call for a movement of change

Top 'The Lottery of Life', Save the Children,
Lowe Brindfors, Stockholm (see pages 50–51)

with the ultimate goal of finding serious solutions for a sustainable future, in which it's not wealth, but wellbeing that defines success.

On the following pages you will see the power behind this movement. I've selected over 120 campaigns from all over the world that show these crises have a creative solution. Leaders of agencies, businesses, governments and NGOs believe in a new and more sustainable future and in the interviews they have shared their best insights with you on how to tackle this transformational tidal wave.

I hope the great work and the great minds of the people I have interviewed will not only inspire you to use your power for good, but also inspire you to inspire those around you. I believe that by sharing work, thoughts and ideas for good, we can inspire each other to do greater good. That's why I'm writing this book. Moreover, I hope you will take personal responsibility and think twice about your footprint. Use your vote as a consumer and citizen and your voice as a professional to advocate change. It's all about giving back – the more you give, the more you get.

This book is a wake-up call not only for businesses, because their financial standing is at risk, but also for creatives because their skills really can make a difference. Most importantly, though, this is a wake-up call for humankind because it's really not about saving the planet, it's about saving ourselves. My belief is, and always has been, that our single biggest relevance is creativity. This book is about great, world-bettering ideas – about our ability to come up with solutions when there seem to be none.

It's time for you to reply.

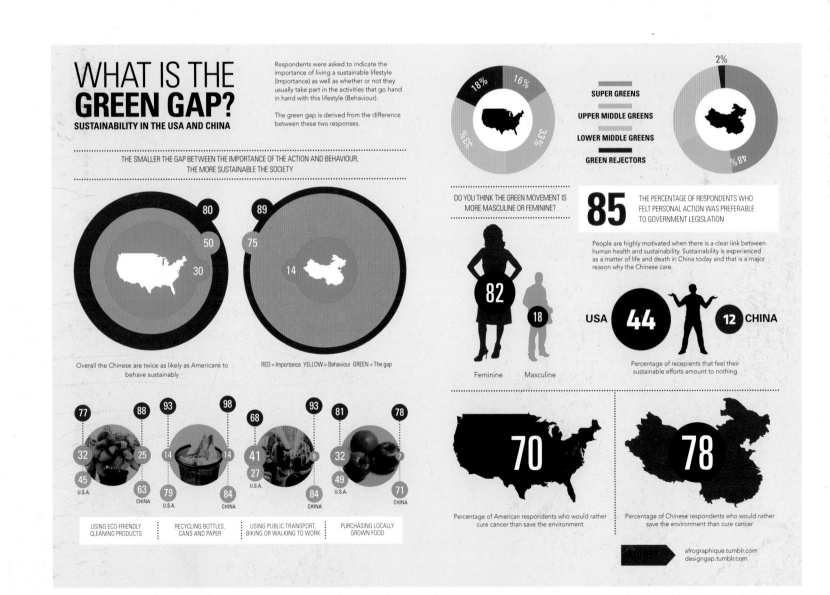

Interview
CONNIE HEDEGAARD

I think raising awareness has to be a continuous effort because people tend to forget.

Connie Hedegaard is the Climate Action Commissioner for the European Union, representing the future of all 500 million citizens. This makes her one of the most important voices internationally when it comes to the climate crisis. She was also instrumental in organizing COP15, which was hosted in Denmark in 2009. After a career in politics (Connie was the youngest ever member of the Danish Folketing, the National Parliament), she moved to journalism before returning to politics again in 2004. At the beginning of 2010 she assumed her current position at the EU. Thankfully, Connie was able to squeeze me into her busy schedule – we had half an hour to chat about how to save the world. While we didn't manage to solve the climate crisis in its entirety, Connie gave me more than enough hope that things are changing for the better. As a fellow Dane, I am immensely proud of Connie's work.

What comes through, when speaking to Connie, is the idea that we need to redefine what we see as growth and that the capitalism of the past has to be tempered with responsibility. While this may sound like a rather obvious statement, we can no longer continue producing goods as if there are unlimited resources from which to make them. This may be something we all inherently know, but it is something that cannot be stressed enough; as Connie said, if consumers are not constantly reminded of a problem then it can lose importance in their minds.

We began by speaking about her goals as Climate Action Commissioner: she is hoping that by 2014 the EU will be the most climate friendly region in the world. **'I think we are on track to prove that you can have economic growth and yet make less impact on the environment and climate and you can create jobs too. It's due to our targets and regulations, but also because of the economic crisis we are overachieving our own target and because of what is happening** elsewhere in the world we are on track to reach that overall vision that I put out.'

While this vision is important, Connie has found it is essential to continue reminding consumers of the climate issues we are facing. It also provides an opportunity for companies to do their part for the cause by disseminating climate-conscious messages through traditional communication channels as well as product labelling. **'I think raising awareness has to be a continuous effort because people tend to forget. If we just take this summer [2011] in Copenhagen, where we normally tend to believe that people are extremely climate aware, people were very surprised when suddenly their basements flooded. They have been warned again and again and again! We know violent precipitation is the form of climate change that would happen in that part of Europe and yet it seems people are still taken by surprise. So it's not enough to raise awareness over a period, you have to do it continuously. And that is why companies have a very big responsibility – also through labelling. Some of these tools that we have will be incredibly important.'**

On the subject of labels, Connie believes that consumers should be empowered through the availability of more information. If they can see how much energy products consume before they make a purchase then hopefully that will enable them to make responsible choices. **'When it comes to big commodity things like, say, a car, I think Europe should have labelling, I think it should be comparable. If I go and buy a boiler or an electronic device I should be able to see what the energy consumption is. That should be a basic standard thing. If I buy a hairdryer or a kettle I should be able to see which is consuming more energy.'**

For Connie, it's also a question of looking at things qualitatively as opposed to quantitatively. We should not be looking at just the numbers, but the full story of a product, through labelling and other avenues. **'It's tremendously important when you buy a car that you tell people what the CO2 impact is, how long it runs on a tank of petrol and so on… When you are now selling or advertising houses for sale, look at how much energy a house uses. Make it visible in all sorts of areas. Personally, I also think that many of these big retailers have huge power when they advertise their products.'** At the same time, it's not just governments that should be taking responsibility, but businesses too. **'Of course, politicians should continue to put out ambitious targets, make the regulations, set the standards – all these kinds of things, but I will say that it's also very, very important that the business community takes part in communicating this message to the consumers…make this an issue not just focusing on price and quantity, but also on this more qualitative side of growth. What we are discussing all over Europe, for instance, is that we need to create more growth. I think the real big question is – what kind of growth?'**

Connie expands on her definition of growth and how we can plot a sustainable course for the future. **'It really matters what kind of growth we create for the 21st century. We cannot continue to create the same kind of growth that we did in the 20th century. I think that leadership is very important, not only from Brussels, but also from national governments to raise this issue. What kind of growth? A much more qualitative kind of growth with less impact on the environment.'**

This raises the question, of course, of developing countries and how they can enable the growth of their economies and improve the lives of their citizens in a responsible way. Clearly, to expect them to withhold growth is unfair. Connie agrees. **'I think that in many of the developing countries it's also about how to mainstream climate into your general development plan. It's much cheaper if you mainstream it from the outset of a project, instead of what we did in the West, where we made the development first and then had to mainstream and build climate into it. They could really skip some generations of technologies and they could avoid replicating our sort of growth. I think that is part of the development strategy in many African and Asian countries.'**

And while we try to grow the world's economy safely and sustainably, another issue that arises is how many products are produced in the developing world and consumed in the first world, with differing sets of environmental and societal laws. How do we ensure that 'green' products in the first world are not produced under terrible circumstances in the developing world? **'I think that's through as tight standards as**

possible – making them accountable for their emissions, having internationally agreed rules. If you're a global company you can't say that your impact is one thing in one country and one thing in another. To bring that to a common denominator is also something that is a topic for Durban – the next international climate conference. [COP17 took place in Durban, South Africa late in 2011.] And, of course, there are some countries that will be resistant towards this, but I think it's very important to pursue a global framework addressing these kinds of issues. I mean, we can do whatever we can in Europe and we are also now expanding it into aviation where we say, OK, if you land in Europe, if you depart from Europe, it is not only European airlines who have to live up to our legislation.'**

Talk turns to the future and whether we will come through our current problems. **'I think it's sometimes strange that man has to experience things… It's not enough to get the warnings, you have to experience the downsides and suffer the consequences and then it starts to dawn on you: "Wow, maybe we should do things in a more intelligent way"…so in that sense I'm sure we will experience that… It always takes much too long for people to react on a grand scale but we are moving in that direction, compared to five years ago when people were only talking about traditional quantitative growth and when this climate agenda was not at all there. I think we have seen in more recent years that things are moving and are moving in the right direction. Take China, they are actually trying to build their cities now in a very different manner. They are putting targets now on how much energy their different sectors can consume, very big things like that. So it is moving, but I think it's moving too slowly. We will be moving in the right direction, I don't think that will be stopped.'**

What is abundantly clear is that we cannot continue moving forward as we have before. Connie elaborates, **'In many respects people have thought more narrowly about the economic part of the crisis, but I think that the crisis has made it very clear that we cannot just continue business as usual. Because business as usual means that part of the crisis we are in grows, so there has to be an open-mindedness to another way of doing things, and many will now have to rethink their business strategies. And there I think the overall green growth agenda is very much on the screen.'**

May the green growth agenda be a topic of discussion for years to come.

TRANSPARENCY

1.

TRANSPARENCY
Why start a friendship with a lie?

'Pizza Turnaround', Domino's Pizza, Crispin Porter +
Bogusky, Boulder (see page 24)

The end of secrecy

The days of corporate secrecy or indeed any secrecy are over. Brands' steps and missteps are increasingly exposed and judged by an online spiderweb of global consumers – around 1 billion of them. It's an all-encompassing force. Just see how websites such as WikiLeaks or social networks have such an impact on governments and global brands.

There is no longer a clear distinction between public or private, as you might have noticed by looking at some of the pictures people upload to Facebook. Some of us have no inhibitions about sharing our most intimate moments or aspirations in a status update or even constantly geotagging our whereabouts. People expect the same openness from brands, institutions and governments. If a company doesn't wear its heart on its sleeve then how can it be trusted?

Time to get naked

You and I become part of that movement when we write a critical online review or post a Facebook comment complaining about a company's customer service. A tweet or comment can attract others with a similar view and put pressure on a brand. The transparent power of the internet is merciless. This is explored in the classic *Cluetrain Manifesto*, where David Weinberger et al. challenge companies to wake up and realize the power of the web: 'Now the Web is enabling the market to converse again, as people tell one another the truth about products and companies and their own desires.' For brands there is simply nowhere to hide and, as advised in the introduction, it's time to get naked.

Don't be afraid to admit your weaknesses

There's nothing more disarming than honesty and in interviewing a great many people for this book it's a word that I kept hearing again and again. You have to take a long hard look at what you would not like your customers to find and then do something about it. Make a clear plan and get it out in the open. Sometimes admitting a mistake is the first step: tell your customers where you've been, where you currently are and where you would like to be and let them help you along the way.

A good example of this came up in a talk with ad legend Alex Bogusky. He mentioned Justin's Nut Butter and how their biggest problem was their wasteful packaging. Justin's were frank about it and reached out to consumers and suppliers and asked for help to solve the problem. The lesson to be learnt is: don't be afraid to admit that you have a problem – in fact you should look for your biggest problem and ask for help. If you don't do it now, somebody will reveal it eventually and then the damage is done. This approach works because you're telling the truth.

MICROSOFT TURNS HUMAN

In an exclusive interview Bill Gates, former CEO and current Chairman of Microsoft, thanked his Channel 9 co-author Robert Scoble for his work on the Microsoft blog: 'You are letting people have a sense of the people here. You're building a connection. People feel more part of this. Maybe they'll tell us how to improve our products.'

'Non-processing Process', Citric,
DraftFCB, Buenos Aires (see page 28)

CITRIC: NON-PROCESSING PROCESS

Nobody's perfect, so admit your work is a work in progress

In the early days Innocent's plastic bottles were made of 25% recyclable plastic and on the label it stated: we're working on the rest. When they later launched a new bottle containing 50% recycled plastic consumers called and congratulated them on their progress: they didn't complain because it wasn't 75% or 100%. Innocent's honesty paid off.

The outdoor clothing company Patagonia has also chosen a genuine approach with The Footprint Chronicles, a site dedicated to the environmental footprint of their products which shows both the good and the bad sides. I can't help loving their product descriptions. Here is one that appears on one of their bags: 'We wanted to be able to price the Chacabuco Pack competitively in a crowded market, but using recycled materials, which are costly, would have put us out of range. So the Chacabuco Pack embodies no environmental innovation.' Patagonia is direct about its flaws, which undoubtedly makes the brand feel more human and appealing.

Work not only on the advertised story, but also on the whole story

The demand for transparency leaves no stone unturned. A must-read is Daniel Goleman's book *Ecological Intelligence*, in which he advocates transparency that covers 'the entire lifecycle of a product and the full range of its consequences at every stage, and presents that information to a buyer in ways that demand little effort...unlike those hard-to-decipher E numbers on that bag of candies.' One guide that helps consumers make better informed choices and drives transparency is Goodguide.com, which shows the hidden impacts

of ordinary consumer products in terms of health, environment and society. Downloading their mobile app will change your shopping habits forever. Another guide, ClimateCounts.org, holds companies accountable for their carbon footprints and willingness to tackle global warming. When consumers can easily scrutinize a company and their brands, the company can no longer rely on the advertised story alone, but have to work on the whole story. This means that new knowledge about 'product lifecycle' and 'ecological footprint' has to be a natural part of your marketing vocabulary and the creative process, and it also forces companies to 'get naked' because the market will tell the whole story in any case.

Hold their hands and guide the consumers

Seventh Generation is a firm believer in transparency. The company sells green cleaning products and is at the forefront of growing consumer concerns, disclosing full lists of ingredients as well as the environmental impact of its products. Customers can watch videos, read about their products or leave a review. Even giants such as the manufacturers SC Johnson and Clorox have opened up and disclosed their ingredients through respectively WhatsInsideSCJohnson.com and Clorox's Ingredients Inside initiative. Although their openness hardly lives up to the level of transparency Goleman defined above, it is certainly a step in the right direction. Being transparent will allow brands to hold hands with consumers and guide them or even educate them. It's a trust-building exercise.

Loosen your tie and be more chatty

You can't ignore transparency, but you can embrace it and blog, tweet and shape your on- and offline presence with your corporate voice. It

HOW HONEST DO YOU DARE TO BE?

Jeffrey Hollender, former CEO of green cleaning product company Seventh Generation, once posted a list on the company's website that detailed everything he thought was wrong with its products and how those shortcomings let down the company's mission. He has since left the company due to a dispute about the company's direction.

fosters a demand from top to bottom for a new generation of employees and CEOs who are open and leave their suit behind and talk like the average Joe. Tony Hsieh, CEO of the online shoe retailer Zappos, has got it right from the beginning – his tweets, equally company-related and personal, have a massive following. One of his tweets, @zappos, reads: 'From now on, any time I'm stuck in traffic I'm just going to pretend that I'm part of a really big parade.' Through his tweets I can feel who the guy is, build a relationship with him, and most importantly he comes across as frank. Perhaps for the same reason, Twitter has launched a service, ExecTweets.com, where top business execs and IT pros are sharing their insights and thoughts.

Microsoft is another company who have chosen a frank approach. In 2004 they launched their corporate video blog, Channel 9, where you could follow life inside the walls of the software giant. Today, any insider nerd or technician with a keyboard can blog, share and post videos. The initiative has quickly attracted thousands of followers worldwide, sparked discussions and added some flesh and bone to a company formerly known for its secrecy. In a period when consumer trust in companies is at a low, knocking down the corporate walls is an important first step in rebuilding the precious relationship between consumer and company.

In the long run, honesty always wins

In an ideal, transparent market the balance shifts from companies to consumers. As a consequence, I can make an informed choice in the supermarket aisles and buy the shampoo that rates best on what matters most to me: health, environment or society. It's a positive reinforcement cycle, what I call the Wheel of Good, which rewards companies for doing good and asks others to improve. The future belongs to those brands that dare to open up, to be honest and embrace transparency. After all, if you want to befriend someone, don't begin your relationship with a lie.

Interview
ALEX BOGUSKY

Interviewing Alex Bogusky is not something you take lightly. This is the man who fronted some of the most audacious ad campaigns in recent memory, the man who was described as the Steve Jobs of advertising. Strange then that it was really quite easy to get hold of him and set up a Skype interview, and strange also that I wasn't interviewing him in his huge office at Crispin Porter + Bogusky (CP+B), but in a little house known as FearLess Cottage.

Alex has recently left CP+B and set many tongues wagging and teeth gnashing in the process. This was the guy who must have sat in on a creative meeting and gone, 'Hell, yeah, we'll make a fragrance for Burger King that smells like hamburgers!' but he's also the guy who wrote *The 9-Inch Diet*, a book about portion control. This dichotomy, this multi-pronged personality is what makes Alex Bogusky one of the most interesting men in (or out) of advertising.

To some, Alex's story is one of hypocrisy (if you believe the zealousness of, well, zealots), but in my interactions with him he seems nothing but genuine and heartfelt. His story, rather than being that of the mysterious conjurer – pulling whoppers out of a hat – is really one of redemption. Having been involved in advertising for a decade and having spoken to many different people on the advertising hamster-wheel, I understand his concerns. I understand the drive to use your creativity for something good rather than to sell more products at the expense of people and the environment. Rather than Alex being a hypocrite, force-feeding fast food to children, he's someone who wants to make amends, to leave the Earth just a little better than he found it.

Alex's new initiatives – Common (a social brand-licensing programme) and FearLess are his attempts to speak the truth and to say what he really believes. He explains the uneasiness he began to feel in his final years at CP+B, **'I would say it was a year or a year and a half where you just start to get a bit uncomfortable, and you're just like – uuuh, I don't know. I'm not able to say what I think about things and I was in this speech and people were asking me questions and it was really hard to navigate.'**

Many people have accused him of being a hypocrite, and even of being a psychopath, which Alex himself admits is quite funny, but in his rebuttal he says something I agree with, **'If you're going to be afraid of being called a hypocrite, then I guess you can never change your mind about things.'** He makes a good point and in the advertising world, where we are taught the importance of a 'Single Minded Proposition', back-tracking is in some ways a form of heresy.

He goes on in the same vein when talking about Al Gore and his tireless efforts to do something about the world's climate crisis (Alex is currently

consulting on Al Gore's Climate Reality Project), **'People like Al Gore are called hypocrites because he's worried about the climate but he also drives a car. If that's what's going to stop us then we're all stopped and there can be no change and that's a tragic problem.'**

As I talk to Alex via Skype, I see the real side to him – a man who is trying to make amends, trying to find a new way to use his considerable talents to make the world better. During the interview a hailstorm started up and, without missing a beat, Alex picked up some of the hail and showed it to me; at other times I could hear a dog barking in the background. I think he's really taking joy in his realness. To hear him talk about the rather huge dent he's taken in salary and how he moved from a life in which everything was set – great job, great salary, no need to prove himself any more – to a life that is much less certain, you appreciate the personal journey he has made and the bravery involved in his decision.

Someone who worked on a global scale, Alex is now enjoying spending his time working on small local projects. He has invested time and money into a bicycle company in Alabama that produces bikes from bamboo and into a peanut butter company called Justin's Nut Butter. They are two small(ish) companies that have values in which Alex believes. This sets the trend for responsible consumption and investment that the world should see more of – people love brands that speak to them and are honest. Alex told me a story about Justin's Nut Butter and their packaging problems: about how when he raised the issue with them they didn't go off and sulk, but changed their packaging for the better – because that's what they believe in.

When talk turns to advertising and the power of doing good we move into some very interesting territory. He speaks about how advertising is moving from a fictional story told to consumers to a dynamic, real-time, honest account of what a company is doing. **'What's most interesting in marketing right now is how you are actually acting as a company… If you can tell a real-time, transparent story about who you are as a company and what you care about and what you're doing, if you can tell that in such a way that it's compelling – that's where marketing is most interesting now… When the consumer is like, I really like transparent companies,'** says Alex, dancing from side to side like a concerned consumer, **'I like companies that do good things! The corporations are like: WHAT? We need some more of that! Where's the consumer going? I want to follow the consumer…'**

Alex sees a chance for advertising to move into business partnership, rather than just acting as a tool to promote sales or increase brand awareness: **'I think if you're in advertising and you're not thinking about corporate structure and you're not thinking about [product] lifecycles then I think you're irrelevant.'** If advertising acts as a go-between for brands and consumers then it has to start being more responsible and, most importantly, more truthful.

I can see, after speaking to him, that Alex is revelling in his new-found truth and this is something we can perhaps all try to emulate, no matter our status. He is a man in search of the answer. He admits that he is not even sure that FearLess and Common have come to full fruition yet – they are still finding their purpose, much like the man himself. He said something great about his motivation and his children, **'I definitely have the ability for a certain amount of time to just take my voice and lend it to things that I think are going to affect my children's future. And when the future comes we can have one of two conversations, they can either say to me: "Thanks, dad, that was awesome", or they can say: "The world is just a shit bag, dad, what did you do to try and stop it?" And I can say I did this, this, this and this. I did what I could and I'm sorry that it turned out this way. I know that conversation is coming and I don't want to be unprepared either way.'**

Given the time difference between Cape Town and Colorado, by the time we were finishing up our interview it was close to two o'clock in the morning for me, but in my tired state Alex said something that gave me hope that advertising for good was here to stay. **'When you take what a typical corporation does with their millions of dollars in advertising and you somehow shape that in a way that it does good, right? That's the highest order of advertising. That's the most sophisticated, brilliant, sexy, hot, cool thing you can do.'**

That's the highest order of advertising. That's the most sophisticated, brilliant, sexy, hot, cool thing you can do.

Domino's pizza crust

> *There comes a time when you know you've got to make a change.*
>
> PATRICK DOYLE, CEO OF DOMINO'S PIZZA

"BORING, ARTIFICIAL, IMITATION OF WHAT PIZZA CAN BE."

"CRUST SEEMED LACKING"

Meredith Baker
Product Manager

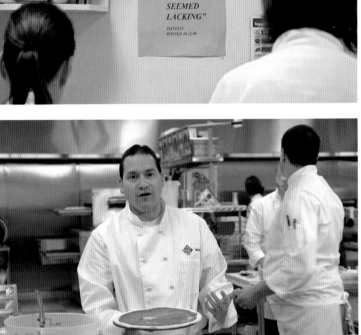

DOMINO'S PIZZA
Crispin Porter + Bogusky, Boulder
PIZZA TURNAROUND

In a brave and radical move, Domino's Pizza admitted to the public that their pizza sucked. Rather than close ranks, as one might expect a large company to do, they spoke openly to their customers and admitted their faults. They then changed their entire pizza recipe from the ground up, allowing customers to see the whole process.

They have also undertaken other transparent initiatives such as 'Show Us Your Pizza', which encourages their customers to take photographs of Domino's pizzas and upload them onto a website. This was part of a promise from Domino's that they would no longer use food stylists and airbrushing to make their pizzas look better in adverts.

In perhaps the most radical of their transparent moves, Domino's started the pizza tracker, which allowed workers in the Domino's restaurants to get real-time feedback from the people who were eating the pizzas they had made. Customers could log onto a website and rate their experience – they could even find out the names of the people who had made their pizza. This was taken to extremes when a billboard was erected in Times Square, New York, showing a live feed of these pizza reviews.

As one might expect, this campaign paid off. While opening up does mean that you have to be willing to take criticism, Domino's has also seen a sharp rise in sales, with a 14% spike in the first quarter of the campaign. Their profits for the quarter immediately after the campaign were more than double those of the previous year. This shows that being transparent and honest is good for business, very good for business.

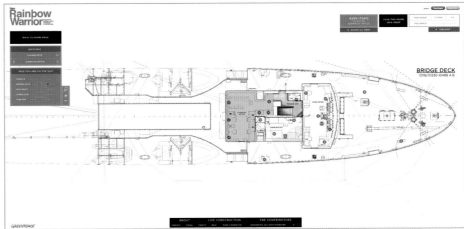

GREENPEACE
DDB, Paris
RAINBOW WARRIOR

Greenpeace is an independent organization and will not take donations from corporations or governments, leaving them reliant on public support. As their boat, the *Rainbow Warrior II*, reached its retirement age, Greenpeace launched a campaign to fund a new member of the Rainbow family and started with a fairly standard method of appealing for donations, but made it so much more than that. Through a well-designed and functional website users can browse the blueprint for Greenpeace's new Rainbow Warrior and decide which part of the ship they would like to buy.

Absolutely everything that the ship will need is for sale. Users can buy anything from a fork (€1) to the ship's wheel (€500). People who donate are given a certificate and their names are put onto a special wall in the conference room of the ship.

By making donations tangible, Greenpeace has made it much easier for people to commit to parting with their money. And the fact that supporters can say, 'I bought one of the desks that crew members on board the *Rainbow Warrior* use', is something of which they can be proud. By allowing their supporters to buy into this idea of independence and freedom – to feel that they have literally contributed to Greenpeace's boat – Greenpeace have turned donors into collaborators and strengthened their brand immensely.

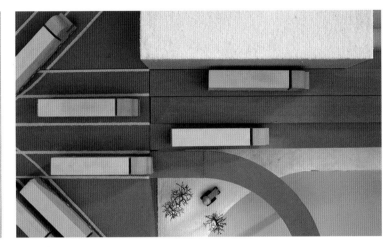

CHIPOTLE MEXICAN GRILL
CAA and Chipotle
BACK TO THE START

In this stop-motion animation from Chipotle Mexican Grill, the US Mexican food chain, we are told the story of a farmer who expands his farm and turns it into an industrial behemoth. He soon learns the error of his ways and returns to his original farming methods – where he is closer to the animals and more in tune with the Earth. The film has a specially commissioned soundtrack – Coldplay's *The Scientist*, sung by Willie Nelson. The song is available on iTunes, with all proceeds going to the Chipotle Cultivate Foundation.

The commercial is a story of redemption, something that speaks to all of us. It also makes the mistakes of the past so obvious that one can't help wondering how we ever allowed farming to get so out of hand. While Chipotle's farming methods are about going back to the beginning, the chain is ready for the future with revenue growing by 23.7% in 2011.

CITRIC: NON-PROCESSING PROCESS

CITRIC
DraftFCB, Buenos Aires
NON-PROCESSING PROCESS

To show how natural Citric juice is,
the company decided to explain their
non-processing process. This series
of print ads shows how in each instance
the production of the juice bypasses
the factory. Through slick, witty
art direction, we see how Citric juice
avoids processing.

It's simple, it's transparent and
it lets consumers know immediately
that what they are getting has not
been processed in any way.

CITRIC: NON-PROCESSING PROCESS

VESTAS
Droga5, New York
WINDMADE

With WindMade, Vestas and their fellow founding partners created the first label of its kind – a label that shows consumers which clean energy source produced the electricity used to make their favourite brands and, in turn, their favourite products. The creation of the WindMade labelling programme means that companies will be able to inform their consumers about how much clean electricity is used for its operations, and consumers will be able to buy products based on their energy 'ingredients'. The label, which can be used anywhere in the world, will display how much wind energy helped make a product. This extra information allows consumers to make an even more informed choice when shopping and rewards brands that use wind energy to produce their products.

In a selfless move, Vestas has partnered with other wind industry members, global brands, NGOs and technology experts to make this initiative happen. Vestas realized that uplifting all wind energy is a positive move for all the players in the game, even if they are traditional competitors or even non-traditional energy customers. As more consumers drive the need for these products, more companies will want to source green electricity, positively reinforcing the entire cycle.

A rising tide raises all the boats.

DAVID DROGA, CREATIVE CHAIRMAN OF DROGA5

2011

Choose Wind.
Power Change.

PEDIGREE
Havas Media, Miami
MY IDEAL DOG

In order to increase brand awareness, as well as dog adoption, across Latin America, Pedigree started 'My Ideal Dog' – a 30-minute TV series on the Animal Planet channel that documented families receiving their adopted dog. A dog psychologist hosted the TV shows, raising awareness about the plight of dogs who weren't adopted. The show also focused on finding the ideal dog for each family. This allowed Pedigree to teach people how to care for their dogs as well as reinforcing Pedigree as the number one brand in its sector in Latin America.

The results were very impressive. Sales of Pedigree increased by 8% and across Latin America people were 15% more likely to adopt a dog than before the show aired. On top of that, 77% of people who watched the show were likely to adopt a dog. This proves that giving people branded entertainment and real content pays off. It's good for the Pedigree brand and it's good for dogs too.

PETA
McCann Erickson, Singapore
THE UGLY SIDE OF BEAUTY

PETA in Singapore wanted to make fashionistas more aware about the clothes they were buying and what the real costs were. Through an innovative use of outdoor media and mobile phones, billboards were produced featuring shoes, bags and belts made from animals. These billboards advertised the products at unbelievable prices, but in order to see the prices people had to download an app and scan a barcode. The barcode was a link to a video showing how the animals were treated before the products were made.

By showing people the horrible conditions animals have to endure just to make pretty shoes or a belt, PETA is making people think twice about their fashion choices. Cruelty is never sexy.

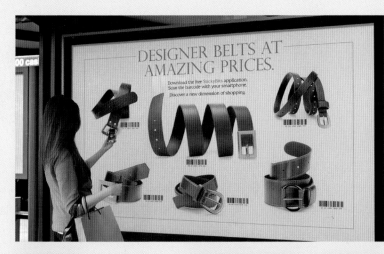

Joaquin Phoenix
for **PeTA**

and so is what they suffer.

while being led to the slaughterhouse.

KNOW THE REAL PRICE.
SHOP RESPONSIBLY.

Visit petaasiapacific.com to learn more
about cruelty-free shopping.

PeTA

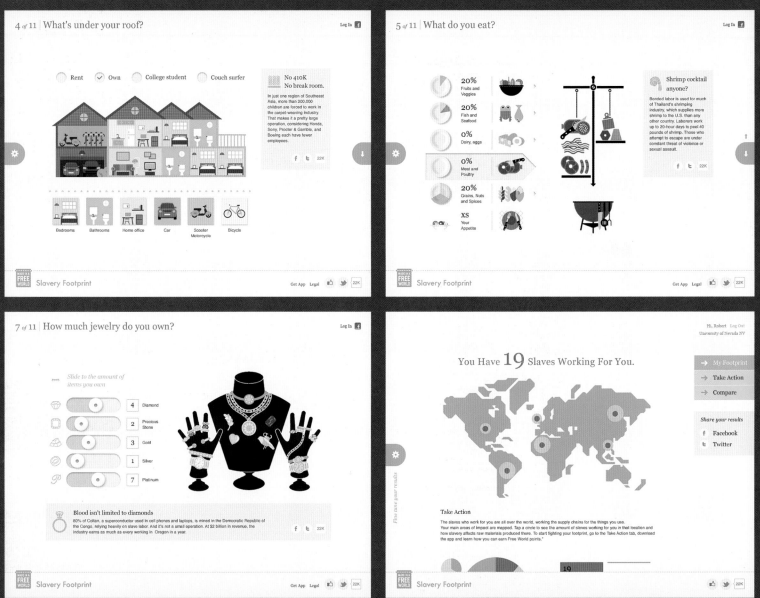

CALL + RESPONSE
Muhtayzik Hoffer, San Francisco
THE SLAVERY FOOTPRINT

Call + Response is an organization that aims to educate people about economic slavery and the shocking conditions under which some products are manufactured. On their Slavery Footprint website you can take a survey that estimates how many slaves you have 'working for you'. As you fill out the survey, you are provided with facts about economic slavery along the way.

There is also a mobile app called 'Made in a Free World', that allows users to enter the name of a brand and look at how ethical, labour-wise, the brand's supply chain is. It checks in on Facebook at two places at once — the store and the brand. These check-ins then appear on 1,000 Facebook pages that have been built to show the slavery impact of various brands. The app then lets users send a note directly to the brands saying, 'I want to know about slavery in the supply chain'.

This note is also posted to Twitter so brands will pick it up as they monitor social media. In addition, the campaign is partnered with MTV in the US to see which university can earn the most Free World Points, awarded for choosing more ethically sourced products.

By creating an interesting, engaging way to give consumers information, this campaign deals with a serious subject in a way that lets people know they can be part of the solution. The aim of the Made in a Free World label is to become a product label like Fairtrade or WindMade — to show which products are made under good working conditions. In the first two months alone more than two million consumers took the survey. This is not the last we have seen of the Made in a Free World label.

 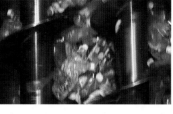  

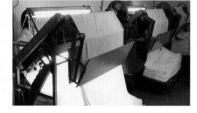   

The national team kits represent an important step in the process to make all Nike products more sustainable.

NIKE

NIKE
BOTTLE T-SHIRT

In a responsible and committed move, Nike rethought the material used to make their soccer jerseys for the 2010 FIFA World Cup in South Africa. They used recycled polyester made from plastic water bottles – up to eight bottles were used per jersey. To make these 2010 national team kits, Nike's fabric suppliers sourced plastic bottles from landfill sites in Japan and Taiwan and then melted them down in order to produce the yarn that was ultimately used for the jerseys.

By doing this, Nike managed to reduce their energy consumption by 30% compared to manufacturing virgin polyester and they prevented just under 13 million plastic bottles from going to landfill sites. This is the equivalent of around 254,000 kg of plastic waste, which could cover 29 football pitches.

This commitment from Nike to produce more responsible apparel is something that can only resonate positively with their audience. Brand moves like this are difficult to fault and do great work to get people believing in your brand promise and environmental commitment. Your brand wins and the planet wins too.

CONNECTION

CONNECTION
How close can you get?

The power of making a personal connection

'A grape stuck in my throat. I couldn't breathe. It was really scary. But I knew a grown-up would help me. Who was clever at first aid. Who knew that all I needed was some hard slaps on the back. Because grown-ups always know what to do. Don't they?' This is the body copy from a print ad for St John Ambulance accompanied by a lack-and-white picture of a girl with closed eyes and her name, Abigail West 2005–2010). The story is fictional, but it places you in the middle of a situation where you could make the difference between a life lost or a life saved: if only you had known first aid. Too often people don't donate because they feel their contribution doesn't matter or don't vote because they don't believe in the weight of their voice. A personal story is a powerful tool to make you realize that your personal contribution or lack of contribution makes a difference. You can place yourself in another person's shoes.

One face helps people to relate to your campaign

Thousands of people being killed by war or starvation in Africa is merely unfortunate, yet one person dying in a car accident down the road is a tragedy. We seem to be able to relate more easily to our neighbour down the road than to 1,000 faceless Africans – whether this is good or bad. This is also true of how the press mostly reports stories based on what is near and dear to us. Unlike a soulless statistic, you can feel and relate to an individual. When margarine brand Flora was running a campaign in South Africa to create awareness about heart disease they wanted people to know that choosing their low cholesterol product was a way of lowering the risk. They didn't focus on the statistics of the high number of deaths, but on an average bloke called Wally: '…a successful 52-year-old businessman, happily married with two children and two beautiful grandchildren. I enjoy playing golf and am a self-confessed sport fanatic.' In talk shows, magazines and blogs South Africans got to learn about Wally and his struggles to change his bad habits and fight off heart disease. When he had to undergo a heart bypass operation the nation tuned in on live TV – a world first. Through Wally's personal story Flora created empathy and understanding towards sufferers of heart disease that resonated with millions of South Africans.

Turn your story into their story

There have never been more opportunities to show what you as a consumer like and don't like, from the Facebook 'like' and Google '+1' buttons to reviews and comments left about a book, movie or travel experience. We humans are social animals and we like to show off who we are and what we stand for, which also explains the success of the Toyota Prius with its iconic eco design that immediately announces to other drivers that there is a green halo over the driver. For the same

'The Difference', St John Ambulance, BBH, London (see page 55)

I was at the pool.
I slipped.
I banged my head.
Blacked out.
Luckily, Dad was there.
I'd be OK.
Dad would know first aid.
He'd know to lie me on my side.
Keep me breathing.

But Dad didn't know.

SAMUEL SHAW ... 2000-2010

You can be the difference between life.
And death.
To find out how search 'life saved'.

% of the world's plant and animal species could be wiped out by global warming by 2050

reason, it's important for brands to think about how their story can be part of their consumers' personal story – how they can connect with each other – whether it's 'I'm eco-fashion conscious' or 'My body is my temple'. The story has to be easy to share, so that it becomes part of the self-portrait people are constantly painting for others to see. For the same reason getting personal has become a commonly used tool in initiatives such as pink breast cancer ribbons or donation programmes in which you receive a personal certificate showing your plot of saved rainforest as a thank you.

Another example is The American Red Cross, which has created a Foursquare Blood Donor badge, allowing blood donors to show their dedication to their online pals – and also help raise awareness about the cause. A similar tactic was used during the Tour de France cycle race when Nike launched a support programme for cyclist Lance Armstrong's cancer foundation Livestrong. Supporters of the campaign could write a personal message on a campaign site and, if chosen, it would be chalked on the very road the riders rode on. One of the messages of support read: 'Pain is temporary. Quitting lasts forever. F. Dreyer!' The personal message was not only shown to the supporters' cyclist idols, but was also televized for the whole world to see: a personal contribution gone global.

Put your audience in the story

What's stronger and more personal than making your story about the person you're trying to reach? Remember the anxiety you felt when reading the St John Ambulance ad at the beginning of this chapter. Online games are a way of amplifying that effect by turning your target group into the main character of a story. One example is Barclays' 56 Sage Street, in which young people can take on roles navigating through economic hazards and learn to save money. The online platform is fundamentally interactive, so you can tell complex stories and still make them compelling, personal and charged with a strong sense of personal responsibility. Banking and money management for young people aren't easy or, for that matter, particularly sexy topics, but the interactive personally driven narrative hooks you in. Another potent and personal medium is the mobile phone, which unfortunately is still to see a powerful creative thrust, but the quality of work is improving all the time.

Clearly communicate your brand's values and beliefs

In the global marketplace consumers have more freedom to choose the brand or cause that matches their values and what they stand for rather than the brand or homeless shelter that happens to be on their street corner. This will drive a development towards more personal brands that strive to deliver a personal experience, a personal service or

IT'S ALMOST LIKE HAVING A CHILD OF YOUR OWN

The Sponsor a Child programme, initially introduced by Save the Children in the 1930s, has spread around the world and evolved along the way. A regular cash donation given to a child in the developing world is rewarded with different levels of personalization such as pictures of the donor child and regular letters. Who has the heart to bail out of that?

a personalized product. In the Transparency chapter I also touch on a trend towards brands using social media such as blogs or Twitter to be more transparent, as well as more personal. It's a must, especially when you're dealing with issues we all care about such as cancer, or what's in our food or our children's food. Enter into a dialogue with people, show them that you care, make them heard and turn them into collaborators. It's a chance to get really close and you'll learn a lot from what they tweet or comment. Your cause becomes their cause.

Connect like-minded people through your campaign

This development has been pushed further by digital media that have revolutionized not only how we connect with others, but also how we can now reach more people all over the world. In the social media campaigns I've worked on over the years I've noticed that if people take an active part in a campaign then not only do they become more attached to a campaign or cause, but they also become connected to each other. With the explosion of the digital realm, nearness is measured less in kilometres and more in the importance of shared values and interests.

A truly personal campaign resonates with many like-minded people, and this is a chance to connect people with people. In the Nike 'Chalkbot' campaign, people would receive a picture of their chalked message

'Team Hoyt', TV3 Spinal Cord and Brain Injury
Telethon, Bassat Ogilvy, Barcelona (see page 58)

'Support Scent', Guide Dogs Australia,
Clemenger BBDO, Melbourne (see page 61)

and GPS coordinates of the location so they could easily share this information with others online. This encouraged them to support the Livestrong initiative. This is exactly what you want: a friend giving another friend a recommendation. It's no surprise that a Nielsen Global Online Consumer survey from 2009 found that the most trusted channel of communication was real friends: 90% of consumers surveyed trust recommendations from people they know. Campaigns should always have a person-to-person dimension and make it easy for people to connect. Andreas Dahlquist, Vice Chairman and Executive Creative Director at McCann Erickson, New York, and the man behind the digital blockbuster 'The Fun Theory', shared this point with me, 'Think social more than digital; how to connect people to people and create some real value in the process.'

The potential of personalization

The potential of a personal strategy brought alive on a digital platform is exciting: the potential scope and reach is mind blowing. You can touch millions of like-minded individuals living very different lives. It's also going to be a lot of fun to see where personalization will be taken in the future. Not only is data about you and me increasingly collected to personalize the web, but digital technology is also increasingly integrated in our cars, houses and even in our food packaging. What good can that connectedness and data not be used for? But don't get lost in technology because, as the St John's Ambulance ad and the Flora case demonstrate, good advertising is always about great ideas that touch people and get them to realize that their actions make a difference. Or as Wally said, after surviving his heart operation, 'Bad habits catch up with you later in life, so don't think, "It can never happen to me!" I hope sharing my story with you will help you make changes in your life today!'

YOUR PERSONAL BEAUTY STATEMENT ON A BILLBOARD

As part of the 'Campaign for Real Beauty', Dove asked women and girls to give their personal perspective on different beauty issues such as 'What makes you feel beautiful?' The answers, submitted via Twitter or SMS, will be featured on a large-format screen at London's Victoria Station, which has an estimated footfall of 350,000 people every day.

Interview
ANDREAS DAHLQUIST

//

We want to support companies that create growth without draining Earth's resources for the future.

//

Andreas Dahlquist was the Executive Creative Director of DDB, Stockholm when it produced Volkswagen's much-loved 'The Fun Theory'. He is now Vice Chairman and Executive Creative Director at McCann Erickson, New York. As the head of an agency spearheading the digital revolution and breaking new ground, he very kindly took the time to speak to me about the digital space, goodvertising and just what it is that can make people change their behaviour. I have been fortunate enough to work with him in the past through the DDB, Copenhagen office.

As with many of the other people I've spoken to, one of the big issues raised is honesty. Advertising can no longer be marketing's shady cousin, offering impossible deals out of a trench coat. It seems we are moving to a place where consumers are expecting more out of advertising, and that can only be a good thing. This two-pronged challenge: that advertising is no longer a disruptive medium and that it needs to offer something of real, honest value at the same time it is something that advertising professionals should ignore at their peril.

We began by talking about the DDB Stockholm office and just what it is that enables them to produce such good work. Andreas stressed the importance of seeing advertising as more than just advertising – understanding that it can broaden the scope of what is possible. **'I think a lot has to do with identifying and attracting the right talent with the right mindset and creating a culture where people feel that they can realize their potential. We have always been very conscious about putting creativity at the centre of everything we do. That might sound a bit clichéd but I honestly think that this industry gravitates towards identifying a formula for what we do and how we do it. First of all there is no formula, and secondly, that really puts a limit on how you can leverage creativity. Creativity in our field, to me, is about problem solving...about understanding how to generate business. And it can come in any shape or form: product development, added services, applications, new inventions, different collaborations, commercials, ads and so on. I think this way of thinking has guided our agency for a long time and, as we witnessed the collapse of the old distribution systems, we found ourselves operating in a world where we truly needed to earn the liking of individuals before we were really off to a flying start.'**

At the same time, Andreas talks about the importance of new ideas and how to make them come to life in an industry that can at times be more restrictive than people think. **'I always fight for ideas I believe in. Also, people tend to judge ideas from what they already know and if you really want to create something new you need to defend those ideas. And on a bigger note, I think it's time to really put** creativity back in the driver's seat in this industry again. We're leaving an age in which knowledge was the most valued asset and entering a new age where innovation and creativity will be the real key to differentiation.' As consumers become more savvy and sophisticated, it's up to us to meet their needs – and Andreas definitely sees advertising as moving from disruption to a real value-adding medium.

The way Andreas sees it, and this is perhaps a more humble stance than that often taken in the US, is that advertising needs to earn the trust and respect of consumers. While earning that trust, he also sees brands and advertising as being able to give people something tangible. **'As a brand I think you really need to earn your place with people. One way of doing it is, of course, entertainment, but there are many others; thinking in terms of creating utility is becoming increasingly successful.'**

When it comes to the digital realm, Andreas reminds us all not to see it as an adjunct to what we are doing, but as a great way for people to share content with each other. It's just up to us to create content that is exciting enough to share – such as 'The Fun Theory', which is the most viral campaign ever. **'Don't wait until you have "figured it out". Everyone is struggling. To a large extent it's a brand new world and there are no rules. And don't treat digital as an add-on. Think social more than digital: how to connect people to people and create some real value in the process.'** When it comes to trying to create something great he has the following advice: **'In general I think the whole notion of mixing two things you didn't necessarily think of as a perfect match to make an interesting new thing is driving a lot of the innovation in many areas at the moment. Mash-up – seeing new possibilities in mixing already existing things.'**

On the subject of social responsibility, Andreas has some interesting insights. Coming from a country as socially forward-thinking as Sweden, he has some great ideas. **'I think we are moving into an area where everyone needs to take on the responsibilities... And when we as individuals accept that responsibility then we don't accept that profit-making companies don't do the same. I think what many people in the post-industrial world are looking for and hoping to see is sustainable growth. We want to support companies that create growth without draining Earth's resources for the future.'**

Moving on from social responsibility, we found ourselves speaking about greenwashing: how to avoid it and one of the cornerstones of the entire advertising for good movement: transparency. **'I think you can't get away with greenwashing in the long run. Everything is far too transparent and the consumers are indeed very capable of making**

that judgment. But I guess it is a good thing to try to eliminate in every possible way the brands that are not honest in their sustainable approach.' The point to be made again is that transparency is not a threat, but rather an opportunity. Brands that are honest are brands that will be successful.

Andreas has a really positive view about consumers, too, something that comes as a breath of fresh air. When I asked him whether the same level of incentivizing and, in some ways, 'gamifying' life, such as we see in 'The Fun Theory' are going to become necessary for consumers to make the right decision, he said he didn't think so. **'No, I think products and campaigns that aim on adding to the world is incentive enough.'**

I hope he's right.

AMNESTY INTERNATIONAL
TBWA, Paris
SIGNATURES

In this award-winning animated film from 2007 we see people in dangerous situations being saved by the power of a signature. As they are just about to be tortured, executed or even run over by a tank they are saved by a signature. A signature becomes a hole through which they can dive and lose their pursuers, or a signature becomes a balloon, so they can float up and away, over the battlefield.

This film succeeds not only in its concept, but also in its execution. The animation is superb, and by taking the signature and making it something so powerful Amnesty International is sending a very strong message. They are confronting the apathy many of us have felt: 'What difference is my signature really going to make?' Amnesty International shows us that, yes, signing a petition can make a difference.

It seems that sometimes all we need is a reminder that our own small contribution can make a difference, and this film gets that message across very well. Amnesty International has always been an organization that relies on the power of signatures and petitions, and here we can see how looking back at their past and their function results in a powerful piece of communication.

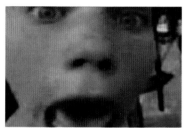

THINK!
Leo Burnett, London
CAMERAPHONE

Think! is a road safety charity run by
the government in the UK. This ad was
one of the first to be shot entirely on
a cameraphone – and it has proved to
be one of the most powerful. It shows
a group of teenagers walking down
the street, having fun, but when they
cross the road, without paying
attention, one of the boys is hit by a car
and flies through the air. The ad ends
with the sounds of the boy's friends
screaming as they run towards him.

Originally this ad was seeded on
the Internet without any branding and
it quickly spread through the network
of teen phones in the country – they
thought it was footage of a real
accident. Only after a week did a
branded version launch on TV and in
the cinema.

By using a medium that teens were
used to interacting with, Think! ensured
that they were spoken to personally.
Speaking to them in a language they
understand means that the message
becomes easier to retain and act on. In
the first week alone, this film garnered
150,000 hits. Research also went on to
show that nine out of ten teenagers
who saw the film said they would pay
more attention when crossing the road.

KINDERTAFEL DUSSELDORF
Ogilvy & Mather, Düsseldorf
DONATE A MEAL

This website for Kindertafel Düsseldorf
acts as an awareness campaign and
as a method of securing donations.
Website users can drag different foods
onto a plate to feed hungry and poor
children in Düsseldorf. Each food type
has a specific monetary value and at the
end users are asked to donate the cost
of the food they have put on the plate.
To encourage you to donate more, there
are some really sad-looking kids holding
up the plates.

This method of 'interactive
donations' makes donations much
more tangible. In a similar fashion
to the Rainbow Warrior website by
Greenpeace (page 25) you can see what
your money can buy. This example also
personalizes the problem facing these
children – it's hard to deny a child
staring up at you.

The simplicity of the campaign also
works in its favour. Users do not have
to take in anything very complicated –
they drag food to a plate and are then
encouraged to donate the corresponding
amount. Simplicity is in some ways
a form of responsibility – by breaking it
down, you make it easier for consumers
to take in the information and then
act on it.

SPENDE EIN ESSEN
Online Spende der Düsseldorfer Kindertafel

DÜSSELDORFER TAFEL   KINDERTAFEL   WEITERSAGEN   TELLERGALERIE   DEIN SPENDEBETRAG

3,80 €

Weiter zur Spende ›

HOME | PROJEKTE | TEAM | KONTAKT | IMPRESSUM | ENGLISH

45

CHILDREN OF THE WORLD
Contract Advertising,
New Delhi
HELP ME READ THIS

Children of the World created a classic piece of advertising of which Marshall McLuhan would have been proud – the medium, in this case, really is the message. With the insight that many of the street children in India who sell newspapers and magazines on street corners are illiterate, Children of the World played on that sad irony.

Tear-off, self-stamped envelopes were attached to each magazine with the simple message: 'help me read this'. The results showed how powerful the communication was: over 300 children were sponsored (a much greater number than in previous years). On top of that, Children of the World was also able to set up makeshift schools across New Delhi. Many people called in and then became volunteers for the programme.

This campaign tugs on the heartstrings and doesn't let go, all for a good cause. By encouraging

people to give their own time to help those in need, it succeeds at every level. When consumers give their time to collaborate with a brand or a cause such as this, someone is doing something right.

DEPAUL UK
Publicis, London
IHOBO

With the 'iHobo' app, Depaul UK, the UK's largest charity for young homeless people, increased awareness of the reasons why people can become homeless, the challenges that the homeless face and how best to help them in a responsible way. The idea of the app is that users look after a homeless person on their mobile phone for three days and try to keep him or her out of trouble. At all times of the day and night, your iHobo needs your attention and if you ignore him for too long he will spiral downwards into drug abuse and unhealthy living. If you ignore him for long enough he could even have an overdose and die.

This app also features in-app donations, a first for the iPhone. When people have spent three days with the 'iHobo' they are prompted to donate – one of the big objectives of the app is to make people aware that simply handing

a homeless person some change doesn't help. By making the problems of homelessness a personal experience for people, Depaul ensures that their message is taken to heart and acted on. Over 600,000 people have downloaded the 'iHobo' app so far, and Depaul's mission of educating people about homelessness has been greatly furthered.

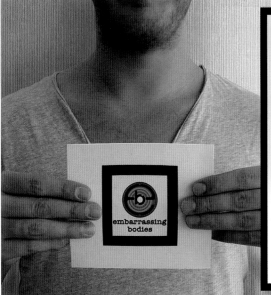

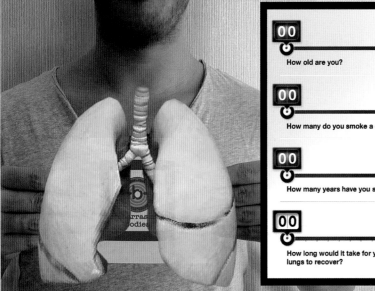

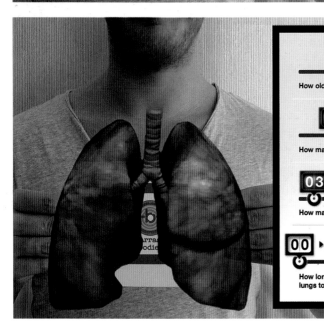

SAPIENTNITRO
AR LUNGS

This augmented reality app from SapientNitro takes the subject of lung disease and makes it painfully personal. Anyone with a webcam-enabled computer or a smartphone can take part – all they need to do is print out the augmented reality tag from the website and hold it over their chest. There are two sliders, one related to how many cigarettes you smoke in a day and one related to how long you have smoked. By moving this around, you can see what effect smoking has on your lungs.

By being so personal, with lungs superimposed over the viewer's chest, this campaign becomes so much more powerful than a Surgeon General's warning or an explicit photograph.

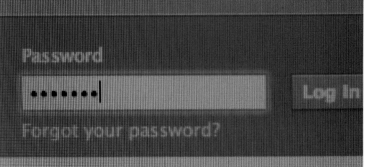

JASON ZADA
TAKE THIS LOLLIPOP

This interactive app from Jason Zada, a TV, digital and music director, highlights the dangers of sharing too much information on Facebook. By agreeing to 'take this lollipop', Facebook users are presented with a personalized video that shows a sweaty, crazy-looking man trawling through their Facebook profile. As he collects information, he sees more and more personal details used – even producing a map he uses to find out exactly where you live.

This deeply personal story shows users just how much information they make public on Facebook and encourages them to think twice before sharing too much. As social media becomes even more entrenched in our lives, privacy issues will become even more important. How much do you have available online for the general public to see?

SAVE THE CHILDREN
Lowe Brindfors, Stockholm
THE LOTTERY OF LIFE

In order to speak to an audience in the developed world, Save the Children introduced The Lottery of Life, which allowed users to see what kind of life they would have lived had they been born in a different country. Users of the site were immediately entered into a lottery and assigned a country. They were then given information about that country and the circumstances in which they would have grown up. This information could then be shared with the user's friends.

By personalizing the experience and giving information about what it would be like to be born in another country, The Lottery of Life forces users to see their lives in a different way. It also encourages them to donate to the Save the Children charity – getting people to imagine themselves in the shoes of another is a great way to get them to empathize. Over 380,000 people embraced the challenge.

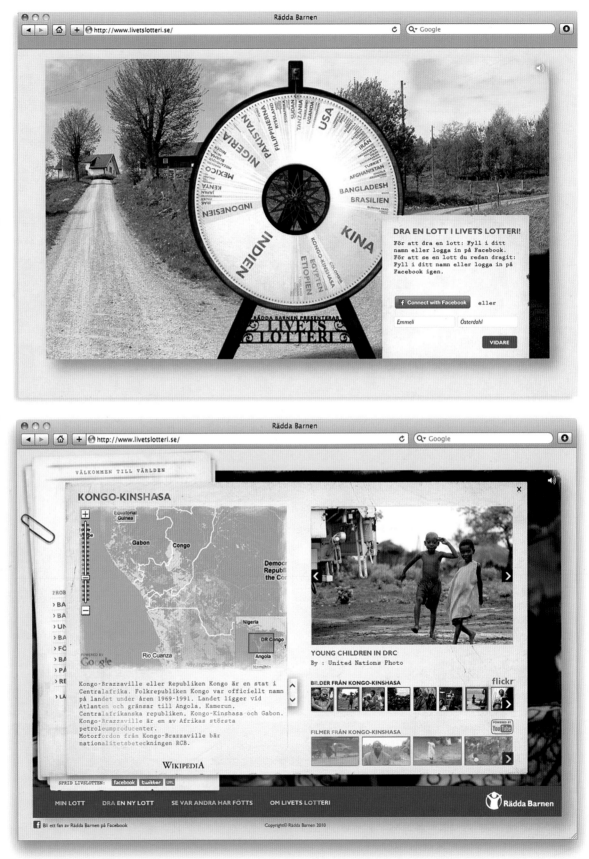

THEY'D LOVE TO MEET YOU

DRIVE DRY
A brandhouse INITIATIVE
DRIVEDRY.CO.ZA

BRANDHOUSE
FOXP2, Cape Town
LOVE TO MEET YOU

This campaign from Brandhouse, the South African alcoholic beverage company, provided a hard-hitting warning for those who still think that drinking and driving is OK. By using the horrors of the South African prison system, Brandhouse ensures that people will think twice before having a few drinks and getting behind the wheel.

South Africa's prisons are known for being overcrowded and for their frightening gangs, and Brandhouse reminds people of that without pulling any punches. The TV spots are filmed like a dating show, with the men describing what they look for in a partner. The camera then zooms out and we can see that they are in fact prisoners speaking about who they are hoping to share a cell with. Radio ads were written as love poems, pushing the point home. Covered in prison tattoos and leering menacingly, these guys are just waiting for someone to be caught for drunk driving.

Some campaigns encourage better behaviour by being positive and funny, while others do it by being personal and visceral – this campaign most certainly fits into the latter category.

OVK
Happiness Brussels, Brussels
LET IT RING

Even though speaking on a mobile phone while driving is dangerous and can lead to an accident, many people still do it. OVK, a charity for the parents of child road victims, wanted people in Belgium to realize the dangers. To do so, they partnered with Garage TV (Belgium's top video-sharing website) and showed people the direct results of their actions.

People could log on to a website and put in a friend's email address and telephone number. The person then received an email that shared the video link. The video, seemingly a typical online video, showed someone driving. While the video was playing, the viewer's phone would ring. If they answered the phone while watching the video they would cause the car in the video to crash.

By personalizing this experience, OVK has ensured that people can see the direct results of talking on the phone while driving. This creative execution also encourages users to share with others and within two weeks thousands of people had already tried it out.

NIKE
Wieden+Kennedy, Portland
CHALKBOT

With Chalkbot, an idea that followed on from Nike's Livestrong initiative spearheaded by Lance Armstrong, Nike showed their ongoing commitment to cancer survivors. Nike enabled people to send messages of encouragement to riders in the Tour de France – these messages were painted onto the roads on the route. Users could either upload their inspirational messages to a website or send them via text message. Where this campaign showed outstanding innovation, though, was the way in which these messages were handled. A robot was designed and built to apply the messages to the road. It then took a picture of each message with the time and GPS coordinates and sent it to the user.

Nike has always been known for its fighting spirit and the same goes for Lance Armstrong and his personal triumph over cancer. It's a reminder and message about what we as humans are capable of if we keep fighting and never lose hope. The campaign was very successful – over 36,000 messages were painted and over $4 million was raised for Livestrong.

A grape stuck in my throat.
I couldn't breathe. It was
really scary. But I knew a
grown-up would help me.
Who was clever at first aid.
Who knew that all I needed
was some hard slaps on the
back. Because grown-ups
always know what to do.
Don't they?

Abigail West 2005-2010

You can be the difference
between life. And death.
To find out how search 'life
saved'.

St John Ambulance
The difference.

THE DIFFERENCE

St John Ambulance, the UK's leading first aid charity, had an important message to convey – that, by applying simple first aid, situations that are potentially life threatening need not be so dangerous. In the UK alone, 150,000 people die every year because of a lack of first aid skills. Their challenge was to get this message across to the public.

Through a selection of powerfully shot and executed print ads they told the personal stories of five people who had died because no one in their vicinity knew basic first aid. Through first-person narratives readers were made aware of how tragic these stories were. Very often, the person who couldn't save them was a family member or someone close, enabling the readers to imagine themselves in the same situation.

As one of St John Ambulance's main aims is first aid training these ads encouraged people to learn more about how they could save lives and how they could be the difference between life and death. These ads also pointed readers to text a number to get themselves a free booklet about five common conditions that can easily be remedied with basic first aid in order to spread education and

St John Ambulance
The difference.

St John Ambulance
The difference.

2. CONNECTION

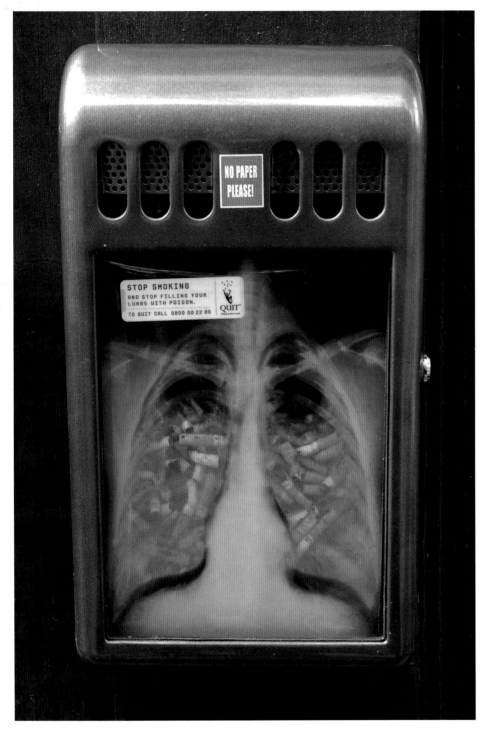

NO PAPER PLEASE!

STOP SMOKING
AND STOP FILLING YOUR
LUNGS WITH POISON.
TO QUIT CALL 0800 00 22 00
QUIT

QUIT
Saatchi & Saatchi, London
LUNGS X-RAY

As the smoking ban came into effect in the UK, cigarette disposal bins became commonplace. QUIT, an anti-smoking charity, took full advantage of this by cornering smokers while they were doing the very thing they were being encouraged to stop. As more cigarette butts and ash were thrown into the bins, the lungs on the bins began to fill up,

showing smokers just what was going into their lungs.

By personalizing the experience and showing consumers what goes into their lungs, this campaign forces them to think and hopefully encourages them to stop. Within the first week alone, calls to the QUIT helpline increased by 50% – proof that this approach works.

REMEMBER A CHARITY
DDB, London
ONE STUNTMAN, ONE LEGACY

Remember a Charity is an organization that encourages people to include charities as beneficiaries in their wills. According to their statistics, 74% of people give to charities during their lifetime, but only 7% of people leave money to charities in their wills. By their reckoning, if the number of people who gave to charity in their wills increased by just 4%, this could mean an extra £1 billion worth of funding for charities.

In order to make people aware of this, they enlisted the help of Rocky, who has been a stuntman since the 1980s. Their reasoning was that no one understands the importance of a will more than a stuntman. For his first stunt Rocky re-created one that had gone wrong early in his career – it had put him out of action for five years at the time. Fans on Facebook could vote how he should do the stunt and, thankfully, he did it with flying colours.

An unexpected idea like this creates a real buzz and a sense of involvement, making the story personal and encouraging people to do good while they are being entertained. It is also a great move away from the more traditional public service announcements (PSAs), which tend to rely on not much more than black-and-white film and a liberal dose of guilt. In the end, this angle worked very well and the campaign generated £1,280,189 of free broadcast PR, reaching an audience of over 83 million. On top of this, searches for 'Remember a Charity' doubled during awareness week and new visitors to the site were up fivefold on an average week. The ultimate goal was to encourage people to leave money to charity and it was successful in doing so – people who remembered the campaign were three times more likely to discuss leaving a legacy with their friends and family and just under 20% of people said they would leave a legacy after seeing the Rocky ads.

Like everyone else, my family and friends will always come first, but I think it would be great if more people, like me, choose to leave a little of what's left to their favourite charity — I know it would make a huge difference.

ROCKY TAYLOR, STUNTMAN

57

2. CONNECTION

Over the past 20 years, Rick Hoyt and his father have participated in over 900 endurance tests and 6 Ironmans.

Team Hoyt

December 19th
Fighting against spinal cord and brain injuries
905 11 50 50

TV3 SPINAL CORD AND BRAIN
INJURY TELETHON
Bassat Ogilvy, Barcelona
TEAM HOYT

To convince people of the importance of donating money to charities that support spinal cord and brain injuries in Spain, the Spinal Cord and Brain Injury Telethon on TV3 told the story of Team Hoyt. Team Hoyt is a father and son long-distance running team that consists of Dick Hoyt and his son Rick. As a result of oxygen starvation to Rick's brain at the time of his birth in 1962, he was diagnosed as a spastic quadriplegic.

Rick and Dick entered their first five-mile race in 1977, with Dick pushing Rick in a wheelchair. Since then, they have competed in over 1,000 races,

including marathons, duathlons and triathlons as well as six Ironman competitions. By covering this story and making it known, TV3 has created a powerful and uplifting piece of work that defies even the hardest hearted person not to be moved. By taking a problem that can feel abstract and making it very real, TV3 is eliciting a personal and powerful response from their target audience, showing them how important it is to donate.

Rick was once asked, if he could give his father one thing, what would it be. Rick responded, 'The thing I'd most like is for my dad to sit in the chair and I would push him for once.'

TEAM HOYT

58

FLORA
Lowe Bull, Cape Town
MEET WALLY'S HEART

Flora wanted to raise awareness about heart disease in South Africa, a country that has a growing obesity rate. Rather than bombard consumers with statistics and information about their low fat margarine, they decided to take a more personal approach. They found Wally Katzke, a man in his early fifties with a history of heart problems, and followed his journey. The story culminated in the live broadcast of his heart bypass surgery on national television.

This two-hour procedure was shown in its entirety as a video insert in the corner of viewers' screens while a panel of experts discussed cardiovascular health in easy-to-understand language. Prior to the procedure, Wally was also interviewed on a local talk show over a period of a few days, spreading awareness of heart disease and the importance of a healthy lifestyle.

This incredibly personal advertising experiment (is there anything more personal than literally looking *inside* someone's body?) not only succeeded in making people aware of the dangers of heart disease, but also helped save Wally's life. He recovered well and is currently living a healthy life and enjoying the time he spends with his family.

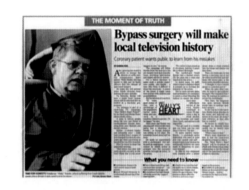

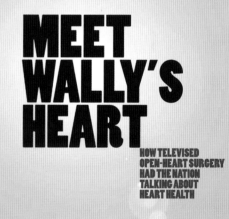

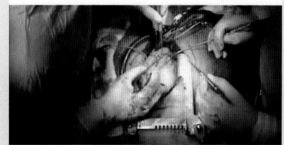

NZ TRANSPORT AGENCY
Clemenger BBDO, Wellington
SLEEP BEFORE YOU DRIVE

By replacing cars with beds, NZ Transport Agency reimagined the traditional car crash ads we have all seen before. These incongruous visuals pull the viewer in and demand his or her attention. We see people who have died in their beds, as if they were in a car accident. There are no pulled punches: we see the blood and the danger.

By personalizing this problem and showing that falling asleep at the wheel can be mortally dangerous, NZ Transport Agency made sure that people who see these ads will think twice before driving again when they are tired.

GUIDE DOGS AUSTRALIA
Clemenger BBDO, Melbourne
SUPPORT SCENT

Advertising is largely a visual medium, so how do you show your support for people who can't see? Guide Dogs Australia (GDA) came up with the perfect solution – to show your support for the blind through smell. People could buy a unisex scent to wear in public, so that blind people could recognize the people who were supporting them.

The goal was to reach women between the ages of 25 and 40, a part of the market that GDA had found difficult to engage with in the past. The results were very positive – the likelihood of supporting GDA within the target market increased by 18%. The fragrance was sold at KIT cosmetics stores across Australia for $5 and all the proceeds went to GDA.

This unexpected use of a medium shows just how much can be done in the field. Advertising a cause or advertising for good does not need to take place online, through print or via any other traditional medium. By allowing people to feel, and smell, that they were personally helping the blind, this campaign shows that anything can be a medium for advertising.

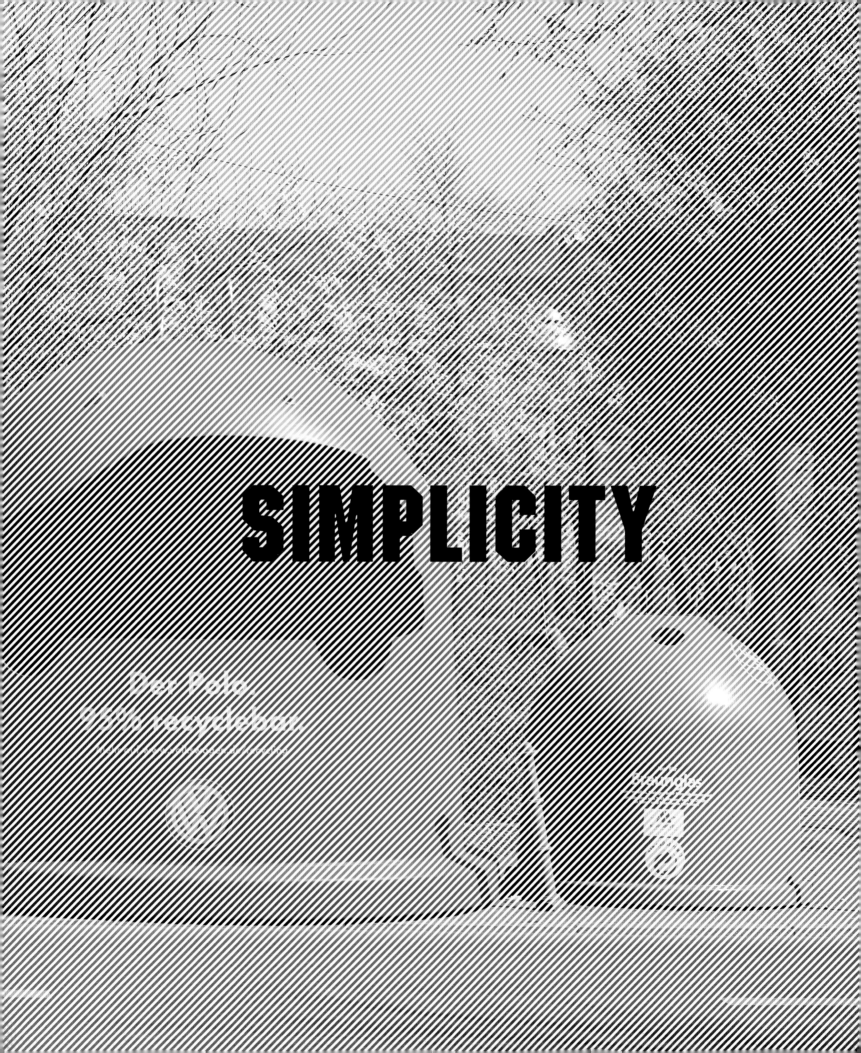

SIMPLICITY

3.

SIMPLICITY
Can it be done more simply?

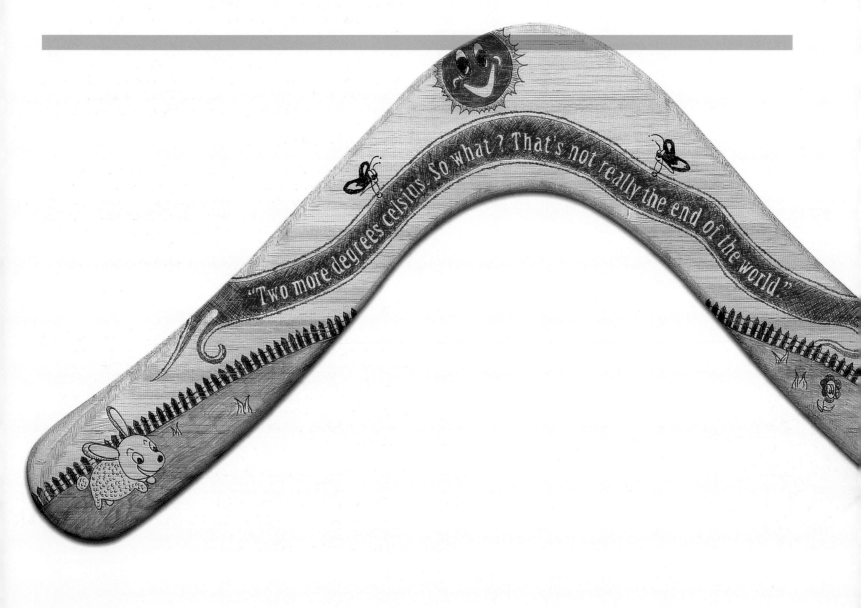

"Two more degrees celsius. So what? That's not really the end of the world."

'Boomerang', Greenpeace,
DDB, Paris (see page 74)

EINSTEIN SAID...

If you can't explain it simply, you don't understand it well enough.

In a complex world simple works

There is growing pressure on companies to be more accountable for their impact on the planet and on people, and the scope of this accountability is continuing to expand as science improves our understanding of the world around us. Consumers become enlightened and empowered, and governments raise the bar. On the other hand, consumers are drowning in information and choices – many supermarkets boast more than 30 types of toothpaste. Even the NGO sector is exploding, with well over 40,000 international NGOs recognized by the United Nations and hundreds of thousands on a national level. How do you make it easy for consumers to understand and support your cause or campaign? Siegel+Gale's Global Brand Simplicity Index from 2011 of 6,000 consumers around the world showed that almost half think their lives are more complex today than ten years ago. The same survey found that consumers are willing to pay 5–6% more for a simpler brand experience or interaction. If you want people to respond to your initiatives, simplicity is a way of making sure that your messages are actionable – that you close the gap between intent and behaviour.

Be as simple as a road sign

There is an increasing need for direction. Think of simplicity as road signage: turn left, hospital, road works ahead. Simplicity leaves out the details and communicates the single most important message. If you look at how Google and Yahoo tried to convey their message in the early years it's no wonder Google won the search battle. Google entered the market with just a search field where Yahoo had a search field and 190 links. Google peeled the redundant layers of information away for signage-like simplicity and the result was: search here.

Help simplify lives

Consumers want brands to make their life easier. In most companies there is a treasure chest of great initiatives hidden in a 120-page long CSR (Corporate Social Responsibility) report only seen by the people who get paid to read it – investors and journalists. Simplicity is translating something you don't understand into something comprehensible upon which you can act. I think one of Al Gore's greatest contributions to the climate debate has been his ability to simplify the crisis so that a broader audience can understand.

Thankfully, technology has also helped make it simpler to navigate the many choices available. Sites such as VolunteerMatch, Network for Good, JustGiving and GuideStar make it easier for consumers to work out exactly which causes they want to support and how. Recently Johnson & Johnson launched a similar initiative through an online widget that brings together everything from volunteering possibilities to ways to donate.

'Engineered for a Lower Impact on the
Environment', Fiat, Marcel, Paris (see page 76)

'It's Your Turn', WWF,
JWT, Singapore (see page 91)

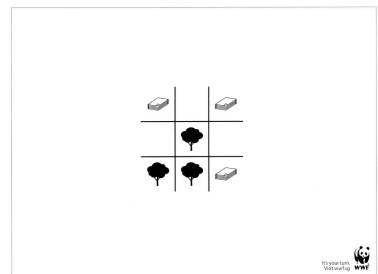

Many mobile apps can help make your life easier or encourage positive behavioural change, such as GE Healthcare's 'Morsel' app, which suggests simple and healthy daily tasks that can improve your life.

Trade comprehensiveness for action

The global retailer Tesco, whose headquarters are in the UK, added a picture of a plane to the packaging of products that weren't locally produced. It's not comprehensive, but it's a symbol that can easily guide a shopper. It's no coincidence that the most frequently recited health messages are a memorable formula such as '5 a day' or 'Exercise 20 minutes a day'. Too often sceptics complain about communication making environmental and social issues banal, but with the sheer amount of advertising messages out there, all demanding attention, you have to be simple. For example, have a look at Fiat's 'Engineered for a lower impact on the environment' ad, which portrays a test car crash and instead of a crash test dummy in the seat there's a Panda. It's a powerful image that transforms a factual message stating the car's low carbon emissions into a touching story of animal (and climate) rescue. What you lose in complexity, you win in effect.

Pick your concept wisely and be ruthlessly simple

There's a reason why simple donation schemes are so successful. For instance, TOMS Shoes: buy a pair of shoes and a disadvantaged child in South America gets a pair. Most successful campaigns have the same cunning simplicity, whether it's WWF's 'It's your turn' ads or Greenpeace's 'Boomerang' billboards. They succeed in communicating a complex message in a simple, insightful way. Simplicity demands more work and resources upfront as it takes time to peel the redundant layers of communication away, but pays off tenfold in the long run.

Begin with an idea or concept before choosing the media or message

Too often the message or media choice comes into the equation too early – making it impossible to simplify the message. Here is an example that cracked the code: 'Project Watch Your Drink' communicated to the very people who could be victims of a drug rape assault. At bars and clubs a cocktail umbrella was put into people's drinks. The umbrella stated: this is how easy it is to spike your drink. It was the right message, in the right place, at the right time, in the right situation. In their book *Marketing Public Health*, Michael Siegel and Lynne Doner Lotenberg refer to these situations as 'openings' and define them as 'the times, places, and situations when the audience will be most attentive to, and able to act on the message'.

Use simplicity to show responsibility

Simplicity is an opportunity that will reward those who get it and leave behind those who continue with business as usual. In a world where resources are scarce I don't need more blades on my razor or 30 brands of toothpaste from which to choose. Simplicity is a new kind of responsibility. I'm not the only one to feel guilty when I've unwrapped 110 grams of ham and thrown out an equal amount of packaging. Or am I? Puma's Clever Little Bag is a simple way of walking the talk of having less impact on the environment as well as less-is-more design wise. Another example is Häagen-Dazs Five which is an all-natural ice cream made out of only five ingredients: skimmed milk, cream, sugar, egg yolks and natural flavouring. It's a product label that is easy to understand and a product that consumers relate to for its days-of-yore simplicity.

Less is more responsible

People are asking themselves, 'Do I really need this?' and, rather than owning something, they are instead looking to share, rent or co-own. Why should everyone in the neighbourhood buy a lawnmower when they only use it once a week and could just as easily share one? Websites such as Neighborgoods, Freecycle and Neighborrow bring borrowers and lenders together – exchanging and sharing products and services. Many like-minded initiatives also exist. BMW and rental agent SIXT offer a car-sharing service called DriveNow across several German cities, and unlike similar programmes they make it easy for you – you can drop off the car wherever you want. Such initiatives are great opportunities for brands to show their responsible behaviour. Seize simplicity as responsibility.

Aim for a simple connection between brand and cause

Amnesty International's cause is human rights. Dove's is promoting real beauty. Volvo's is safety. It's important to remember that simplicity makes it easier for consumers to take in, retain and then act on a message or idea. If you're a brand such as Volvo, known for safety, how can you passionately campaign for safety? Traffic safety is obvious, but what about employee safety? What about safety from post-buying stress as with Hyundai's Assurance programme? During the economic recession Hyundai promised Americans that they could return their newly bought car if they got fired within a year of purchase.

Simplicity is one of the hardest disciplines to crack, but if done right it can be a powerful tool for change, turning communication into action. The world is complicated enough as it is and if you can make it simple for people to act or engage with your brand or cause, or even show people the way to a more simple and responsible life, you will definitely have loyal followers.

IT'S SIMPLE: TALK TO YOUR CUSTOMERS

Starbucks have educated their employees to become cause ambassadors and it makes sense. While I'm waiting for my coffee, I'm primed to hear about Fairtrade. Ensuring simplicity is as much about choosing your media wisely as it is about the message – and nothing beats the power of word of mouth.

Interview
MORTEN ALBAEK

Morten Albaek is a writer and an academic, and was a banker in a former life. He was the youngest ever Senior Vice President of Danske Bank, a leading bank in Northern Europe, but was dealt a life-changing blow when his father passed away at the age of 64 – Morten was just 32 at the time. He realized then that if he were to live as long as his father then he was already half way through his life. This made him reassess his life and what he wanted to do with the next 32 years; through coincidence, kismet or divine intervention he found himself in talks with Vestas. Soon after that he took a job as a Senior Vice President there. I was lucky enough to speak to him about 'WindMade', an ambitious new project from Vestas, his views on the business world and sustainability, and the challenges facing wind energy in the future.

We began by talking about WindMade, the first initiative of its kind to show customers which products are produced by wind energy and which aren't. WindMade is one of the first large-scale projects in this field that is at once generous, transparent and collaborative. Morten explains it as follows, **'WindMade is the world's first global consumer label for wind energy – or actually for any single energy source. The effort was spearheaded by Vestas, but was founded by a collection of global partners including the WWF, UN Global Compact, Bloomberg, PricewaterhouseCoopers, Lego and the Global Wind Energy Council. WindMade is not just a labelling programme, though – it is a movement. It is designed to catalyse markets for renewable energy above and beyond what the industry and the political system has managed to do to date. They want to give consumers a choice that they don't have when they go down to the supermarket in Delhi, Berlin, Sydney, Cape Town, Beijing, Rio or Portland – and that is to choose between a product that is produced by an energy source that is sustainable and not ruining the planet, namely wind, and a product that doesn't disclose what energy is used to produce it.'**

This is something that had been brewing at Vestas for a while. **'We started noticing a couple of trends a few of years back. The first trend had to do with our customers. Traditionally, we sell our wind power plants to utilities and large energy companies whose core business is to develop and sell energy. But we soon saw that non-traditional customers, mainly global corporations that were thoughtful about their energy footprint, were starting to invest in wind farms and become more active in energy procurement. The second trend we noticed was that the average global consumer was becoming more knowledgeable about the type of energy used to power their world. They wanted to know how their favourite products were made, including the type of energy used to produce them. It is like wanting to know nutritional information about the foods you choose to eat every day.'**

WindMade helps the brands we know and love tell this story to the global citizens who are ready to listen.

Vestas is spearheading a new type of capitalism, in which the entire industry is integral to success. By laying down their swords (for now) competitors in the wind energy game are working together to improve the entire industry and thus the world. Everyone wins on all levels – from financial growth through to knock-on effects for the environment. 'WindMade is designed to enhance the entire market for wind energy by activating new customer segments. Its success depends on creating a foundation of credibility and by building trust with the companies and consumers we want to involve. By creating an independent non-profit organization that has the support of our industry and other partners such as the UN and the world's most trusted environmental NGO, the WWF, we have created a much more powerful tool than just a traditional marketing label.'

The WindMade mark is not only designed to help consumers make more conscious choices, it also allows greater transparency. 'One of the key elements of WindMade is that it's clear and easy to understand. A consumer will know exactly what source of energy was used to make a product or to power a company. We have a strong belief that the model for WindMade will easily translate to other renewable industries and we definitely envisage a family of "clean-made" labels developing in the near future... WindMade and other "clean-made" products will have impacted the entire supply chains, changed the consciousness of consumers and helped lead to an increased supply of renewable energy to the world.'

At the launch in New York towards the end of 2011, WindMade had already been adopted by several leading companies, including Motorola Mobility, Deutsche Bank and Bloomberg. It seems as if WindMade is off to a promising start.

Vestas itself is proud to be one of the greenest companies in the world, with a large workforce that prides itself on passion and commitment. At the same time, they are all optimistic and fiercely positive. 'I, as well as my more-than-22,000 colleagues at Vestas, believe that mankind is born sensible and when sensible people are exposed to facts, information and new insights – in other words enlightened – their sensibility will be activated and their behaviour will change, and as a consequence the world will change... It is an incredible privilege and deeply inspiring to work in an organization where, due to the purity of what we do, the purposes of capitalism – efficiency and revenue and returns – and the core meaning of humanism, which is namely putting the wellbeing of people first and above anything else, are truly merged and interlinked.'

Despite Vestas's ardent belief in what they do they still encounter issues when dealing with the government and also in terms of the pace at which Vestas would like to grow. 'I believe that the lack of long-term, consistent policies from governments is really detrimental to swift progress in terms of the new energy future. People often talk about the subsidies for renewables, but in reality these are dramatically trumped by the subsidies of fossil fuel industries. How many people know that in 2009 and 2010 fossil fuels received approximately $400 billion in subsidies and renewables only $37 billion? It is hard to be competitive when we aren't competing on equal terms. Transparency into subsidies for all energy industries is drastically needed.'

With luck governments can address these issues, and hopefully the pressure to change can come from consumers. Morten thinks that consumers are the answer and that advertising has a big role to play in disseminating positive, empowering messages and maintaining honesty. 'It is clear that consumers want the trust, not just information that makes them feel good. Advertising will have to find a way to remain creative without deceiving consumers. It will have to offer creative transparency.'

At the end of our conversation I hear a sobering, pragmatic thought – one that tells me we will all be more like Morten in the future as we attempt to put right the wrongs we as mankind have done. 'I would much rather compete with other wind companies in a thriving wind market than in one that is non-existent.' Long may Morten and Vestas be competing.

% of girls say magazine models influence their idea of a perfect body shape

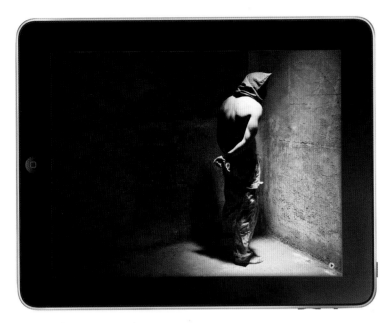

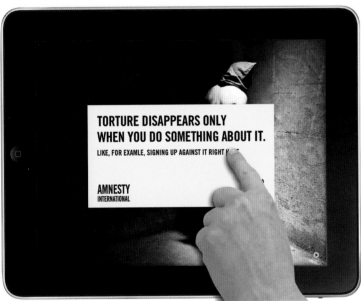

AMNESTY INTERNATIONAL
TBWA, Berlin
IPAD AD

In a bold use of the iPad's multi-touch functionality, this ad for Amnesty International shows you quite literally that human rights abuses cannot simply be wiped away. As these ads appeared in the tablet edition of *Die Welt*, a German publication, users would try and swipe them away to get to the next page. What the user found out was that the ad would only be disabled after repeated swipes: copy came up that reminded them that human rights abuses were not something just to be ignored or swept away.

By observing the way the iPad (and other tablets) work, Amnesty International has created an ad that has great impact. It breaks the experience of the user in a way that is hopefully not too annoying and should mean they retain the message. The simplicity of this ad also makes it powerful — there are no involved levels of meaning that users have to decode, it is just the action of wiping away abuse.

ASICS
Babel, São Paulo
BOOTS AGAINST RACISM

In a football mad country such as Brazil the professional players are incredibly famous, but football had become a staging ground for recurring racist demonstrations. ASICS wanted to send out a positive message, and found no better way than getting one of the most famous soccer stars in Brazil, Loco Abreu, to play a game of soccer while wearing a pair of boots where one boot was white and the other black.

ASICS placed just one newspaper advert on the day the match was being broadcast live across Brazil. The levels of fanaticism about football in Brazil meant the message was seen by millions of people across the country and was picked up online, spreading across blogs and news sources. This sent a powerful message that anybody who truly loves football will not stand for racism.

El Loco Abreu will play with these boots. Because racism shouldn't win.

sound mind, sound body

71

DEUTSCHE STIFTUNG
DENKMALSCHUTZ
Ogilvy & Mather, Frankfurt
BEGGING SCULPTURES

The German Foundation for Monument Protection (Deutsche Stiftung Denkmalschutz) was faced with a problem. Funding was dropping and the upkeep of cathedrals and sculptures was suffering. First people had to be made aware of the problem and then they had to be encouraged to donate.

In order to hammer the point home, replicas of the affected sculptures were made and put to work — begging. They were placed in subways and pedestrian underpasses, with a piece of cardboard asking for money for their historical monuments. The campaign worked incredibly well — not only was it unexpected, but it also increased donations to the German Foundation for Monument Protection by 40%.

By harnessing the power of the ambient medium (small-scale ideas that don't cost vast amounts of money, but can still reach large numbers of people), this campaign personalized the plight of monuments in an unexpected way. This is also an example of advertising that can turn a potentially dull subject into something engaging and exciting — something from which many fundraising campaigns could learn.

BRAILLELIGA
Duval Guillaume, Brussels
BLIND CALL

Brailleliga, a Belgian charity for the blind, came up with a simple, elegant and clever solution to a problem that plagues all of us. We've all been in the situation where our mobile phone is in a bag or a pocket, and it is unlocked. Invariably, it will end up calling the first number in our phone book. This means Aaron, Alice, Andrew or Arthur will get a call and be able to hear nothing but ambient noise, and we'll have to pay money for a call that went nowhere.

But what if those blind calls could be used to help the blind? Brailleliga gave people a number to put into their phones and asked them to save the contact as 'A Blind Call', which will generally put it as the first contact in a given list. Then, whenever a blind call was made by mistake the call costs would be donated to a charity for the blind.

This creative, yet simple, execution meant that people responded very positively. Every call logged donated no more than €0.75. Some of the thousands of people who called the line went as far as to phone it on purpose, just to donate money to the blind.

WATCHYOURDRINK.COM
TBWA, London
**DRUG RAPE AWARENESS
UMBRELLA**

This simple, effective and in some
ways downright scary idea for Project
Watchyourdrink.com shows how a very
small object can have a huge impact.
Finding an umbrella in your drink with
a printed message saying, 'This is how
easy it is...to spike your drink' shows
you just how easily it could happen if
you let your drink out of your sight.

One can only imagine the effect this
could have on you: the knot of fear in
your stomach as you search the bar,
wondering who managed to drop the
umbrella into your drink without you
noticing. Of course, this is the kind of
experience you would tell your friends
about too, spreading the message
cheaply and effectively.

WWF
Leo Burnett, Sydney
EARTH HOUR

Earth Hour began as an initiative for the WWF in Australia and has since become a worldwide phenomenon. It originated in Sydney in 2007 and is now observed in over 130 countries around the globe. Some of the most famous landmarks are turned into a communications platform as their lights are turned off to create awareness. This is a big statement since we are used to seeing these monuments bathed in light at all times.

People are asked to turn off their lights for one hour from 20:30 to 21:30 on the last Saturday of March every year as a show of solidarity. Businesses, homes and landmarks such as the pyramids of Giza, the Eiffel Tower in Paris, the Empire State Building in New York and Christ the Redeemer in Rio de Janeiro all have their lights turned off. By allowing people around the world to collaborate with Earth Hour and feel

they are making a difference, Earth Hour ensures that the buzz around the idea can continue to grow. Earth Hour is not just about turning off lights: all those who participate are encouraged to see it as a sign of their commitment to showing leadership and finding solutions to the environmental challenges facing our planet. It is the simplicity of this idea that makes it so creative – all it involves is turning off lights.

ENGINEERED FOR A LOWER IMPACT ON THE ENVIRONMENT
THE LOWEST CO$_2$ EMISSION CAR RANGE IN EUROPE

ENGINEERED FOR A LOWER IMPACT ON THE ENVIRONMENT
THE LOWEST CO$_2$ EMISSION CAR RANGE IN EUROPE

FIAT
Marcel, Paris
ENGINEERED FOR A LOWER IMPACT ON THE ENVIRONMENT

Fiat took a fairly standard image in car advertising and subverted it with visually arresting executions: using an endangered animal to drive the car.

Fiat is the industry leader in terms of having the lowest carbon emissions in the European car market. By taking this carbon emission statistic, something that can be a little dry and boring, and equating it with something emotional, such as an endangered species, a powerful message is created. With visually arresting executions like this, consumers will take on board the message that Fiat is environmentally responsible. This means Fiat drivers feel proud of their choice and encourages car-buyers to consider a Fiat.

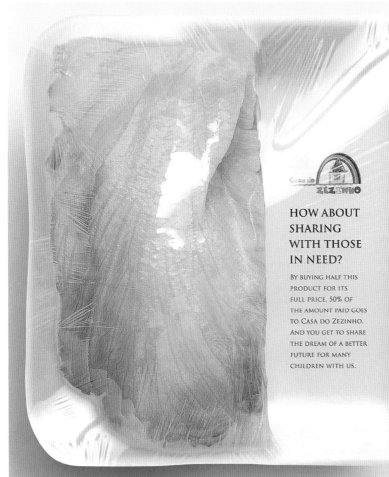

HOW ABOUT SHARING WITH THOSE IN NEED?

BY BUYING HALF THIS PRODUCT FOR ITS FULL PRICE, 50% OF THE AMOUNT PAID GOES TO CASA DO ZEZINHO. AND YOU GET TO SHARE THE DREAM OF A BETTER FUTURE FOR MANY CHILDREN WITH US.

CASA DO ZEZINHO
AlmapBBDO, São Paulo
HALF FOR HAPPINESS

This simple and powerful idea from Casa do Zezinho, a Brazilian NGO that focuses on low income areas, has such a strong impact in the supermarket that it cannot be ignored. Two local chains partnered with Casa do Zezinho to make this campaign happen and, with the help of children who benefited from the NGO's work, they cut various food items in half, but packaged them as usual. The supermarket chains provided the food, ensured the quality was up to standard and provided transportation and storage throughout the campaign. Customers shopping in these supermarkets were encouraged to buy half of what they would usually buy, but for the full price. The other half of the money was donated to Casa do Zezinho.

It is worth noting that these food items were displayed without any additional promotional material or communication, leaving the choice up to customers. And, by the end of each day, almost all of the halved products had been sold. On top of this, the campaign proved doubly effective, as donations to Casa do Zezinho were up 28% compared to the previous year.

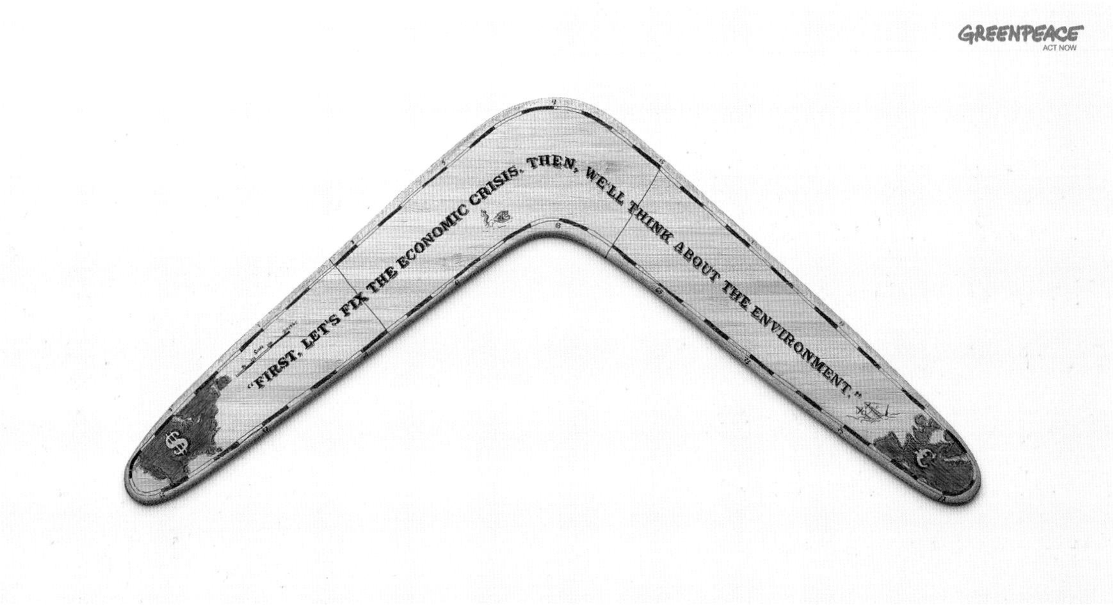

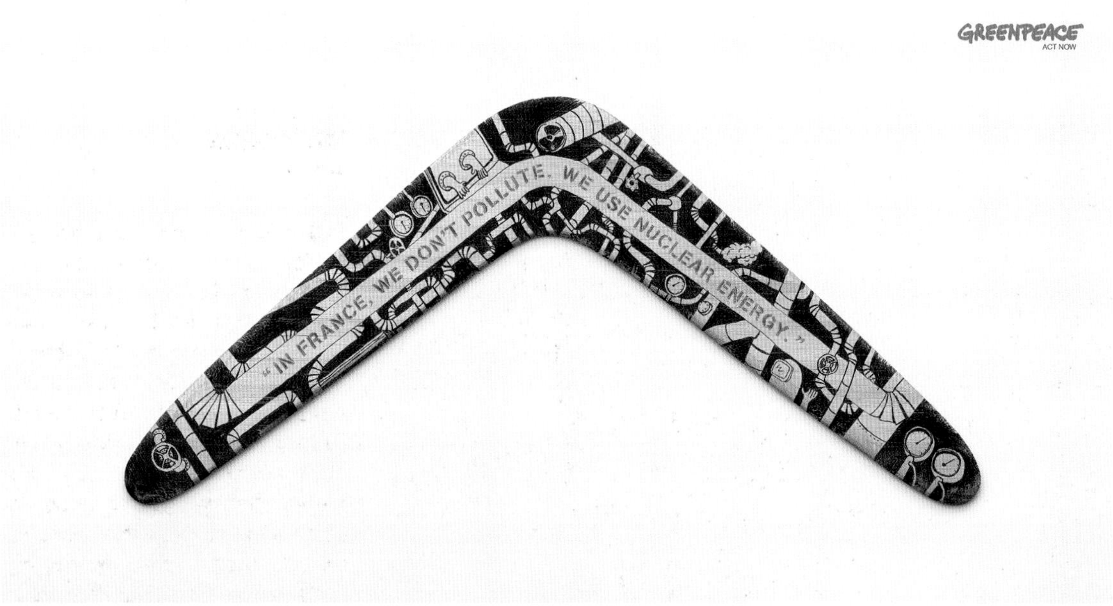

GREENPEACE
DDB, Paris
BOOMERANG

These billboards were created by Greenpeace in France to remind people that environmental apathy quite literally 'comes back to you'. By dealing with issues such as pollution, water usage, recycling and nuclear energy, these billboards provide consumers with something that is thought-provoking and visually interesting.

By being both insightful and simple, these executions speak directly to consumers and expose just how shortsighted climate ignorance really is. The messages on these boomerangs are feelings we have all felt or considered at some time or other. By personalizing such problems, Greenpeace makes it easier for consumers to act on them in a way that will be beneficial to the environment and to themselves.

The legalization of marriage for gay and lesbian couples in Vermont is certainly a step in the right direction, and something worth celebrating with peace, love — and plenty of ice cream.

WALT FREESE, FORMER CEO OF BEN & JERRY'S

BEN & JERRY'S
HUBBY HUBBY

To show their support for the passing of a law in Vermont that allowed same-sex marriage, and in partnership with the organization Freedom to Marry, Ben & Jerry's renamed their Chubby Hubby ice cream Hubby Hubby. For an entire month in Vermont, the renamed packaging featured the wedding of two men in tuxedos as opposed to the usual, plainer packaging. They also announced a special sundae that was available in their stores as part of the celebrations.

As a company that has always had a social conscience this was a great move for Ben & Jerry's — it showed people that they really care about social issues and are willing to speak out about them. The campaign generated massive buzz and press coverage, reaching an estimated 430 million consumers.

unicef❤
united states fund

DURING **WORLD WATER MONTH,** GO OUT TO EAT, DONATE A MINIMUM
OF $1 FOR TAP WATER, AND A CHILD IN NEED WILL HAVE 40 DAYS OF CLEAN WATER.

 unicef   **TAP PROJECT**

TO FIND A RESTAURANT OR DONATE NOW, UNICEFTAPPROJECT.ORG

UNICEF
Droga5, New York
TAP PROJECT

The UNICEF Tap Project started in 2007 as an initiative in New York. Restaurant goers were encouraged to donate $1 on World Water Day for a glass of tap water that would usually be free. All funds raised support UNICEF's efforts to bring clean and accessible water to millions of children around the world. Although this started in just one city on one day, it has now spread across all 50 states in the US with thousands of restaurants participating every year during the month of March.

By choosing to portray their message at a relevant time (when water is being ordered), UNICEF has ensured that they can encourage people to donate. If a glass of water is usually free and you are asked to pay just $1 for it, during one month a year, it is hard to refuse. This has proven to be a very powerful tactic – since its inception in 2007, the UNICEF Tap Project has raised just under $4 million. Just $1 can provide healthy water for a child in need for 40 days – the campaign has provided a lot of clean water for a lot of people.

It is the insight into human behaviour that makes this simple idea so successful – there is no real way that someone could justify not paying for a glass of water in these circumstances, especially when they consider how many free glasses they would have had in restaurants over the years. At the same time, this initiative benefits everyone – the consumer who wants to make a difference but doesn't want to put himself or herself out too much, the restaurants who can prove their dedication to making the world a better place, and the children who can drink clean water and live better lives as a result.

TROPICANA
DDB, Paris
ORANGE-POWERED BILLBOARD

After three months of meticulous planning and many, many oranges, Tropicana released the world's first orange-powered billboard. It had no connection to the power grid and was powered solely by the acidic juice from oranges connected with wires to zinc and copper electrodes.

This execution lives up to the promise of Tropicana orange juice – it's natural. It uses no electricity and does not have a negative environmental impact. This simple and creative idea ensures that it will be memorable in the minds of consumers too.

The challenge was to make the melting of ice caps relevant to children in a tropical part of India such as Kolkata. An ice cream seemed the most compelling medium to do this in a simple and engaging way. It was a demonstration that had an element of surprise and made children empathize with the issue immediately.

OGILVY

AICMED
Ogilvy, Kolkata
MELTDOWN

AICMED is an Indian NGO that focuses on environmental preservation. With this campaign they wanted to raise awareness among children about the climate crisis and the melting of the polar ice caps. In a simple and innovative move, AICMED partnered with Kolkata-based Rollick ice cream to produce special ice lollies.

Once children had eaten the ice lollies they could see a picture of a lifeless-looking polar bear with the message, 'When polar ice melts, they die. Stop global warming.' This made children aware of the crisis at an early age, hopefully starting on a path to live responsibly. As a result, 91% of all participating children promised to prevent global warming and over 300 children also joined AICMED as summer volunteers. Not bad for an ice cream.

Don't talk about it — do it.

KEMPERTRAUTMANN, HAMBURG

MISSING CHILDREN'S INITIATIVE
Kempertrautmann, Hamburg
GERMANY WILL FIND YOU

In Germany, 100,000 children and young people are reported missing every year. To raise awareness about the Missing Children's Initiative and to get the public involved, Mark van Bommel, the captain of Bayern Munich, ran on at the beginning of a match in 2011 without a child escort. Instead, he was carrying a poster with a picture of a missing girl and a link to the Missing Children's Initiative's website.

The match was broadcast live to 15 million people in over 40 countries and helped to give momentum to the 'Germany Will Find You' campaign. Since then, over 120,000 people have joined the campaign's Facebook page to show their support and to help find missing children. This proves that a simple, actionable message and a clever choice of media can be the best way to get a positive result.

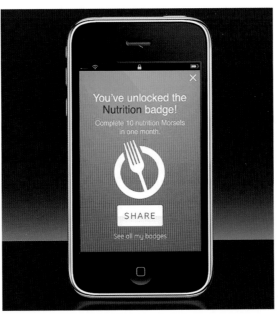

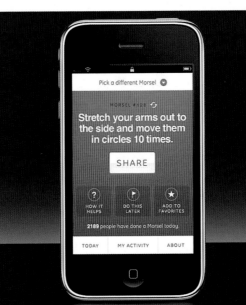

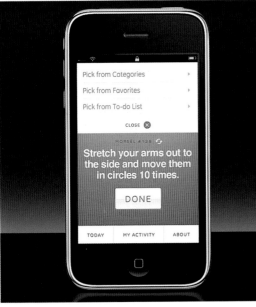

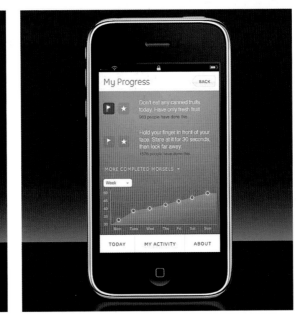

GENERAL ELECTRIC
Big Spaceship, New York
MORSEL

As part of their Healthymagination marketing thrust General Electric created the 'Morsel' mobile app, which encourages users to do one small thing per day that will contribute to their health. It can be anything, from having a good stretch to drinking a soothing cup of camomile tea or making a stir-fry with tofu as opposed to red meat. The idea is that by creating a collection of small things they can do, people using the app can live healthier, happier lives.

This is a simple initiative that reminds consumers constantly that General Electric is concerned about their wellbeing and overall health.

It always pays to remember that it's better to let consumers get involved and feel they are making a difference than to push marketing messages at them. This collaborative approach makes General Electric a brand that cares for consumers' wellbeing, one that consumers can partner with to make their lives better. To date, the website claims that over 350,000 morsels have been completed by users of the app. This adds up to a lot of healthy living.

The Polo. 95% recyclable.

VOLKSWAGEN
DDB, Berlin
THE CAR RECYCLING DROP BOX

Volkswagen had something to say about the new Polo – it is 95% recyclable. They needed to work out how best to show this and decided to make the world's first car recycling drop box. This stunt didn't actually allow people to recycle their cars, but a handy link pointed them to a website that taught them more about Volkswagen's eco-friendly recycling programme.

By putting an advertising message like this in this setting, Volkswagen did something very clever strategically.

Those who regularly visit recycling depots have a much higher chance of buying a car based on its recyclability, and with an unexpected and simple idea Volkswagen pushed consumer engagement. This is the type of campaign that gives consumers a 'smile in the mind', like all good traditional advertising, but in a non-traditional way.

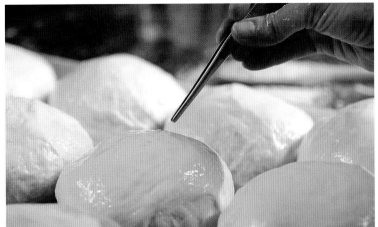

WIMPY
MetropolitanRepublic, Johannesburg
BRAILLE BURGERS

To make customers aware of the Braille menus available in all of their restaurants, Wimpy, a fast food chain from South Africa, started a viral campaign using hamburgers as their medium. Targeting the three largest institutions for the blind in South Africa, they delivered hamburgers to the people there, but they were hamburgers with a difference — the sesame seeds on the top of each burger bun spelled out a message in Braille. Each message was a description of the burger to help the recipients really 'see' their food. One of the messages reads: 100% pure beef burger made for you.

Wimpy estimates that through targeting these three institutions, with just 15 burgers, they reached in the region of 800,000 blind people across South Africa via Braille newsletters, screen-reader emails and word of mouth. Added to this is the positive halo seen by sighted people when they watch the campaign clip. Only the hardest of hearts could not be moved by this personal, emotional and creative campaign.

MCDONALD'S
Leo Burnett, Chicago
FRESH SALADS

In order to remind customers about the healthiness and freshness of their salads, McDonald's in Chicago decided to build a billboard that literally showed the quality of the produce. A vertical garden was created and planted with 16 different types of lettuce (all of which appear in McDonald's salads) and over a period of three weeks the billboard sprouted to spell out the words. During this period even sales of lettuce seeds went up in Chicago – proof of the impact of this ad.

Simple, effective and creative, this billboard encompasses what all outdoor advertising should be.

PUMA
Fuseproject, France
CLEVER LITTLE BAG

In an attempt to reduce their impact on the environment, Puma launched the Clever Little Bag in April 2010. After nearly two years of research and development, Puma, in conjunction with renowned industrial designer Yves Behar, were ready to show their new shoe packaging to the world. And in the end it wasn't a box at all – it was a bag.

The Clever Little Bag uses 65% less cardboard than traditional shoeboxes, has no laminated printing or tissue paper, takes up less space than traditional shoeboxes and weighs less, which means that shipping costs are cheaper. On top of that, it replaces the plastic retail bag, giving consumers a nifty little thing to carry on their arm.

Choosing bags rather than boxes not only reduces transport costs, but also reduces carbon emissions, electricity and water usage. No longer will muddy running shoes be such a burden to carry around. This bag strikes the perfect balance between desirability and environmental impact – it is something fashion-conscious people would be happy to be seen using, while still being kind to the environment. It also proves that Puma walks the talk when it comes to the environment, providing tangible results.

It's time we put boxes to good use, by not using them.

PUMA

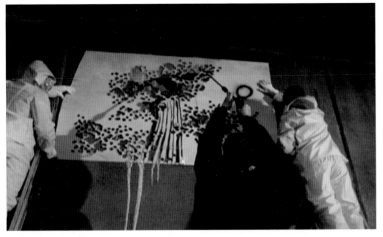

CLOROX GREEN WORKS
DDB West, San Francisco
THE REVERSE GRAFFITI PROJECT

How do you launch a 99% plant-based green cleaning brand in a way that shows your commitment to the cause, but still creates enough buzz? Clorox Green Works answered this question with the Reverse Graffiti Project in San Francisco. A 43-metre (140-foot) long section of wall at the entrance to San Francisco's Broadway tunnel was selectively cleaned in order to form a mural of indigenous plant life.

Both buzzworthy and a demonstration of the product's benefits, this execution succeeds brilliantly. The site is seen by 20,000 people every day as they pass by in traffic and it is still visible. Paul Curtis, the artist commissioned by Clorox to do the project, made a good point, 'Seeing how dirty a wall is by cleaning it in this way, it kind of gets people immediately.' Unfortunately, people are so used to seeing dirt

and grime in big cities that it's only by removing it that people can be made aware of it.

By doing something so closely related to their own product, Clorox Green Works has created a piece of advertising that is more than the sum of its parts.

LOTUS LIGHT CHARITY SOCIETY
Grey, Hong Kong
UMBRELLA BAGS

The Lotus Light Charity Society wanted to raise awareness about the shortage of water in Northwest China. They decided to put one of the symbols of Buddhism, the umbrella, to good use. Umbrella bags were placed in busy shopping centres, so that people could put their wet umbrellas in them. Printed on each bag was a message about the water shortage (most drinking water in the region is collected from rainwater), and images of a bowl, a cup or a bucket were seen to fill with water from the wet umbrellas.

Making shoppers aware that drops of water could help alleviate the drought in Northwest China led to such an increase in donations that more than 5,300 water cellars were built in 2009, benefiting over 20,000 people.

Getting a message across in a tangible and simple way makes it much easier for people to act on the information given. The thought that the water that came off your umbrella is the same amount one person would be able to drink for a whole day is more than enough to spur you into action. Or it should be.

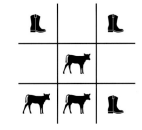

It's your turn.
Visit wwf.sg WWF

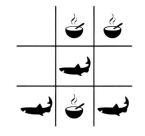

It's your turn.
Visit wwf.sg WWF

WWF
JWT, Singapore
IT'S YOUR TURN
▬

In these ads from the WWF we see
games of noughts and crosses (or
tic-tac-toe, depending on where you're
from) that highlight the consequences
of your choices or, as I like to put it,
the backstory. Calves play against
boots and crocodiles play against bags.
The WWF's message is simple: it's
your turn.

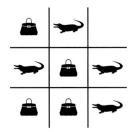

It's your turn.
Visit wwf.sg WWF

COLLABORATION

COLLABORATION
How can you work together?

Collective will

The environmental activist Al Gore makes an important point about the challenges ahead: 'It is now abundantly clear that we have at our fingertips all of the tools we need to solve the climate crisis. The only missing ingredient is collective will.' We are all in this rocking boat, whether you're a CEO of a large corporation, an employee or a worried mother – the threats and possibilities will affect your everyday life, from rising food and petrol prices to allergies affecting your children. This gives brands an opportunity to turn target groups into collaborators and work together towards a common goal.

This is not about you, but about us

You have probably sat next to someone at a dinner party who rambles on and on about him or herself. It doesn't work for people – and it doesn't work for brands. You have to move from self-interest to common interest. In the last decade collaborative models have been appearing everywhere, from sites such as Wikipedia, a user-generated encyclopedia, to eBay or Craigslist where buyers and sellers meet. It really shouldn't be such a strange notion – and the advantages for brands, people and the environment are indisputable.

Work together to solve common issues

Collaboration is rewarding in itself. Several scientists, among them Jonathan Haidt, professor of psychology at the University of Virginia, argue that natural selection is not only about survival of the fittest, but also about group competition: it is the most cooperative, altruistic group that wins and passes on their genes. Recent brain science adds to these findings and shows that altruism triggers a chemical reaction in the brain that rewards cooperative behaviour. You might recognize this feeling from playing team sports or giving a stranger a helping hand. If your brand can create a collaborative environment then the pros are many.

Brands should be looking for touchpoint issues where they can't solve the problem alone – so that through active participation from consumers one plus one equals three. Many products have a more harmful impact in the hands of consumers than when they are produced. A good example is Ariel's 'Turn to 30°' campaign. Procter & Gamble, the parent company, carried out product lifecycle analysis of washing detergents and found that 85% of the energy usage was at the hands of consumers. Not only did Ariel invent a washing detergent, Ariel Cool Clean, that could wash effectively at lower temperatures, but they also encouraged consumers to help the environment by turning their machine down to 30 degrees. A study later concluded that approximately 85% of UK consumers

claimed Ariel's campaign was the main reason they now washed at a lower temperature. The incentive in the campaign was the money consumers could save on energy, but the reward for Ariel was grateful (and loyal) consumers. A win for both parties.

Create a feeling of collaboration

Charlie Denson, President of the Nike brand, has spoken about the importance of shifting towards a collaborative approach: 'Consumers want to be part of a community, whether it's a digital community or a virtual community, or whether it's a physical community. They want to feel like they're part of something. They want to be engaged.' Nike has most definitely achieved that goal by launching their Nike+ platform, co-created with Apple, where runners can track and improve their running as well as meet, share and encourage other runners. It's not only about building a loyal following, it's also good business. Runners using Nike+ are more likely to buy Nike products and it is estimated that 40% of Nike+ members who didn't previously own a Nike product ended up buying one.

It reminds me of a story about a visit the American president John F. Kennedy made to the Cape Canaveral space station in the 1960s. On the tour Kennedy met someone in janitor's clothing and asked him, 'What is it you do here?' He replied, 'Make a living.' Kennedy met a second person dressed in janitor's clothing and asked him the same question. He replied, 'Mr President, I'm helping to put a man on the moon.' Such a feeling of togetherness is invaluable for a campaign.

Open up to your consumers and ask for their input

The most talked about campaigns at the moment use buzzwords such as crowdsurfing, crowdsourcing, crowdfunding or any other word that can follow the word crowd. It's all about collaboration – and asking people to help out. The coffee chain Starbucks has used crowdsourcing with much success to help develop new products and services. The online portal 'My Starbucks Idea' posed the question, 'You know better than anyone else what you want from Starbucks. So tell us. What's your Starbucks Idea?' In the first year alone 75,000 ideas were submitted and out of those 25 were implemented. Opening up for product development has not only made Starbucks one of the most admired brands on Facebook, but has also generated 25 ideas that resonate with the target group. Think about the costs if those 25 ideas had been found through traditional channels such as a research and development process with subsequent research and analysis to document the ideas' validity with the target group. Starbucks successfully combined a brilliantly engaging marketing initiative with product innovation, and the advantages tick many boxes.

BECOME A SOCIALLY CONSCIOUS MICRO INVESTOR

Crowd funding or micro finance uses the contribution of individuals to fund projects such as charity work or the making of upcoming bands' records. One such organization is Kiva where you can lend from as little as $25 to a charity project you like and get repaid if it is successful.

The input from your consumers is worth more than research

Crowdsourcing is also a brilliant way to increase the chances of a campaign's success. By inviting people to join the early stages, you can test different concepts before committing fully and you can build engagement. People tend to be much more passionate about campaigns they have had a say in shaping than about campaigns that are just pushed at them. If, for example, you are going to make a campaign encouraging people to reduce their use of plastic shopping bags, then it might be a good idea to ask for their opinion rather than just rely on traditional research. It might turn out that people actually think those shopping bags should be banished altogether, a sentiment that is growing in some countries.

There are some exciting initiatives around. Fiat Brazil took crowdsourcing to a new level when they not only engaged customers in the early stages of the campaign, but also invited them to participate in the entire process of building a car – from initial brainstorming to the finished product and marketing. The name of the car, the Mio, which means 'mine' in Italian, highlights the advantage of crowdsourcing – when you're part of something you feel a sense of ownership, and believe that your contribution matters. The car is just as much yours as it is Fiat's. The campaign line reads, 'A car to call your own.' What stronger relationship could you ask for in a campaign?

Be ambitious about what you can solve together

The jeans company Levi's also set out on a big mission they couldn't achieve alone: to transform an entire city. Under the appealing message, 'We are all workers', they helped revive the steel-mill town of Braddock, Pennsylvania, where the population of mainly blue-collar workers had hit hard times. Many had lost their jobs as production moved overseas. This campaign was not only intended to help Braddock, but also to turn its revival into a symbol of hope across the US. The city's mayor, John Fetterman, said, 'The level of services it's going to provide for the next 30 or 40 years – that's invaluable and priceless.' It might seem like good old philanthropy, but Levi's wasn't just giving money away – they were building a strong business case shown by an increase in sales of their Work Wear collection for men. A win for the cause and for the brand.

Create different levels of collaboration

It's important to consider how to create collaboration with graduated tasks. In any team or group there will always be people who are more involved than others, from the tag-along to the true activist. With the licensed cause marketing initiative Product (Red) the tag-along can simply buy a product and feel part of the club. The activist can part not only with cash, but also spare time, by participating in concerts and (RED) Nights, watching *The Lazarus Effect*, a documentary about HIV-positive people, and much more. Asking people for their time is a huge request and anyone doing so should always remember to answer the question: what's in it for them?

Tap into the trend of collaborative consumption

At no other time in history have so many people had such material wealth. This gives your brand an opportunity to bring forward sustainable solutions. Average consumers have so many possessions – clothing, microwaves, gaming consoles and golf bags – that they need attics, basements or even out-of-home storage. Even more stuff is thrown away and most products don't even last a year. Other products barely

get used. In most American households you'll find a power drill, but on average they're only used for 15 minutes throughout their entire lifetime. What a serious waste of resources! For the same reason, people are beginning to ask themselves, 'Do I really need this?'

The pioneering 'Common Threads Initiative' was launched in 2011 by Patagonia with the campaign line, 'Because the greenest product is the one that already exists.' They encourage consumers to take a pledge. Yvon Chouinard, Patagonia's founder and owner, explains the effort: 'This programme first asks customers to not buy something if they don't need it. If they do need it, we ask that they buy something that will last a long time – and to repair what breaks, reuse or resell whatever they don't wear any more. And, finally, recycle whatever's truly worn out.' This is also known as the five R's of sustainability: reduce, reuse, recycle, repair and reimagine. To further the effort, Patagonia has partnered up with eBay and opened a store where used Patagonia products can change hands.

The internet has made these new consumption models much easier and websites such as NeighborGoods, Freecycle and Neighborrow bring borrowers and lenders together to exchange and share products and services. Many like-minded initiatives also exist. Tool-sharing sites seem to be ballooning. Many brands, such as BMW and rental agent SIXT, who offer a car-sharing service called DriveNow across several German cities, see an opportunity and – unlike similar programmes – with DriveNow you can conveniently drop the car off wherever you want. Even when it comes to the short-lived 'must-haves' of the fashion industry, collaborative models such as Rent The Runway can be found. Brands have a great opportunity to encourage similar collaborative behaviour or consumption. Think about how you can be part of this movement either with existing products that can be reused, shared or lent out – or by inventing new ones.

The more the merrier

More brands today are breaking the traditional boundaries of competition, and working together to solve important problems that they couldn't solve alone. At its heart Product (Red) aims to bring companies and consumers together to put an end to HIV and AIDS. Brands joining Product (Red), such as Apple, are literally turning their products red to show their support. For every product sold, a certain amount of money goes to the cause. The clever use of the colour red is a benefit for companies as they can easily signal their social consciousness, and at the same time Product (Red) makes it easy for consumers to support a cause they believe in while also signalling their social conscience to their peers. You can almost hear the first sentence of a longer dialogue: why do you have a red iPod? What I like most about Product (Red) is how it succeeded in bringing companies together around the table instead of competing with each other. If more companies work together to find better solutions, the impact can be world changing.

If you want to go far, go together

Coming up with clever collaborative campaigns and strong community-based ideas or products is not just a task to be left on the table of a marketing director or left to the Corporate Social Responsibility department – it should be an all-encompassing business philosophy, internally as well as externally. The world's biggest company, retailer Walmart, is working together with suppliers to cut the amount of sugar, salt and trans fats in their food. They've also launched a Personal Sustainability Project where they encourage their employees to live healthily, including anything from quitting smoking to doing sports.

There is a growing movement all over the world, involving everyone from government leaders to business leaders to all of us, whose message is that we want to solve these problems, we want to be part of the solution. Now it's up to you to bring these forces of change together. I'll end this chapter introduction with an African proverb: if you want to go quickly, go alone. If you want to go far, go together.

Interview
HANNAH JONES

Hannah Jones, a major player in the world of brands and sustainability, is Vice President of Sustainable Business and Innovation at Nike. Her work with Nike has been groundbreaking, pushing the Oregon-based giant forwards into a sustainable future. First we talk about Hannah herself and her motivations for joining the business world – she studied philosophy and worked in the media industry before joining Nike.

'I saw that there was a role to be played within business, effecting change and helping businesses to look at their environmental and social impact in a different way.' It is this personal drive that makes Hannah so powerful in this field. 'I am profoundly concerned that we are not doing nearly enough to shift the way in which we run our lives, our communities and our economies in the face of scarce natural resources, climate change and social inequity. I have a huge sense of urgency about the need for change, and I see political systems failing us.'

When we speak about how she sees the future – because, let's be honest, we are not guaranteed a smooth ride in the next few years – Hannah offers a glimmer of hope. 'I'm a pessimistic optimist. I always believe in our capacity for change and innovation, but I am deeply concerned about how long it will take for us truly to change our behaviour and wake up. I am concerned it will take a huge disaster to which the systems will have to react.' I must agree with her: worldwide collapse is not the motivator we are looking for in this fight.

Moving on, we talk about where the responsibility lies in this issue – is it the public, the governments or the brands and corporations themselves who should step up? Again, we see that we are going to need to band together to face the coming problems. 'I think there's a collective responsibility to effect system change. Companies will need to decouple their growth from scarce natural resources. To do that, though, companies also need consumers, governments and civil society to effect change. So the real responsibility we all have is to collaborate in a very different way and all pull the levers we can best control or influence.' So the message is that if we all do what we can then we can make a difference. Hannah outlines how she sees it. 'Just doing one thing can make a difference – but depending on where you sit, what you do and the life you live it will be different. But if I had to highlight two things, they would be how we vote and how we consume. Using one's personal power to send a signal of intent is key.'

From there, we turn to the prickly issue of Nike's labour practice scandal in the 1990s. Hannah, admirably, owns up to it and speaks plainly. This embodies Nike's warrior spirit and shows how transparent Nike is willing to be. 'It was the start of our journey, and it was a pretty painful one. The accusations of using child and underpaid labour were the most visible, but there were many other issues about the way our business worked, from the way we sourced materials to the way we designed products, to the way we transported and sold them. Attacks made us vulnerable. And while being vulnerable was uncomfortable, it was also our greatest gift. It made us ask questions about ourselves. It made us change how we behaved, how we listened and how we collaborated. It led to a tidal wave of change that would revolutionize our business.'

This drive to be more sustainable, to lead the athletics market and to be the leading sportswear brand in the world is tempered by the pragmatic need to collaborate to improve our collective future. When asked about Nike's direct competition, Hannah says, 'Nike is on the offense, always. Our CEO always challenges us to measure our success against our potential and not against our competitors. And, in any case, we either win or lose together when it comes to sustainability, so we're intent on working with the rest of the industry to collaborate on effecting change… There is a time for competition, but when it comes to sustainability we see no conflict. These issues are far bigger than Nike. It will take the entire industry to render this current model of reliance on natural resources obsolete… If we can show that a successful company can also champion sustainability, it can help bring others in the industry along.'

Hannah continues, speaking about collaboration and generosity, 'We believe it's a company's responsibility to use the influence of its brand to drive towards a sustainable future. One of the symbols and engines of the old economy was patents. Your secrets were your own; they were your competitive advantage. We know that often this isn't true anymore. Nike believes it is our responsibility to share as much of our sustainability IP as we can to help fast track innovation. This is why we created GreenXchange and released 400 of our patents. This is why we released our Apparel Environmental Design Tool to the industry… A year later we have ten companies involved, including Google, Best Buy, IDEO and Yahoo. We are starting to hold "collaboratories" to bring academics, companies, NGOs and individuals together to start leveraging the IP.'

When it comes to sustainability and advertising for good, Hannah doesn't see it as a function of marketing, but as something that influences a company's entire structure. Transparency and sustainability are non-negotiable in this model. 'It goes beyond collaborating with the marketing department – Sustainable Business and Innovation (SB&I) is integrated into every aspect of the business at Nike. And it goes both ways: our brand marketing team integrates closely to

You'd better be buff if you're going to be naked.

amplify the work of SB&I. Nike Better World, our first consumer-facing message about Nike's SB&I work, is a good example of this… [It] is about speaking to consumers about our commitments. To thrive in a world where resources are constrained, where people and governments and systems are fully connected, where sustainability is an imperative, not a choice, and where transparency is requisite, we believe we need innovation. Disruptive, radical, jaw-dropping innovation. That kind of innovation is not going to come only from within. It will require the best of what we've got, along with unlikely partnerships, collaborations and open innovation with Nike's consumer base… Nike thinks about how we communicate with the consumer and the dialogue we want to have with them. We think about how our conversation needs to be rooted in authenticity, and reflect the work that is being done. So we don't talk about advertising for good or green marketing. We're not interested in proving our green credentials. We're interested in the conversation and whether it can be a vehicle for change and the building of a movement in its own right.' A view like this, where a large corporation admits its responsibility and wants to inspire change, makes me truly believe that together we will be able to overcome our current crisis.

Hannah leaves me with a final thought it would be criminal not to share. 'Transparency is the new inevitability. But to quote Don Tapscott, "You'd better be buff if you're going to be naked."'

FIAT
AKQA, London
ECO:DRIVE

Fiat has always been known for producing nippy and efficient cars and they also have the lowest carbon emissions of any car brand in Europe. With Fiat's move to green, their problem was finding a way to communicate this to young, digitally savvy consumers. Research found that many consumers felt they were being targeted as the root of the problem, yet in the majority of campaigns drivers were not given an active role in the process. As a result Fiat launched eco:Drive.

Eco:Drive enabled Fiat owners to use a USB stick to collect data drawn from more than 32 sensors in their cars. This data could then be transferred to the driver's personal computer, so they could analyse their driving and access tutorials on how to change their driving to save fuel.

Currently more than 53,000 drivers are using eco:Drive and together they

have saved 3.8 tons of CO_2. In addition, drivers have saved over £3 million worth of fuel. Fiat benefited too – eco:Drive has won 12 industry awards and generated over 7,000 press articles, the equivalent to a media spend of £10 million.

By simplifying a mass of information and making it easy for drivers to understand and change their behaviour, Fiat created something that enables drivers to collaborate with them to make the world a better place: a win for all stakeholders.

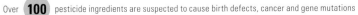

This is completely different to the usual design process, which is entirely hidden and secretive.

PETER FASSBENDER, MANAGER OF FIAT'S DESIGN CENTRE

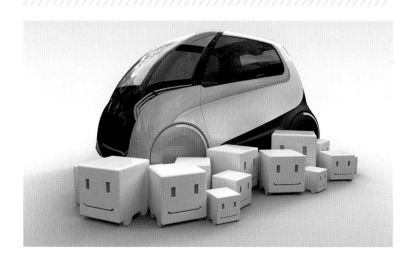

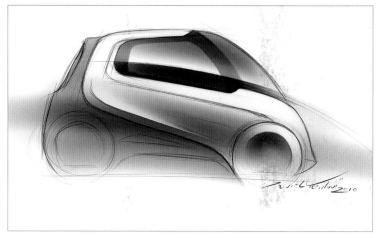

FIAT
AgenciaClick Isobar,
Rio de Janeiro
MIO

In a world first, Fiat Brazil opened up their entire car production process — from conception and design to execution — to the public, allowing consumers to be involved with the project by submitting ideas about what they wanted in a car. The Fiat design team built the car based on these ideas. By allowing consumers to collaborate with the brand, not only have they produced a car that people would like to own, but they have also actively engaged in meaningful conversations with their consumers, and continue to do so.

By September 2011 the Fiat Mio website had received over 2 million visitors, nearly 50,000 comments had been posted and over 10,000 ideas from 160 different countries had been submitted. These levels of engagement are unprecedented in the automotive world and show just how much people would like to be involved with brands and product development.

In late 2010, the first concept of the Mio was unveiled at the São Paulo motor show, showcasing the work of everyone who was involved in the project. It is uncertain whether Fiat will eventually produce the car, but as a branding and information gathering exercise it has worked immensely well.

Fiat can hear first hand what consumers are looking for in a car, while allowing them to feel that they can be a real part of the Fiat brand. The environment was unsurprisingly important to the people contributing — the Fiat Mio is an eco-friendly car, which is just 2.5 metres (8 ft) long, making it slightly shorter than the well-known Smart Fortwo.

LAFA
Ester, Stockholm
WHERE WILL 100,000 CONDOMS END UP?

LAFA (the Stockholm County Aids Prevention Programme) wanted to raise awareness about the increasing number of cases of AIDS in Stockholm, to change the associations people had with condoms and to prevent disease. Rather than focus on the negative aspects – if you don't wear a condom, you could have an unwanted child, contract an STD or die, they concentrated on the positive aspects. This campaign admitted that sex was fun in a way that was not sleazy, sexist or sordid.

100,000 free condoms were given away – each one individually numbered. People were encouraged to share their stories of how the condoms were used online in order to increase this feeling that using a condom can be something enjoyable rather than an annoying or embarrassing interruption.

The results were overwhelming. The blog that chronicled the stories of the condoms was visited by over 110,000 people from Stockholm (more than double the campaign goal). The campaign made 37% of the target audience more positive towards condoms and by July 2009 reported cases of chlamydia were down 13% compared to the previous year.

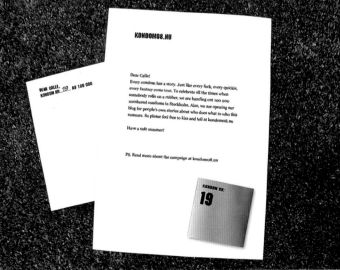

MCDONALD'S
Leo Burnett, Sydney
NATURE TRAYS

In order to reduce the amount of litter around McDonald's restaurants, McDonald's decided to put the problem in the hands of the consumer. Rather than the usual paper insert in their trays, various environmental scenes were printed on the paper. They showed consumers, quite literally, what their rubbish would look like if it was thrown away in the wild. The message immediately relayed how rubbish can ruin natural environments.

McDonald's aim was to reduce litter around their restaurants and in turn reduce complaints from residents in the surrounding areas. By collaborating with consumers they succeeded on both counts, with complaints from local residents dropping by 25%.

It pays to remember that many products can be more harmful in the hands of the consumer than in the hands of the producer.

LEVI'S
BBDO West, San Francisco
CARE FOR OUR PLANET

——

Levi's introduced the 'Care for our Planet' tag after realizing that a large part of the environmental impact of their products was at the hands of consumers. The care tags inside the garments encouraged the end-users of their products not only to wash their clothes at a lower temperature and line dry where possible, but also to donate their clothes to Goodwill once they were deemed used. Goodwill would then sell the clothes in its stores to help fund job-training programmes, community based programmes for people with disabilities and employment placement services. This initiative is good in two ways: it encourages end-users to consume fewer resources and to prolong the life of their clothes.

With the knowledge that nearly 24 billion pounds of clothing go into US landfills each year, Levi's realized that there was a gap in doing good. It is a shame to think that perfectly good clothes are left to rot and take up landfill space when there are people out there in need. This responsible consumption initiative from Levi's shows that they are on trend not only in terms of their fashion, but also in terms of their care for the planet.

By getting their consumers involved and allowing them to feel like they were part of the solution and not the problem, Levi's has done some powerful brand building. For a consumer to feel they are part of your brand is a great way to reinforce positive associations and hopefully do some good at the same time.

As a company, Levi Strauss & Co. is committed to building sustainability into everything we do.

JOHN ANDERSON, CEO OF LEVI STRAUSS & CO.

LEVI'S
Wieden+Kennedy, Portland
WE ARE ALL WORKERS

In this campaign from Levi's, we see the company returning to its original market offering – rough and ready workwear for the common man. Confronted with the battles of blue-collar America, Levi's decided to take on a battling steel town and turn it around with the help of the locals. Welcome to Braddock, Pennsylvania.

Levi's invested in the town to help it revive itself and used people who live there as models for their new workwear range. Levi's has found an unassailable position in the constant quest for credibility that many brands find themselves pursuing. Not only are they using real people, but they are also reminding everyone where they came from.

The practice of going back into a brand's history to find a truthful story is a powerful way to create great advertising that tells consumers the truth and can also do good. The stories we see played out across this campaign are honest, personal accounts of life in the Rust Belt – the industrialized states of the US that are now battling with poverty and a lack of work. What better way could there be to show your commitment to the working man than Levi's position?

GARNIER
Lodestar Um, Mumbai
100% RECYCLED NEWSPAPER

In order to educate India's growing youth population about environmental issues, Garnier launched the World's First Newspaper on 100% Recycled Newsprint in partnership with the *Times of India*. This campaign encouraged Indian youth to submit green and sustainable ideas to a dedicated website. For every idea submitted, Garnier would buy 10 kg of used paper. This paper was then used to produce a special edition of the *Times of India* made entirely from recycled paper. It was released on World Environment Day in 2010.

By engaging young people and encouraging them to collaborate with Garnier and the *Times of India*, Garnier allowed the youth to feel they were taking charge: that they were part of the solution. Environmental awareness was increased among the target audience (4.1 million youths participated in the campaign) and awareness of Garnier increased by 80%. This idea has now been taken on by Garnier in other countries, as a way to increase green awareness and encourage collaboration with their target audiences. Most importantly, over 5,000 ideas were

submitted, resulting in 50 tons of paper being recycled – the equivalent of 1,200 trees.

ENTEGA
DDB, Berlin
SNOWMEN AGAINST GLOBAL WARMING

Entega is Germany's second largest supplier of green energy, but they are not very well known. Their challenge was to achieve nationwide awareness of the Entega brand and their ethos – and on a small budget that did not allow the use of traditional media.

And so they did the unexpected – they encouraged the public to come and build snowmen as an awareness drive for global warming. Perhaps nothing could be a better symbol of the problem of global warming. People responded very well to the call – 20,000 people arrived to build snowmen and to collaborate with Entega. It gave Entega a chance to explain what they do and talk about the problems caused by global warming.

The event was so well received that the German government allowed the snowmen to stay for the entire winter. They had originally only agreed for the snowmen to be there for three days. As a result of this, the event was featured all over the German media and Entega's website unique visitor numbers increased by 300%. This case is so remarkable because it ticks so many boxes. People donated their own time to a cause that raised awareness for others and was not just about the cause itself, but also about a brand that has at its core the need to fight for that cause.

ELECTROLUX
Prime and United Minds, Stockholm
VAC FROM THE SEA

In an innovative initiative, Electrolux made five fully functioning vacuum cleaners from plastic garbage reclaimed from the sea. The purpose was to highlight the huge problem our seas face from pollution and garbage, and to raise awareness about the lack of recyclable plastics available on land. Built upon the base of Electrolux's UltraOne Green vacuum cleaner, made from 70% industrially recycled post-consumer plastics, this initiative not only raised awareness about plastic pollution, but also about the UltraOne Green.

Electrolux collaborated with local clean-up teams to create vacuum cleaners that represented the North Sea, the Indian Ocean, the Mediterranean Sea, the Pacific Ocean and the Baltic Sea.

According to Electrolux, this campaign has already reached over 250 million people and they hope to reach even more, touring the vacuum cleaners across the world.

By partnering with a cause in synergy with their market offering, Electrolux has created a very powerful piece of communication – their products clean your home and at the same time Electrolux cares about cleaning up the oceans. This initiative also proves that they walk their talk – if they had just written a cheque to get a tax write-off, somehow it wouldn't have the same impact.

By building and exhibiting a limited number of UltraOnes made from plastic debris such as shark-bitten bottles, we hope to highlight a pressing issue while breathing life into the subject of recycled plastic.

CECILIA NORD, VICE PRESIDENT, FLOOR CARE SUSTAINABILITY AND ENVIRONMENTAL AFFAIRS AT ELECTROLUX

5.

COMPASSION

Why are you in this world-bettering business?

The ice cream producer Häagen-Dazs is all about the 'finest and purest ingredients' and crafting them into the best ice cream, sorbet and frozen yoghurt ever. They are passionate about what they do, so when they launched their 'Help the Honey Bees' campaign to save the diminishing bee populations, they did it to guard the exact ingredients in their products. Fewer bees means less pollination, which means those ingredients that are so important to Häagen-Dazs won't be available. Selling ice cream is not that different from saving bees.

Align your passion with your compassion

For Häagen-Dazs there was a clear match between its passion, its product and the cause – and you believe their efforts to be genuine. Their passion matches their compassion. It feels right. Being perceived as passionate is about gut feeling, whether your consumers feel you are walking your talk. Always make sure to align your products, your brand and your passion with your compassion, otherwise your efforts won't ring true. Now think about Paris Hilton: does her support for breast cancer ring true?

In his book, *Start with Why*, Simon Sinek says you should start by answering a fundamental question: why are you in this business? His theory shows that successful brands and leaders communicate differently from the rest of us. They communicate from their heart and out, sharing the why, their vision, their philosophy and their passion before talking about facts and USPs (Unique Selling Propositions) as though they are important ingredients of a greater scheme.

Sinek argues that as consumers we don't buy what a company makes, but why they do it. Looking at Häagen-Dazs as an example, there are hundreds of different ice cream brands, so for me it really is no surprise that 'why you do it' matters more than the ice cream itself. As consumers expect your brand to make a difference for people and the planet, it simply changes how you should sell and position products. In the 1940s the concept of a Unique Selling Proposition was introduced, but as three toothpastes became 300, the idea of a USP has become diluted. Moving on from USPs, in the 1960s came the introduction of Emotional Selling Propositions (ESPs), which in my opinion helped to flesh out brands more than ever before.

In today's new, responsible market, I believe you should consider what I call Compassionate Selling Propositions (CSPs): how the real differentiator is the difference you want to make in people's lives, how you can prove to people that you care not only about them, but also about what they care about too. By doing this, brands add a powerfully beating heart to their pre-existing flesh and blood.

Opposite 'Problem Playground', Honda, Wieden+Kennedy, London (see pages 124–25)

'Grrr', Honda, Wieden+Kennedy, London (see page 127)

THE EMOTIONAL SELL

'What drives behavior in a complex world is emotion. Emotions are an important determinant of economic behavior, more so than rationality.'
Dr Daniel Kahneman, Nobel Prize winning economist

When a brand takes on a greater responsibility, consumers reward them with greater affection. It's all about standing up for what you believe in, even if you're standing alone. So ask yourself this question: why are you in this world-bettering business?

Hate something, change something

When Honda was working on its new series of diesel engines in 2003 it wasn't about just another engine in the making. The chief engine designer Kenichi Nagahiro went to work each morning with a clear philosophy: I should change things I hate – like diesels. The result was the new 2.2 i-CTDi diesel engine, known for its performance and quiet, clean operation – not what you would expect from a diesel engine. The quirky, animated 'Grrr' commercial with the lovely, catchy tune, 'Hate something, change something', reflected Nagahiro's passionate belief that this wasn't just another engine. Honda wasn't selling an engine, they were selling a passion, but moreover compassion for the world – they wanted to change the bad in this world to good. It's a philosophy, something I as a consumer can believe in and want to be part of. The 'Grrr' commercial became one of the most successful virals of the decade and was seen by millions. Would that have happened if Honda had communicated the superiority of the engine and how it could help you save fuel? Other campaigns from Honda such as 'Problem Playground' have followed by challenging environmental problems with a visionary and belief-driven take on life. I like this approach – it's more along the lines of 'we're working on it', rather than claiming world-bettering abilities, which for most car companies can be seen as a bit of a stretch. I don't doubt Honda's compassionate intentions because what they do is infused with value, belief and a world-bettering attitude.

Make your message feel right

Recent brain science has also found evidence that messages from brands that convey passion and emotion, rather than facts, have a greater chance of triggering a sale or a decision in favour of the brand. This is because emotional messages connect with a part of the limbic brain called the amygdala, which governs feelings such as trust, loyalty, fear and desire and, more importantly, decision-making, but not language. Factual messages, on the other hand, speak to the rational side of the brain: the prefrontal cortex. This is why when campaigns appeal to our rationality with messages such as 'save money on fuel' we have an easier time explaining our decision-making process in words, whereas when confronted with an emotional message there is seldom a better answer than 'it just feels right'. This is because the amygdala doesn't have a capacity for language. For that very same reason, passionate and compassionate brands are more successful – they target the decision-making part of the brain directly, if perhaps unknowingly.

Find your answer to the why question

If you can't answer that all-important 'why' question – few can – then think about how you can change step by step, from product to product, moving from rational facts to conveying compassion. Your brand is like a person, just as full of flaws, missed opportunities and possibilities as you and me. See it as a midlife crisis and take your time to find a good sea-facing bench and do some serious pondering. If your brand is not well known, see it as an advantage. If you're known for something bad, then remember Honda's catchy tune, 'Hate something, change something'. When the British retailer Marks and Spencer was faced with criticism and falling sales in the past decade, they succeeded in changing their ways, step by step. Nike were heavily criticized because of their

FROM SELF-INTEREST TO SHARED INTEREST

It's not just doing good that makes you a compassionate brand, otherwise the problems many brands face with CSR could be solved by simply writing a cheque to a charity. You have to go out of your way to prove to people that you're working in their interest instead of your brand's self-interest.

dubious labour conditions in the late 1980s and early 1990s and changed for the better – a journey that may have given them an early advantage over their competitors and means that today they are at the forefront of sustainable and responsible retailers.

Is your compassion genuinely anchored in your company?

Volkswagen isn't known as a compassionate, green company, but they, like Honda, launched their greenish initiatives with compassion – and success. 'The Fun Theory' campaign introduced Volkswagen's BlueMotion technology with the bold claim, 'We at VW believe doing the right thing should be fun' and consumers loved it. This was a refreshing message in a cluttered marketplace, with an aim to make a difference for all of us in a less boring way. Still, the European operations of VW have recently run into trouble for their anti-climate change lobbying and slow progress on fuel efficiency. Greenpeace is campaigning against them under the slogan, 'Join the rebellion and turn VW away from the dark side!' With Greenpeace's reference to the dark side in the film series *Star Wars*, it might be a lesson for VW that intentions are not always enough. Be sure that your compassionate vision is rooted in reality and remember to take one step at a time.

I don't want low emissions, I want a better planet

A global survey in 2010 from Edelman, the public relations agency, showed that the majority of consumers are buying into 'belief-driven' brands where a societal purpose is part of their DNA. The survey finds that, globally, 86% of consumers believe a business needs to place at least equal weight on the interests of society as on the interests of the business itself. This is an opportunity for brands to translate what they're passionate about into compassion. If you're not passionate about what

you do or the changes you want to make, how can you expect others to follow you? If you're not able to answer the 'why-are-you-in-the-making-the-world-better-business?' question then your intentions might not seem as deeply rooted as other brands. If your passion doesn't translate into compassion then your communication might risk being perceived as greenwashing. The more compassion you convey, the more affection you'll receive. As consumers, we are not as rational as we would like to believe. Science has proved that we make the majority of our decisions based on gut feeling and emotion rather than cold, hard facts. In other words, I'm not in the market to buy a car that emits just 133.7 g/km, I want a brand that aspires to make the world better.

'The Fun Theory', Volkswagen,
DDB, Stockholm (see page 120)

Interview
MIKE SCHALIT

We will never knowingly lie or create false promises, or deviously manipulate or pollute.

Mike Schalit began his advertising career by failing as a rock musician and, thankfully for the rest of us, has proven to be rather good at the whole advertising thing. Having never heard him rock out, I can't pass judgment on his face-melting ability, but his accolades in advertising speak for themselves. He is the Chief Creative Director of Net#work BBDO, one of South Africa's top advertising agencies. He has been named South Africa's best creative director for 11 consecutive years and even though he's been inducted into the South African Advertising Hall of Fame he is by no means done. Mike has recently started the MAL Foundation, a non-profit advertising agency that is perhaps the first of its kind in the whole world. He explained it further, **'So a few of us are taking some time out to explore some new ways to try find a way of repackaging our skills and our passion for ideas into a truly sustainable way of working. We've made our living courtesy of the ad world. So that's the skill set we're using to put something back into the world around us. In any case, doing good is good business. So whether we work with brands, communities, big environmental challenges or little everyday issues, this is hopefully a humble beginning towards a more sustainable future for us all.'**

From Mike's responses, I can see the way his mind works – how it pings from subject to subject. Coming from South Africa, a country with much work to be done in terms of helping the poor and where there is huge scope for brands to do good, Mike is incredibly passionate: **'Brands can make such a difference to communities. Enhancing lifestyles, inspiring ambition, fuelling growth and development. And then, talk about creating a real connection, people begin to vote with their feet (or was that pay packets?). Hello, brand ambassadors. As communities, in turn, then make such a difference to the growth of those brands, it is a self-perpetuating cycle of good that ensures** that there is a future. A sustainable one at that – for all.' I ask him about the poorest of the poor – whether worrying about the environment and sustainability is a developed world luxury. **'It all depends on where you are in the food chain. If I am hungry I will not give a shit about litter or recycling. But if I need electricity and it is cheaper and easier for me to get it via solar heating, bring it on, brother.'**

This leads us to talk about one of his works, the Nedbank solar-powered billboard, which was put up in 2007 and is still supplying a local school with power for their kitchens. **'It is still up and running now as we speak – 1,200 needy little ones are getting nourished, day in, day out. Nedbank is truly making things happen. Their ad is communicating and invigorating – powering the community *and* their brand. And there is another one now working just as hard for a Rehab Centre in the Cape Flats, harnessing wind turbines… We'd stumbled upon something and it isn't just caring, but daring. It's about changing things, making life better, with a cutting edge idea.'**

Talking to Mike about his agency I can see how important honesty is in this vanguard of responsible advertising. I love his wry answer when I ask him what work they will and won't do. **'We will never do cigarettes as they are addictive and kill. And my co-founder suffered the loss of a parent to the guiles of nicotine. We constantly evaluate everything else against honesty, transparency and the environment. We will never knowingly lie or create false promises, or deviously manipulate, or pollute. That is why, after 17 successful years, we are still a medium-sized agency. Viva to that.'**

When the conversation turns to advertising for good and saving South Africa (and, of course, the Earth), Mike has some great insights. **'It is actually your responsibility and mandate as a corporate citizen (to say nothing of your commitment as an individual) in South Africa to put something back into society. For the privilege of being part of building a vibrant new democracy, for the consciousness of making up for the baggage of an evil past – it's all part of creating a new balance, of redressing inequalities. The "haves" tipping the scales for the "have-nots".'** We move on to talk about who holds the responsibility for making the world a better place: governments, brands or people. **'Every single one of them – therein lies the real power to change things, when it becomes everyone's responsibility. It is a partnership. We all need each other. A "whole of society" approach is mandatory.'**

At the same time, it's important that any work that brands do is not needless philanthropy or empty giving. **'It's all about aligning the essence of the brand with the problem. What does a particular cause really need that our brand happens to offer? The strengths** of the brand and what the brand is actually able to deliver can then be leveraged to make a real difference… Imagine what could happen if more corporate social investment harnessed creativity to make a difference beyond short-term handouts and token charity. Inspiring the nation to change the future, enhancing the value of their very own brand whilst creating a sustainable link between brands with purpose and society.'** Mike makes a great point and it's something we are going to see proved time and time again in the future – doing good is good for business.

For those brands that still think they can get away with outdated practices and not caring about the consequences of their actions, Mike has the following warning, **'They will certainly lose the opportunity to create a very real competitive edge. A generous brand is a brand with purpose, it's a brand that genuinely touches people. Not exactly rocket science as to which brand will gain the loyalty and value at the till. And, of course, a brand that enhances communities is a brand that creates a sustainable future – for the people and itself.'**

To finish off, I think it would be best to quote Mike, in turn, quoting Winston Churchill, **'We make a living by what we get, we make a life by what we give.'**

CORONA
JWT, Madrid
GARBAGE HOTEL

In 2008, Corona launched the Save the Beach project to preserve one European beach each year. Building on this, they wanted to create something with a buzz that would remind people that if they didn't clean up after themselves then all the beaches across Europe would be full of garbage.

So, in a world first, Corona built a hotel made of garbage. The hotel opened its doors in Rome and then Madrid, using 12 tons of garbage collected from beaches across Europe. People could book a night in the hotel and then tell Corona about their experience. The idea gained serious traction and led to news coverage in 180 countries. The Danish supermodel Helena Christensen even spent a night in the hotel and shared her experiences and thoughts.

As a beer known for good times and beach party fun, Corona has strengthened their brand far beyond one or two lacklustre beach clean-ups. This campaign shows their compassion for the environment and was built on an idea that was powerful enough to be spoken about and shared all across the world.

The philosophy of this hotel is to expose the damage we are causing to the sea and the coastline… We live in the era of trash and we are running the risk of becoming trash ourselves. Do we really want this world?

H. A. SCHULT, ARTIST WHO DESIGNED THE HOTEL

One out of every three bites of food an average American eats is directly attributed to honey bee pollination.

HELPTHEHONEYBEES.COM

With Häagen-Dazs's 'Help the Honey Bees' campaign, the brand aligned itself with a cause that fits its offering: a great way to do good and build your brand at the same time.

The campaign addresses Colony Collapse Disorder (CCD): bees are mysteriously disappearing and leaving empty hives behind. As well as using honey, Häagen-Dazs uses fruits that are pollinated by bees, so it makes perfect sense for them to get behind the bees. They have shown how committed they are to this cause by creating a website full of information, a special ice cream whose the proceeds go to bees, and a Bee Board (composed of entomologists and specialists in CCD). The honey bee

issue has even been discussed in Congress in the US – a direct result of Häagen-Dazs's efforts.

By supporting a cause that is in synergy with their product, Häagen-Dazs does good and reinforces their offering to consumers at the same time. Every brand can find a cause to get behind. Without a doubt, food and water aid charities will always need funding, but who's going to save the bees?

Nature needs honey bees. We all do. After all, they're responsible for pollinating one third of all the foods we eat, like the cherries and pears that make our all-natural ice cream so delicious. But they're disappearing at an alarming rate. Learn how to help at helpthehoneybees.com
Häagen-Dazs® Vanilla Honey Bee

honey, please don't go

Häagen-Dazs
made like no other®

hd ❤ hb
Häagen-Dazs loves Honey Bees

VOLKSWAGEN
DDB, Stockholm
THE FUN THEORY

How do you get people to change their behaviour and do the right thing, especially when the right thing is a little bit more difficult than the usual way of doing things? The answer is to make it fun. This is exactly what Volkswagen did in Sweden. Through the implementation of four public interventions they showed that doing good can be fun too – that driving an eco-friendly car need not be dull. To begin with, 'The Fun Theory' installed the Piano Stairs, the Bottlebank Arcade and the World's Deepest Bin. They were documented and then turned into a viral campaign shared on YouTube. With the Piano Stairs, stairs in a busy station were rigged to play a tune as people walked up or down them, discouraging them from using the escalator or lift. The Bottlebank Arcade turned recycling into an old-school arcade game and the World's Deepest Bin made an amusing cartoon-like sound of something dropping deep into the earth.

The fourth execution was the Speed Camera Lottery, part of a competition for 'The Fun Theory' that asked consumers to submit their own ideas on how to make doing the right thing more fun. A normal speed camera documents all the drivers who are under the speed limit. Using the money collected from speeding fines a lottery was set up and a portion of the money collected was given to a random person who drove past the camera below the speed limit. Not only was this idea fun, but it also had a positive result – the number of people speeding on that road dropped by 15%.

This passionate approach was understandably good for business too – Volkswagen improved their market share in the eco market from 8% to 14.7%, an increase of 87%. And to top it off, sales of the Passat EcoFuel rose by 106%. In the end Volkswagen Sweden raised their share of the auto market from 10% to 13%. So how can you use fun to encourage your consumers to do the right thing?

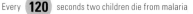

THE ZIMBABWEAN
TBWA\Hunt\Lascaris, Johannesburg
TRILLION DOLLAR CAMPAIGN

The *Zimbabwean* newspaper was set up in 2005 when journalists were exiled from Zimbabwe for reporting unfavourably on the Mugabe regime. The paper was produced outside the country to avoid government intervention, but in 2008 the Zimbabwean government placed a 55% luxury import duty on all newspapers produced outside the country in the hope of crushing The *Zimbabwean*. In order to get the newspaper (and the truth) into the hands of the Zimbabwean people, the paper had to be subsidized by people living outside Zimbabwe.

Rather than explaining the complicated reasons for Zimbabwe's collapse, the paper chose to use the most tangible, real result of Mugabe's mismanagement – the Zimbabwean dollar, which had been rendered worthless by inflation. By printing on Zimbabwean banknotes (some in denominations of 100 trillion dollars), they could show the world just how bad it had become. This resulted in trillions of dollars being handed out to the public and the first-ever billboards printed on money (which was still cheaper than printing on paper).

In the first week of the campaign alone, The *Zimbabwean* website received 2 million hits and raised awareness about Zimbabwe's financial plight. The import duty has since been lifted, but the newspaper is still produced outside the country and trucked in to avoid censorship by the Zimbabwean government.

BUNDABERG RUM
Leo Burnett, Sydney
WATERMARK

After Queensland in Australia was devastated by floods that started in December 2010, Bundaberg Rum, a stalwart of the Queensland landscape, stepped in to help. After their own distillery (which was situated in Queensland) was drained of the floodwaters, they set about making Watermark, a limited edition rum. It sold out within a week of going on sale, prompting a second run soon after.

In order to promote the rum and lift the spirits of the 4.5 million Queensland residents who had been affected by the floods, Bundaberg went to the 16 worst hit towns and put a watermark on the walls of the pubs. To launch Watermark, they also staged 16 music festivals in each of the areas, with festivities starting at midday on 16 April.

As a brand that is so intrinsically linked with the area from which it comes, this move from Bundaberg shows a dedication and compassion for Queensland that cannot be faulted or doubted for one second. All proceeds from the sale of Watermark went directly towards rebuilding Queensland, with an immeasurable boost to the way Australians see Bundaberg Rum.

When Watermark went on sale, people queued up for over 96 hours to buy it (this is longer than people queued for iPads).

LEO BURNETT

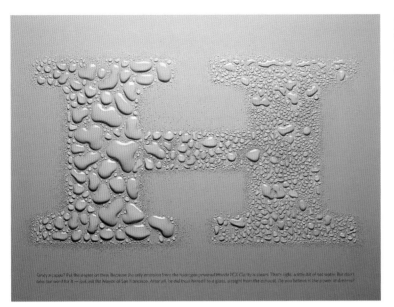

Fancy a cuppa? Put the engine on then. Because the only emission from the hydrogen-powered Honda FCX Clarity is steam. That's right, a little bit of hot water. But don't take our word for it — just ask the Mayor of San Francisco. After all, he did treat himself to a glass, straight from the exhaust. Do you believe in the power of dreams?

HONDA
Wieden+Kennedy, London
H

To let the public know about their new hydrogen-powered vehicle, Honda released this print advert, telling people that the only emissions from the car were hot water and steam.

The simple execution and snappy copy reminded consumers of Honda's belief in innovation and caring for the environment. This ad plainly shows Honda's commitment to and passion for 'The Power of Dreams'. If you are a brand who does good then there is nothing wrong with letting people know about it.

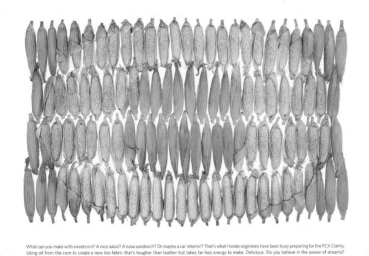

What can you make with sweetcorn? A nice salad? A tuna sandwich? Or maybe a car interior? That's what Honda engineers have been busy preparing for the FCX Clarity. Using oil from the corn to create a new bio-fabric that's tougher than leather but takes far less energy to make. Delicious. Do you believe in the power of dreams?

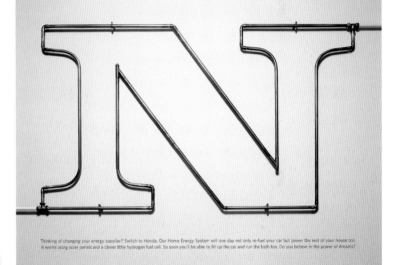

Thinking of changing your energy supplier? Switch to Honda. Our Home Energy System will one day not only re-fuel your car but power the rest of your house too. It works using solar panels and a clever little hydrogen fuel cell. So soon you'll be able to fill up the car and run the bath too. Do you believe in the power of dreams?

Dinner for 3 billion guests. Where do you start? Rice is good, especially as it forms the staple part of half the world's diet. Problem is rice plants are prone to wind damage. So Honda engineers have grown a shorter, hardier version, which means bigger harvests and fewer people going hungry. Do you believe in the power of dreams?

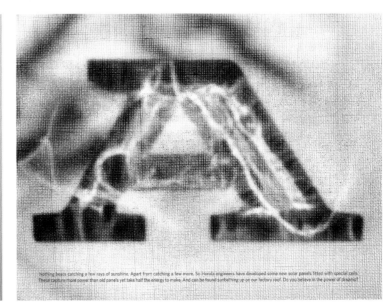

Nothing beats catching a few rays of sunshine. Apart from catching a few more. So Honda engineers have developed some new solar panels fitted with special cells. These capture more power than old panels yet take half the energy to make. And can be found sunbathing up on our factory roof. Do you believe in the power of dreams?

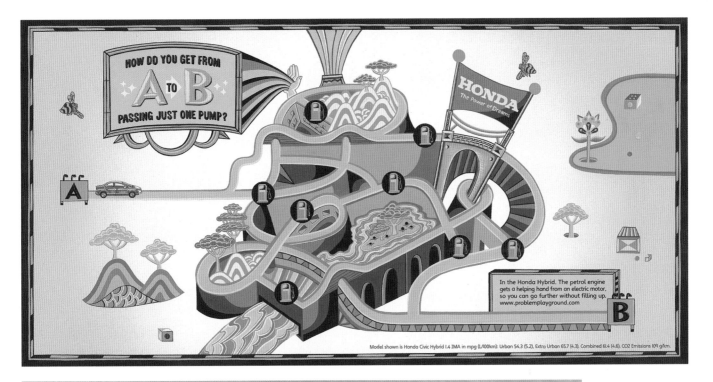

HONDA
Wieden+Kennedy, London
PROBLEM PLAYGROUND

In order to make the public more aware of their hybrid cars and sustainable efforts as a company, Honda launched the 'Problem Playground' campaign. The TV spots feature Honda engineers taking on oversized puzzles such as Rubik's cubes – we can see how good they are at solving problems and how much fun they have doing it. The campaign is also supported by a website that helps consumers learn about Honda's initiatives and, among other things, how to calculate how much money they could save if they bought a hybrid car.

A line from their TV spot sums up Honda's positive, can-do attitude perfectly, 'When you love solving things, isn't every problem a playground?' Taking on the task of saving us from the climate crisis isn't a small thing, but with their positive, can-do attitude and proven ingenuity, Honda puts forward a trustworthy positioning.

HONDA
Wieden+Kennedy, London
GRRR

Can hate be good? Can hate effect positive change? Honda asked us this question and found that, actually, it can. When Kenichi Nagahiro, Honda's chief engine designer and inventor of the renowned V-Tec engine, got up to announce Honda's new diesel engine to the European market he said something that in time was to spark a movement, 'I hate diesels'.

Honda took this sentiment to heart and built their entire ethos around it. What if hate can be a positive force? Nagahiro's hatred for diesel engines – their noise, dirtiness and emissions –

pushed him to improve upon Honda's diesel engine, making it better, cleaner and quieter. And so the 'Grrr' campaign was born, with the catchphrase many of us may have heard, 'Hate something, change something'.

But this campaign wasn't really just about engines: it was about how people can change the things they don't like. It stood out in its category – we don't often see car ads that don't show a single car – and it pushed the boundaries of car advertising. As proof of its crossover appeal, the song in the ad was played on the radio and was

even released as a downloadable ringtone. And as proof of how well the philosophy was received, a drug rehabilitation centre in the UK even incorporated this philosophy into their treatment programme.

NIKE
Wieden+Kennedy, Portland
BETTER WORLD

Nike Better World is Nike's umbrella
term for all of their projects for good.
It includes a TV commercial made solely
from recycled Nike ads, soccer jerseys
made from recycled plastic bottles and
Nike's GreenXchange programme, which
aims to share sustainable business
ideas and patents across companies.

Coupled with Nike Better World is
their Considered Design Initiative.
Considered Design puts Nike at the
forefront of performance-based sports
products with a reduced environmental
footprint by reducing waste during the
design and development processes, as
well as using environmentally preferred
materials and eliminating the use
of toxics. For example, in 2011 alone,
Nike expected to divert the equivalent
of more than 440 million PET bottles
from the waste stream.

Of the big three sports brands, Nike
seems to be at the forefront of doing
good and trailblazing the way for sports
brands to provide performance on the
field and for the environment as well.
They have translated their passion
for winning into a world-bettering
compassion. From shoes designed for
Native American feet to refurbishing
basketball courts in New York City, Nike
has taken the position of being a brand
that not only cares for your physical
body, but also for all aspects of your life.

If a sports brand can show its
commitment and expand its scope to
transcend running faster, being stronger
and beating the opposition then there
is hope that brands really can do
something to change the world for
the better. What Nike also manages
to do with all these initiatives is to
throw down the gauntlet to the other
sports brands out there – are they up
to the challenge?

TIDE
Saatchi & Saatchi, New York
LOADS OF HOPE

Tide makes laundry detergent and in times of crisis the Tide Loads of Hope programme moves into disaster-stricken areas and helps people out with something they know a lot about – washing clothes. A mobile laundromat that can wash up to 300 loads a day is sent in to provide free laundry services to communities affected by disaster. The clothes are washed, dried and folded for free so that families in crisis can focus on bigger things.

In the US the Loads of Hope programme visited New Orleans after Hurricane Katrina in 2005, Baton Rouge after it was hit by hurricane Gustav in 2008, and even Haiti after the earthquake in 2010. By the beginning of 2011, Tide had washed over 49,000 loads of laundry and helped more than 35,000 families.

This commitment is very powerful and by providing something simple that is within the gamut of Tide's offering, they will never over-promise or provide people with something that feels foreign to the Tide brand. Using your own brand values and offering to do good can sometimes be more powerful than attaching yourself to a cause that might be incongruous with your offering.

When families face disasters, they are often deprived of the most basic needs – food, water, shelter and clean clothes. Clean clothes are an integral part of who people are and help people feel like they have a piece of their daily life back.

SAATCHI & SAATCHI

CREATIVITY

6.

CREATIVITY
What if?

THINK BIG, THINK WORLD PEACE

Filmmaker and actor Jeremy Gilley aimed for what seems impossible: an International Day of Peace. His three-year struggle bore fruit in 2001 when the United Nations officially acknowledged 21 September as Peace One Day. A documentary was made to chart his efforts, which culminated when both sides in the Afghan conflict put down their arms for one day.

The power of a big idea

I'm a strong believer in the transformational power of ideas: big ideas, bold ideas, even scary ideas. Several big ideas have dominated history and left their mark on us – religion and capitalism, for example. Some ideas such as hard-line communism eventually fade away quietly and others such as conscious capitalism fragment and evolve into new ideas. Today, the creation and domination of ideas is not only reserved for the select few – priests, politicians or the wealthy – if you have a big idea then the internet enables you to share it with the world and share it with immediate effect. For brands, the internet is an opportunity to take to the stage with their idea.

If your idea is big enough, then you have the potential to touch billions of people. If your idea is bold enough, you might be able to change the very essence of consumerism. On Black Friday in the US, Patagonia launched a series of print ads that challenged consumerism run amok with a headline stating, 'Don't buy this jacket'. These ads should make consumers think twice about buying something new and instead make them consider reusing their existing wardrobe. We, in the marketing industry, are not inventing new medicines or securing new energy sources, but what we can do is use our creativity and communication skills to plant a seed of change in people's minds and show them a sustainable future awaits, if they want to come along.

Challenge your thinking by asking 'what if?'

Big ideas shake up the status quo. Be curious and begin your search by asking 'what if?' The question forces you to ignore the established rules, defy conventional wisdom and imagine the impossible. Force yourself to keep inquiring. Nothing is too stupid and everything is possible. The team behind the Gatorade 'Replay' campaign dared to ask those questions and the odd one out that ignited the idea was, 'what if Gatorade were a sports network and not a beverage brand?' The result, as you might know, was a TV series where men, now in their thirties, could replay a football match from their high school days that had ended in a disappointing and unfulfilling tie.

If you're not asking the right questions then you will never find the right answers. What if it becomes more fun to do the right thing? The answer could be VW's 'The Fun Theory'. Or what if people could see the real effect of antiretroviral (ARV) drugs? The answer is the film *Selinah* where you see the miraculous recovery of an HIV positive woman on ARVs. Out of 100 'ifs' that perfect idea might be in there. There is no formula for creativity, but it helps to be curious and to challenge the established way of thinking. It is no different from any other industry asking a big, daring question, just like Apple did when they asked

Opposite 'Xylophone', NTT Docomo
Drill, Tokyo (see pages 152–53)
Above 'Replay', Gatorade, TBWA\Chiat\Day,
Los Angeles (see page 146)

'The Voice', Reporters Without Borders,
Publicis, Brussels (see page 151)

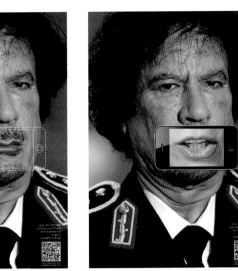

'The Power of Wind', Epuron
Nordpol, Hamburg (see page 145)

'what if music was truly digital?' The answer was the iPod, which
revolutionized the entire music industry.

Use creativity to stand out

As the competition to have a more responsible voice becomes fiercer,
creativity is your single biggest differentiator. According to a study from
the research institutes IPA (the Institute of Practitioners in Advertising)
and Thinkbox, ads that win creative awards are 11 times more efficient.
The IPA Director Janet Hull explains it well, 'The efficiency of highly
creative campaigns is growing – the more creative you are, the more
you get for your money. And the effectiveness of these campaigns is
growing; greater creativity enables greater consumer engagement, so
the importance of generating surprising or inspiring content should not
be overlooked.' The advantages of creativity are so obvious and the
cases so plentiful that they cannot be ignored.

Be a problem solver

Above anything else, you should be a problem solver, not just an art or
marketing director. If you can push your communication from creating
awareness to actually solving the problem, then real value and tangible
outcomes are created. It's a move from words to a solution. That's exactly
what the WWF did when they wanted people to print less and invented
a new document format, the .wwf file, which cannot be printed. They
solved the problem at its root, whereas other anti-print campaigns have
been forgotten as the media pressure has weakened. Toyota's mobile
app 'A Glass of Water' had the same problem-solving approach – by
making the car's fuel consumption visible to the driver. People do change
their behaviour if they can see it matters. Social or sustainable innovation
where the core business idea does good is of enormous value and shows

that the traditional media approach is not always the answer and very
seldom the solution.

Always challenge the media

Everything is communication. If you look at advertising's sister industry,
design, you can see that design has outstripped advertising in some
ways – taking on the task of saving the world early on and expanding
the definition of what design really is. For example, whether you are
designing a toothbrush or a city, they are both 'design'. You have to go
on the same journey and with great stamina pursue an all-encompassing
view in which everything is and can be communication. If you want to
stay relevant in consumers' lives, you have to evolve, especially as it gets
harder and more expensive to build relations in traditional media. In a
campaign for WWF's Earth Hour, the world's most famous monuments
were turned into a communication platform as they turned off their lights
in order to create awareness for the cause. This highly visible action
generated massive press coverage.

The 'what if?' question can also help you make everything a medium,
everything a possibility. In a fundraising drive for Guide Dogs Australia
the answer to the 'what if?' question was selling a scent so people could
smell of donation. This meant that a blind person could tell you were
supporting them through smell. Creativity finds solutions where others
haven't even considered looking (or smelling).

Use the responsible marketplace as a canvas

The backstories of products and companies are increasingly moving to
the forefront of their relationships with consumers. How a TV is made
and what it's made from might be as important as the story you're

A CASE OF COKE SAVE LIVES

ColaLife is an organization with a real, life-changing idea: Coca-Cola has the biggest and most far-reaching distribution network in Africa, so why not use this to deliver essential medicines to remote villages? A test project is underway in Zambia and you can follow the progress on their site colalife.org.

advertising. This is an opportunity to expand the creative canvas and look for ideas in new places, from how the product is produced to how consumers throw it away. This approach also demands a great deal of curiosity: the product or the company should be questioned as if by a sociologist studying an indigenous tribe. Don't take any answers as a given. Vestas, the wind energy company, together with Droga5, found the idea of listing wind as a product 'ingredient' by looking at the lifecycle and backstory of products and making them known. Through this clever move WindMade became a product label and they made it easy for consumers to choose a product made with renewable energy, like wind, instead of a product with a hidden energy backstory most likely involving fossil fuel or atomic energy. You might need new knowledge to ask the right question, but hopefully this book will help shed light on some of the pitfalls and possibilities in the responsible revolution. Just as our industry is slowly beginning to master digital media, the responsible market also has its learning curve. The earlier you adopt this way of thinking, the more distance there will be between you and your competitors.

Great campaigns have a great answer

The answers to the 'what if?' question are many. Use this question as a tool to think bigger. As the examples above show, great campaigns have a great answer. The creativity of advertisers has done enough to sell Coca-Cola in the furthest corners of the world, but now think about what good could be achieved if that skill and acumen was used to educate African women about disease prevention and basic hygiene, or teach the industrialized world's consumers to act more responsibly and more sustainably. Now it's up to you to answer that call with world-bettering creativity.

One of ColaLife's ingenious methods of distributing medicines

Interview
DAVID DROGA

David Droga is currently one of advertising's biggest players. With his agency, Droga5, he has created an independent agency that is cleaning up at awards shows and pushing the boundaries of how much good advertising can do. Coming from Australia, with a mother who is an environmental activist and a father with an astute nose for business, David tells me that his father always wanted to rule the world and his mother wanted to save it, and I can see these traits coming through when we speak.

David is without a doubt a driven man. He's been in the advertising industry for decades and is still one of the hardest-working people around. As many people who work in this industry will know, advertising is not a job you leave at the office and David uses that restlessness and drive to push the boundaries not just of what advertising can do, but also of what advertising is. Initiatives such as the Tap Project (page 80) and Million (page 185) show a deep understanding of communication and how advertisers' skills can be used to make the world a better place.

The Tap Project, in particular, is very close to David's heart in terms of its impact and reach. **'It very much transcended regular advertising, for me, and it set a precedent of what I want to try and achieve in advertising, which is: yes, we're an idea-generating company and we're in the business of marketing and building brands, but it's very much coupled with using our creativity for good or, as I always say, creativity with a purpose. [It's about] transcending the disposable nature of advertising and [proving] that it's the size of the idea not the size of the budget that is what is at stake now.'**

David told me that one of his proudest moments was being at Cannes in 2011 and seeing that the Tap Project had been taken on in other countries, where other agencies were doing creative work for it that he

///

If brands want to play a genuine part in society, then they have to contribute to society.

///

knew nothing about. 'It had nothing to do with me and I was so proud that this idea is far bigger than us, far bigger than this, and now it's moved into different countries as this real, genuine, potentially amazing thing…seeing other agencies seeing that as a creative opportunity… I've got more pride from that than I did with all the Grands Prix and everything else – not saying that there's anything wrong with Grands Prix… The thing about the Tap Project is that, as an agency, it's done more for the morale and the ethos of who we are internally, in terms of personal pride, when we talk at the dinner table about what we do. It's unbelievable. It accentuates my belief that all the biggest ideas are grounded in the everyday and the very obvious.'

Bearing these initiatives in mind, David sees the communications industry as having a powerful role to play not only in broadcasting positive messages, but also in making a lasting contribution. 'The world is conscious of its contribution, of what it does. The industry is conscious of the messaging and the footprint that it has out there and brands want to put their best foot forward. The collective brain power and strategic power and all the will and energy of our industry can be transformational. I know we're greasing the wheels of capitalism and we do a bloody good job of that but the imagination and creativity – it's going to be one of the things that changes the world. I really believe it. Some of the biggest issues facing us will be solved by scientists and doctors, and thank heavens for that, but there are other things where if we tackle problems laterally then we can contribute a little bit, even if it's one percent or two percent or whatever, I mean how spectacular is that?'

For David, it all boils down to honesty and action. Brands and companies have to walk their talk in order to be accepted by the new, aware consumer. 'If brands want to play a genuine part in society, then they have to contribute to society. Now I'm not saying that the responsibility for everything falls on every brand, but if you profit from housewives and mothers then you should play a role and contribute to their lives… The industry has changed drastically – the principles are the same, but it's moved from what you say to what you do. And that's how you'll be judged. And I'm not saying that suddenly a soda company has to solve leprosy, but you know if you want to be a global business and you actually want to reap the rewards of that. The thing is…with governments, they have huge amounts of money but they go where the votes go. So they only have to be seen to act every four years, whereas consumers vote every day. Every single day that they make a purchase, they are voting, in essence. So brands have to have a more day-to-day contribution to the world.'

David's vision for Droga5 is ambitious, outrageous even, but there's something about his drive and his determination that you cannot deny. 'I want to build the most influential creative company in the world. I know that's a ridiculously ambitious thing to say, but that's my goal. By influential, I mean at a size where we can effect change. Where we can contribute to industries, build brands, ensure social change, social good, influence pop culture, all these types of things. I want to feel that whatever category we're put in we can effect some positive change [and] I want to see that our ideas outlast media budgets… We want to be the best at getting better.' Given the track record of Droga5 – four Cannes Titaniums in five years (the most Titaniums won by an agency ever), they are a horse you'd be a fool not to bet on.

When it comes to advertising for good itself, David has the following advice and opinions. He suggests you start by asking the following questions: 'What's the reason for your brand's existence, beyond making money? What is its place in the world? It's not just what you say, but what does your brand do? What is the body language of your brand? That's what I always say. How it acts, more than what it's saying… My favourite saying is: this industry was built around us making wrapping paper for 50 years, yes, we still make the wrapping paper but we can start affecting what's in the box as well. And that excites me no end.'

I'll pass on David's challenge and ask, 'What are you going to put into the box?'

The communication strategy was built on an insight that Sweden has millions of bad storytellers. All children love it when their parents tell them stories, but a good story is hard to ad lib. It easily disintegrates into a mish-mash of princesses, fish-fingers and things that happened at work that day.

DDB

MCDONALD'S
Prime PR and DDB, Stockholm
BOOK HAPPY MEAL

The Happy Meal from McDonald's has been a marketing boon for the company for years, with movie tie-ins and toys that harness the might of children's pester power. But what if the toy given away with a Happy Meal was a book – something that could encourage children and parents to bond rather than something forgotten after a day or two and thrown away?

McDonald's in Sweden answered this question by launching the Book Happy Meal in 2009. Supported by the Swedish royal family and with a website where parents could build their own wacky stories to tell their children, this campaign went far beyond cheap little toys. As with all promotions at McDonald's, Book Happy Meal had to prove its worth and sell at least as well as other Happy Meal programmes during the year. The good news was that it went on to become the highest selling Happy Meal in Sweden in 2009.

At a time when many countries are becoming critical of Happy Meals – they have been banned in San Francisco, for example, this proved they may still do good. As well as promoting sales, it also provided stimulus for the Swedish publishing sector – 920,000 books were distributed, which meant a spike in children's book publishing of 26%. On top of that, PR impressions peaked at 10 million – more than the entire population of Sweden, which proves that doing good in a creative way can get you noticed.

STUDIO BRUSSEL
Mortierbrigade, Brussels
THIRSTY BLACK BOY

When Studio Brussel, one of Belgium's largest radio stations, wanted to raise awareness for their yearly charity drive, Music for Life, they enlisted the help of a young black boy. To highlight the point that every 15 seconds a child dies from a disease contracted due to a lack of drinkable water they decided to use the glasses of water we see on live television. On Flanders's most watched TV station, the black boy ran into shot on live television, thirstily gulped down the water in the presenter's glass, then ran off again. None of the presenters knew beforehand that they were going to be interrupted.

This idea soon became contagious and the word spread, as people asked, 'Have you seen the thirsty black boy on television?' The idea was then splashed all over the internet and was featured on YouTube, blogs and marketing websites. Once excitement and curiosity had reached a fever pitch, all that was left was to let people know the cause the boy was representing – Music for Life.

It was incredibly effective and in just six days € 3.3 million had been donated to help provide people with drinkable water, proving that ideas don't need to cost much to garner a great return.

DUNLOP
Dentsu Razorfish, Tokyo
MELODY ROAD

Dunlop Falken Tyres in Japan created an innovative way to encourage drivers to slow down – they built a road that plays a tune if you drive over it at a certain speed. By cutting grooves into the road at specific intervals they changed the pitch of the sound created as a car drove over them. Cleverly, they made the optimum speed to hear the tune 40 kilometres per hour.

By gamifying everyday life, Dunlop ensured that people would take the time to realize that driving slowly and safely can actually be a rewarding experience. Giving people positive feedback for good behaviour (rewarding them with the joy of a song 'played' by the road) instead of using negative feedback (fining people for driving too fast) created stronger associations with driving safely and with Dunlop itself.

As this road became better known, tourists drove to the Nagano Prefecture just to try it out. Accidents decreased and at the same time Dunlop increased positive associations with their brand. Everyone was a winner.

"MELODY ROAD" is a road which is a little bit different than usual.

By making a groove on a road paved by asphalt, a beautiful melody appears by a friction.

This MELODY ROAD turns out to be a safety awarness.

we have designed a new road sign, and set up.

40km/h で走行中

And it came out to be popular as a tourist attraction.

THE WILD BIRD SOCIETY
Beacon Communications, Tokyo
VOICE OF ENDANGERED BIRDS

In order to raise awareness about endangered birds in Japan, The Wild Bird Society created limited edition vinyl records that sampled the real calls of four critically endangered birds in Japan – the Japanese red-crown crane, the albatross, the stork and the yellow-breasted bunting. These sampled birdcalls were mixed into contemporary dance tracks and the records were placed in hip Tokyo record stores. In order to raise awareness and drive desire for the records, the number of records produced for each bird correlated with how many birds were estimated to still be alive in the wild in Japan.

Results proved very positive, as local DJs picked up on the records and began playing them across Tokyo. Also, all the proceeds from sales of the records went back to the Wild Bird Society. This creative use of media shows that a good idea will always win through and – at the same time – anything can be advertising.

Cake took a rather dull fish with a serious ethical issue and applied a humorous approach. In French, Colin (pronounced Colan) sounded sophisticated. In English, Colin is a very normal, everyday forename. The combination of genuine retail news, humour and great imagery on the limited edition packaging secured over a week of national and international news coverage, debate and word of mouth.

CAKE

SAINSBURY'S
Cake Group, London
MIND THE POLLACKS

In order to encourage sales of a sustainable fish species and make customers aware of their sustainable credentials, Sainsbury's rebranded an entire species of fish. The pollack fish, which is sustainably caught and scores high in terms of taste, is not well known and doesn't always sell well, even though Sainsbury's is the UK's largest retailer of pollack.

With a tongue-in-cheek poke at the UK's obsession with French cuisine, the pollack was rebranded as the 'Colin' (pronounced 'Col-an' with a French accent). It was also repackaged and put into 30 stores across the UK. This rebranding resulted in a 68% increase in sales of pollack across all Sainsbury's stores during the course of the rebranding exercise.

Not only did this campaign raise awareness about Sainsbury's sustainable fishing initiatives, but it also made the British media discuss the British obsession with French gastronomy, turning the issue into a reaffirmation of national pride. Not bad for a fish.

All it took was an unbelievable offer and halfway credible signage to convince New Yorkers to gladly hand over all sorts of ridiculously intimate personal information.

CRISPIN PORTER + BOGUSKY

MICROSOFT
Crispin Porter + Bogusky, Boulder
THE DOT CONS

In order to highlight the safety features of the new Internet Explorer 8 (IE8), Microsoft set up three fake business fronts: a bank (The Greater Offshore Bank & Trust), The Inheritance Store and a charity for a Nigerian 'prince'. By advertising these fronts as real businesses, Microsoft was able to get people to divulge all kinds of sensitive information. Each interaction was documented by hidden cameras to show people just how easy it is to be scammed.

As IE8 offered unique online security features compared to other web browsers, this was the perfect way to show people how greed can make something that is too good to be true seem like a viable option. By doing this, Microsoft not only makes people aware of the benefits of IE8 in a creative and amusing way, but also reminds everyone to be more aware of their online security and shows how vulnerable your personal information can be, whether you are an IE8 user or not.

EPURON
Nordpol+, Hamburg
THE POWER OF WIND

How do you show the power of wind without being obvious and create an advert that holds the attention of consumers and spreads a positive message about wind-powered energy? Epuron did just that with this ad. By personifying 'the wind' as a lonely man who cannot connect with people (he is constantly pushing their hats off their heads and turning their umbrellas inside out), Epuron shows us that wind can actually be put to good use in the right situation.

Rather than preaching to consumers or trying to use guilt, this advert actually gives viewers an enjoyable experience. This is not the type of ad that disrupts your life and demands that you pay attention – instead it straddles the line between entertainment and advertisement. This is something you would share with your friends because it's that good.

Epuron has succeeded so well with this ad not only because you feel a real emotional connection with this man, but also because they have managed to personify an intangible force of nature so effortlessly. The reveal at the end brings such an 'a-ha' moment that you can't help but smile. Woven into this story, a traditionally 'dry' subject becomes so much more powerful as a tool for educating people about wind power.

GATORADE
TBWA\Chiat\Day, Los Angeles
REPLAY

What happens if you reunite a group of guys who last played together in high school and are now in their mid-thirties? This was the question asked by Gatorade for their 'Replay' project. Based on the insight that every athlete has one game he or she wishes could have had a different outcome, Gatorade trained up two teams who had last played to a draw in 1993.

Not only did this campaign reinforce Gatorade's commitment to the values of sportsmanship and competition, it encouraged men of that age group to get more active. The men were trained for 90 days and many of them lost over 25 pounds. Some improved their health so much that they no longer needed their high cholesterol or blood pressure medication.

This campaign not only did good for the public, but Gatorade reaped great rewards too – regional sales of Gatorade spiked by 63%. It was also named one of CNN's top stories of 2009, generating over $3 million worth of news (not advertising) on a media spend of $225,000 – that's a return on investment of 14,000%. 'Replay' has now become a documentary TV series, broadcast to 90 million households, showing the power of a great idea.

Every day entire forests die for paper.

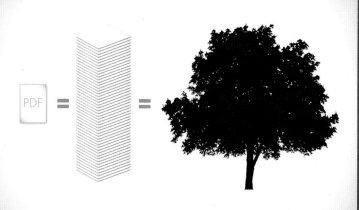

SAVE AS WWF, SAVE A TREE

WWF
Jung Von Matt, Hamburg
SAVE AS WWF
▬

As a great way to discourage people from printing out documents unnecessarily, the World Wildlife Fund (WWF) launched a downloadable app that meant you could save documents as a wwf file. This '.wwf' file extension saves the document as an unprintable pdf. You can spread the message by sending a wwf file. Once you've saved a document as a wwf, the icon of the document changes to reflect the format and a page is added to the end, explaining the purpose to people who are encountering the campaign for the first time.

By encouraging people to spread the message, you are allowing them to feel like they are doing their bit for the cause – there have been more than 50,000 downloads of the app. The

WWF has really attacked this problem at its root – if you are unable to print something because of the very nature of the file then you will certainly take notice, whereas other anti-print campaigns have often lost steam.

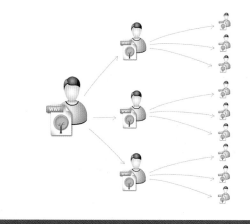

Selinah has AIDS

She agreed to be filmed every day for 90 days
So that her story might help others

Day 90

Day 1

The effects of AIDS can be reversed

Help us provide the treatment
that can give someone a second chance

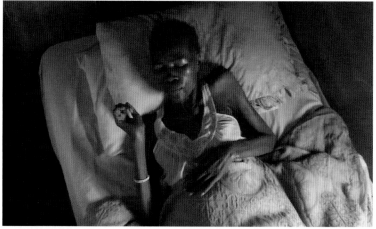

THE TOPSY FOUNDATION
Ogilvy, Johannesburg
SELINAH

The Topsy Foundation is a South African charity that provides antiretroviral drugs (ARVs) and care for AIDS patients. Their aim was to create a TV ad that would tell people what they do, explain how important ARVs are for AIDS patients and encourage them to donate. Topsy used a simple yet heart-rendingly powerful execution with the insight of the 'Lazarus Effect' – the fact that ARVs can return AIDS patients to full health in as little as 90 days.

In real documentary footage, a woman named Selinah is shown in time-lapse photography over 90 days. From being thin and skeletal she returns to full health, with plump cheeks and a contagious smile.

As a result the Topsy Foundation saw a 52% increase in the number of patients coming to them for treatment and have seen an increase in the number of volunteers coming forward to help AIDS patients. On top of that, they have also seen a knock-on effect with an increase in donations for AIDS orphans as a direct result of the advert. It has also been used in a large number of hospitals as an education tool, and was shown at the 2010 AIDS summit in Vienna.

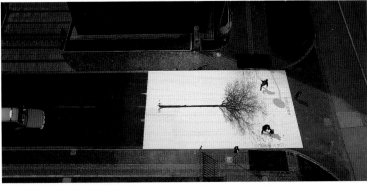

THE CHINA ENVIRONMENTAL
PROTECTION FOUNDATION
DDB, Shanghai
GREEN PEDESTRIAN CROSSING

This campaign started out with seven executions in Shanghai for the China Environmental Protection Foundation and quickly spread to 132 roads in 15 cities across China. The message was to ask people to walk more and drive less, hence pedestrian crossings were used as the medium of choice.

A canvas was laid across pedestrian crossings, with the image of a leafless tree printed on it. Sponges with a green, environmentally friendly and washable paint were placed on either side of the road under the traffic lights. As pedestrians walked across, the paint took to their shoes and they then populated the tree with leaves as they walked.

In terms of results, this campaign achieved great things – over 3.9 million people walked across the pedestrian crossings and general awareness of environmental protection rose by a massive 86%. These canvases were also exhibited at the Shanghai Zheng Da Art Museum, highlighting their importance in China. Encouraging consumers to collaborate with your brand in a fun, exciting way and to create something for a good cause is a great way to increase engagement and ensure that your message is retained well.

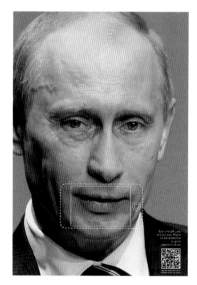

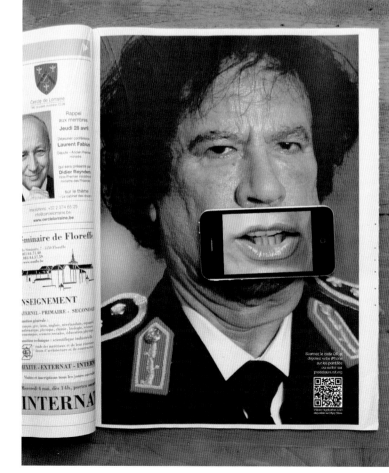

REPORTERS WITHOUT BORDERS
Publicis, Brussels
THE VOICE

Through an inventive use of a QR code and a smartphone, viewers of these print ads could access what are best described as 'special features' for the ads. These ads feature three prominent international politicians who disallowed press freedom (Muammar Gaddafi, Mahmoud Ahmadinejad and Vladimir Putin) and the use of a smartphone enables users to hear the real story. The QR code points them to a website where the user can place their smartphone over the mouth of the politician. A video recording of a mouth speaking then plays over the mouth of the politician.

The video is of a journalist telling the real story of what was happening in Libya, Iran or Russia – highlighting the importance of press freedom. Without knowledge of a country's situation, international supporters cannot act. After viewing the video, users were redirected to a site that highlighted press freedom issues around the world and helped provide the information people needed to make informed decisions about press freedom. Users were also asked to donate to Reporters Without Borders so they could fight for press freedom around the world. The creativity of these ads and their inventive use of new technologies make them engaging, memorable and easy to act on.

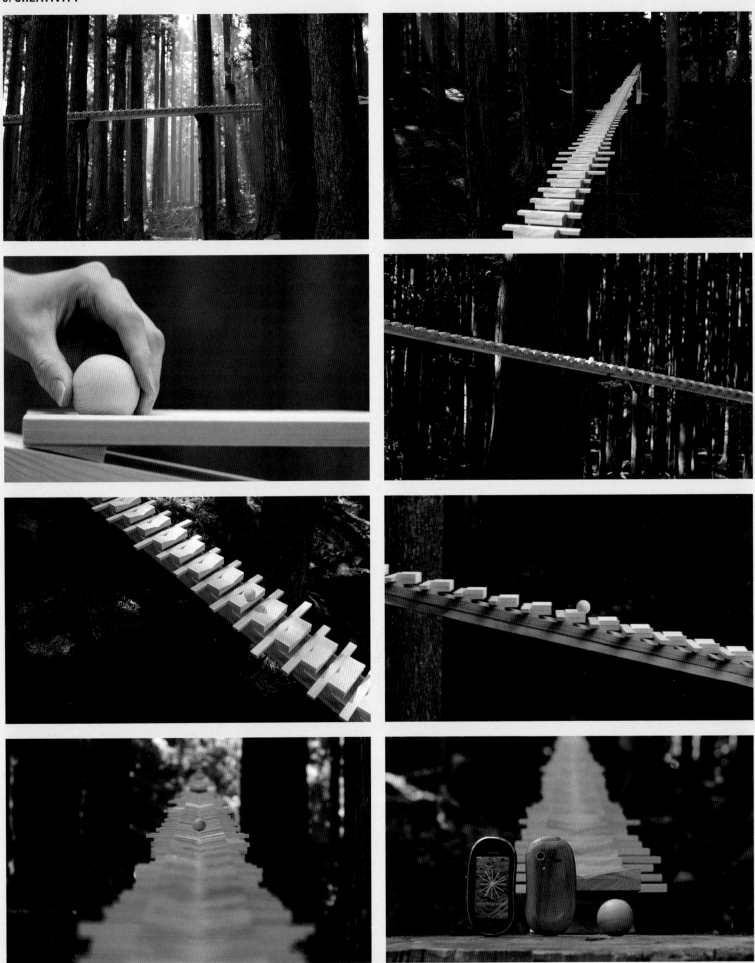

NTT DOCOMO
Drill, Tokyo
XYLOPHONE

In order to launch their new phone with a wooden backing, NTT Docomo built a fully working xylophone out of sustainably forested wood. It was created on a hill, which allowed a ball to be set in motion from the top, playing Bach's Cantata 147 as it hit each block of wood on the way down. It was entirely handcrafted by Japanese artisans and no visual trickery or audio enhancement was used in the making of the film.

By creating something so simple and so beautiful, NTT Docomo gave consumers a great film and a reminder of the beauty of nature. The phone itself is a desirable design object, as well as a reminder to stay in touch with nature.

TOYOTA
Saatchi & Saatchi, Stockholm
A GLASS OF WATER

Toyota wanted to support environmentally friendly driving and suggested that people should drive as if they had a glass of water on their dashboard. If they can drive in such a way that they don't spill any of the water, i.e., driving smoothly without accelerating or braking too sharply, they can save up to 10% of fuel.

Rather than encourage the messy idea of literally driving with a glass of water on the dashboard, Toyota released the 'A Glass of Water' app for the iPhone. It uses the iPhone's accelerometer to mimic the movement of a real glass of water. Users can track their progress and see how much water they have spilled. The information is then uploaded to Toyota's website, so users can compare their results with those of others.

By challenging drivers to drive both economically and safely, Toyota have succeeded in incentivizing responsibility. This not only benefits the consumer, but also reinforces the idea that Toyota is a brand that is concerned about the environmental impact of its products. As proof that doing good is good for business, research conducted after this app was released showed that the number of non-Toyota owners who would consider buying one rose by 150%.

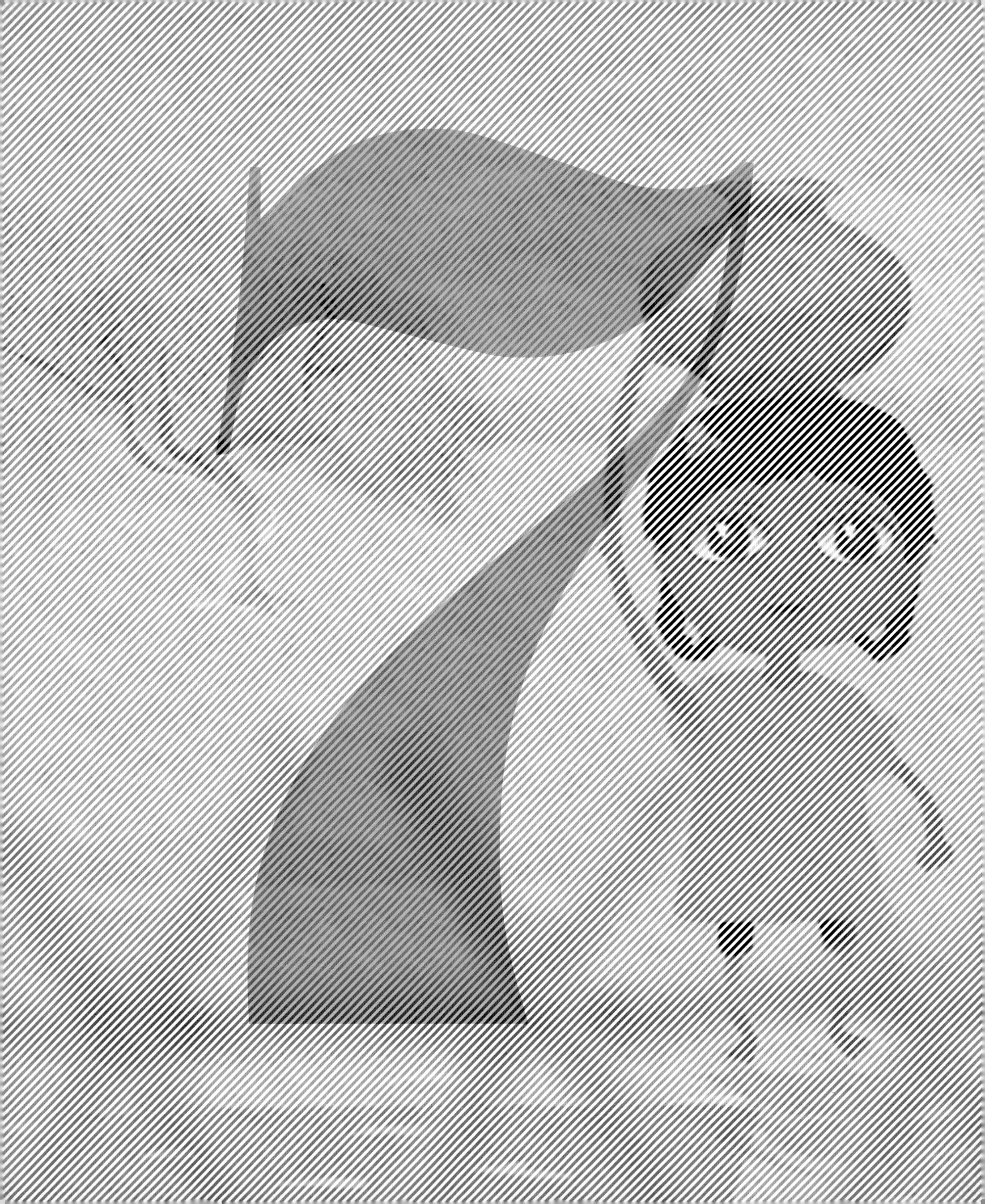

CONTAGIOUSNESS

CONTAGIOUSNESS
What is at stake?

Thanks to the internet and increased global interconnectedness, brands have the chance to touch more people than ever before – but this is also a great responsibility. A tweet about a corporate misdeed can spread like ripples in the water and potentially grow into a tsunami of people demanding justice. The internet is truly democratic and gives the ultimate power to the people. Today's empowered consumers see themselves as co-creators. They would rather verify product claims online and gather information from peers than trust an ad. For brands this is a chance to open up and allow ongoing conversations and greater engagement with your brand, instead of pushing messages at people.

Good news travels fast

Good news really does travel fast. If you're supporting a cause or your brand has a purpose at its heart then people are more willing to get involved. In 2010, Edelman's 'GoodPurpose' study found that 66% of global consumers would recommend a product or service with a good cause behind it and 64% stated that they would share positive opinions and experiences. This is compared to just 33% of global consumers who are willing to punish a brand by either sharing negative experiences or refusing to buy its products. It is no wonder that many cause campaigns thrive through social media – for instance, the 'Pepsi Refresh Project'.

The secret of contagiousness

Malcolm Gladwell's 'Tipping Point' theory, as illustrated in his book *The Tipping Point*, outlines how an exclusive, well-connected few are the ones who start epidemics of change. Others such as Seth Godin argue that it's not about the hand-picked few, but about you and me, as well as anybody else who can ignite a trend. Then there are the in-betweens and the viral and social media agencies with their recipes of success and promises of earned media and cost savings. At the end of the day, who can really foresee a potential blockbuster? It's difficult to trust those who claim to be able to do so, but there is an old, simple solution: the power of the story. The only thing that's changed is the toolbox and the available media.

Aim for high stakes

'So what's at stake in that story of yours?' is the question any Hollywood producer would ask, staring at you analytically through the glasses balanced on the tip of his nose. Showing what is at stake is absolutely crucial – you need to give people something to fight for. If there's nothing at stake then why should your audience care what happens? Why should they even consider passing the story on? Think about what can be at stake: honour? Children's health? Our planet? Love? The Metropolitan Police made people play for the highest stakes in

ARE YOU READY TO LEAD?

'Tribes need leadership. Sometimes one person leads, sometimes more. People want connection and growth and something new. They want change. You can't have a tribe without a leader – and you can't have a leader without a tribe.'
Seth Godin

Opposite 'Digital Death', Keep a Child Alive
TBWA\Chiat\Day, New York (see page 169)

'The Grid', Nike, Wieden+Kennedy
and AKQA, London (see page 168)

'A Girl Story', Nanhi Kali,
StrawberryFrog, New York
(see page 162)

their anti-knife campaign: you star in an interactive story in which picking up the knife is a matter of YOUR life or death. The anti-knife campaign story, released on YouTube, connected with youngsters and was viewed more than 2.5 million times.

The 'Keep a Child Alive' campaign was also a matter of life or death. The deaths of famous people, from Princess Diana to Michael Jackson, have always been cover-story material and the campaign played off that fact. Alicia Keys, the musician and co-founder of the initiative, asked other celebrities to sacrifice their digital lives in order to save a real one on World AIDS Day. A-listers such as Pink, Usher, Elijah Wood, David LaChapelle and others stopped their digital lives: this meant no Facebook updates or tweets until $1 million had been raised for the cause. Not only did the campaign create an enormous amount of digital buzz, but the $1 million was raised in just six days.

Make your story challenge conventions

In the early 1960s, jeans became a symbol for feminism and the modern woman. There was a strong story behind the movement. Those cotton trousers were a clear statement to the other sex: see, we're equal. The jeans were a symbol that rocked the status quo – there was a lot at stake. In the same way, Dove was able to connect with women and girls around the world with their 'Campaign for Real Beauty' because they dared to tell a different story and challenge the existing rules of beauty advertising. Dove's 'Evolution' is one of the most successful viral films ever with millions upon millions of views because it openly revealed the dirty tricks of the beauty industry.

Make your story or product spreadable

Great stories connect with people – but the stories that become truly contagious are those that connect people with people. Like the flu, great stories can potentially infect an entire population, moving from mouth to mouth, person to person. You just have to look at some of the earliest myths or religious narratives that created a following, a movement, a tribe, a related web of like-minded people who follow the same belief. In today's digital media landscape you have new tools at hand that make sharing easier. What you need to look for is how to make your idea social, or, in other words, how to connect people with people. In fact, most digital media have built these sharing features into their functionality like a share button or comments section. Just one click from your audience and your story is shared with potentially hundreds of people – the average person alone has 128 Facebook friends. The campaign 'How hetero are you?' succeeded in using Twitter as a platform to create a spreadable story, challenging people's perceptions of homosexuality (see page 166). As well as stories, products can be spreadable too, and, as I argue in the introduction, the Wheel of Good plays its part in leveraging sustainability to the mass market. Reebok (the Adidas-owned company) has taken on the challenge to deliver a $1 trainer to the Indian market, where two-thirds of the population have a very modest income. The shoe is still in development, but the goal is to produce the trainers locally and sustainably, elevating people from no shoes or bad shoes to a better quality alternative.

Turn sharing into your core story

Instead of adding sharing as an element to your campaign, you can make it more contagious by making it the core story. The charity Nanhi Kali and its clever online cause marketing campaign 'A Girl Story' (see page 162)

MAKE YOURSELF USEFUL

'As a brand I think you really need to earn your place with people. One way of doing it is of course entertainment, but there are many other ways. What is being increasingly successful is thinking in terms of creating utility.' Andreas Dahlquist, Vice Chairman and Executive Creative Director at McCann Erickson, New York

did just that. To advance the story, people needed to donate a certain amount so that the next part of the narrative could be unlocked; it also indirectly asked you to share the story with your friends. The Facebook game WeTopia is another example. Players within the game can create and manage their own villages and make a real-world donation for any virtual purchase. When trees or vitamins are bought, for example, one of the game's partner charities will donate the same item to their cause. So while having fun, you're doing social good.

Be useful

If you want people to share your campaign, you might want to make it useful or design it to add value to people's lives. It's an effort people will reward you for, and who wouldn't share something useful with their friends? The Nike 'Grid' campaign succeeded in motivating people to run more by gamifying real life. Competing runners were encouraged to claim one of London's 48 postcodes – whoever ran the furthest in the game period won the most points. People's results were immediately shared online with their friends. These types of campaigns often have great longevity and real community-building potential.

The power of connectedness

Contagiousness is not confined to the online world. Historically, the women's liberation movement was a powerful force, long before people could send tweets to each other. Stories essentially spread from mouth to mouth – the online world has just made it easier and faster, and the reach is astonishing. Stories that previously would have taken months to spread, maybe even years, can travel the world in minutes and reach millions of people all over the globe. Many of today's problems can be solved by communication – such as educating people about saving

resources and improving the understanding of hygiene. Brands have the unique ability to encourage people to change their perceptions and practices for the better (or worse). Dare to raise the stakes of your story and reach out and connect people with people and the grim but real story of our blue planet, faced with overpopulation and a war on resources, might actually find that happy ending. Yes, there's plenty at stake.

Interview
ROB SCHWARTZ

Rob Schwartz is Chief Creative Officer of TBWA\Chiat\Day, Los Angeles and has been involved in two of the most interesting campaigns for good in recent memory: the 'Pepsi Refresh Project' and Gatorade 'Replay'. I was lucky enough to prevail upon his kindness and secure some time in his schedule. Somewhere between the US and China, he answered my questions – the first interview I've done at 30,000 feet.

What Rob had to say about advertising and doing good reveals that there is much change afoot in advertising. What is most interesting is the movement from seeing advertising as a stand-alone marketing tool to just one of the many touchpoints of a holistic marketing approach. It's not about what brands say, but it's really about *everything* they do, their actions and their attitude. When asked about consumers looking for more socially conscious campaigns from brands, he made the following point, **'I don't think consumers necessarily want more socially conscious campaigns, what they do want is more socially conscious actions from brands.'**

It boils down to honesty and it goes further than the rather trite 'walking the talk'. It's about brands doing the right thing – all the time. **'Honesty is the best policy. Always.'** This is a far cry from the clichéd view of advertisers as hucksters who don't care about the consequences, as long as they shift product. He references a quotation from the CEO of PepsiCo, Indra Nooyi, **'While you had to do good business, you also had to do some good.'**

This is something that he made sure happened with the 'Pepsi Refresh Project' (pages 188–89), where Pepsi pulled out of Super Bowl advertising for the first time in just over 20 years. It turned out to be a masterstroke. In his own words, **'In the end, Pepsi got the most buzz of any brand on the Super Bowl, because of the bold move to be off it. The gamble definitely paid off.'** There's something to be said for a campaign being spoken about because of what it chooses *not* to do. The 'Pepsi Refresh Project' put aside $20 million to be used for socially conscious projects for good and provided people with tangible results they could believe in, an important part of any campaign in this field. **'Campaigns for good work best when there's a real need and a real way for a brand to make some impact. "Pepsi Refresh" gave people a voice. It brought people together to hear problems and share solutions.'**

When we get on to Gatorade 'Replay', we find ourselves talking about media choice and the importance of asking the right questions. **'What if Gatorade were a sports network and not a beverage brand? You ask a different question, you get a unique answer.'** It was this unique viewpoint that enabled TBWA to create the Gatorade 'Replay' campaign (page 146), telling high quality stories, helping people improve their

I don't think consumers necessarily want more socially conscious campaigns, what they do want is more socially conscious actions from brands.

health and encouraging viewers to do the same. Interestingly enough, it began as a TV show and only then became an advert – another way that we are seeing advertising shrug off the mantle of being an annoying, disruptive medium.

There has always been a place in the minds of consumers for advertising that they enjoy and these days it's easier than ever to share it. **'Big budgets are okay, but big ideas are better. Big ideas on big TV is where my head is at. People still talk about and share ads that they love. TV spots travel on Facebook and Twitter.'** Rob understands the power of ideas, because really they are advertising fuel. At the same time, those ideas must be supported by great stories. **'The big learning for me on Gatorade 'Replay' was about storytelling. The "rebirth" of the athletes is a timeless universal tale. It's why people love it. As humans, we love the "rebirth" plot. That's why there were so many *Rocky* sequels! *Rocky* is all about a fighter's rebirth.'**

The scope of advertising and branding is expanding, and this means that advertising agencies have to start re-imagining what it is they can offer. **'There is also a place for non-traditional and branded events, be they shows or live events. We believe everything a brand does is media… Your owner's manual has to be as cool as your TV spot.'** On the subject of social media, Rob cautions against seeing it as a panacea for all your advertising problems. **'Social media is great, but it can't work alone. You need TV as well. Each media drives the other. And don't forget, people tweet when they watch TV. It's simultaneous, not sequential… I think it's best to approach social media not as an intrusion, but as part of the conversation. "Listen before you tweet" is one of my golden rules.'** When we move on to the web and how to leverage the immediacy of its content delivery, Rob said, **'There is so much good content existing on the web, I think it's a good idea for**

brands is to create a "meme fund" – set aside some money in the budget to partner with or invent with the web's content creators.' As the interview turns to advertising for good and the inevitable cries of 'greenwashing' we will always hear, Rob says something that gives me hope. **'I feel that "greenwashing" is the official campaign idea of the cynics. The world is screwed up. People can be selfish. Anything that shakes people a bit to think outside their bubbles is good.'** At the end of the day any good thing that a brand does is better than it doing nothing. At the same time, when it actually comes to making the world a better place Rob reckons it's a partnership between brands and consumers. **'It takes both. You can't have a brand without consumers. And consumers have a worse world without choice. Brands have a unique position. They can fill the gap where governments leave off. And if every brand did a little bit of good, it would dramatically move the world forward.'** When he puts it like that, I couldn't agree more.

NANHI KALI
StrawberryFrog, New York
A GIRL STORY

In many parts of India, girls are often seen as unwanted or as a hindrance. This feeling that they are unimportant can follow them into adulthood and lead to a life of prostitution or servitude. Here Tarla's life is mapped out through interactive YouTube videos.

In order for the story to progress and for new chapters to be unlocked, though, certain donation levels have to be met. This mimics real life in that girls like Tarla cannot move forward with their lives without the help of others. Through an innovative use of YouTube, the stories can be told seamlessly, with Tarla moving from one to another, eventually being able to gain an education.

This story is told so personally and, because donations from the audience are needed in order to move forward, the viewer feels as if they are really making a difference. Of course, donating to a charity always makes a difference, but seeing it played out like this, with these interactive videos, makes it much more tangible and rewarding.

Tarla's story will progress only with audience donations that unlock new chapters within the YouTube film series, just as each girl at Nanhi Kali depends on donors to progress in their education.

STRAWBERRYFROG

TAKE THE KNIFE

DON'T TAKE THE KNIFE

THE METROPOLITAN POLICE
Abbott Mead Vickers BBDO, London
CHOOSE A DIFFERENT ENDING

In 2011 the Metropolitan Police in the UK launched an online anti-knife crime campaign. In a choose-your-own-adventure style YouTube experience, users watched videos from the perspective of a teenage boy and were given a choice right at the beginning – to take a knife or leave it at home. The interactive videos showed the consequences of the teenager's actions. No matter what choices you make, if you take the knife with you then things end badly. Twenty-one films were made, with ten possible endings.

By using the functionality of YouTube in a new, unexpected way, the Metropolitan Police ensured that people would spend time exploring the videos. This was borne out by the results of the campaign: a 2.1% click-through rate on the viral video trailers, compared to an industry standard click-through rate of 0.2% on rich media banners. The number of viewings of the campaign on YouTube are now approaching 3 million.

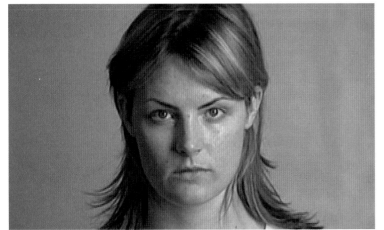

DOVE
Ogilvy, Toronto
EVOLUTION

Dove's Evolution viral spot showed in detail how an average-looking woman could be made to look like a supermodel through the powers of Photoshop and digital retouching. Dove re-created what takes place during a normal shoot, with hair stylists, make-up artists, photographers, lighting technicians and retouchers, and allowed viewers to see just how much work goes into making someone look like this.

The response was overwhelming and spearheaded Dove's 'Campaign for Real Beauty'. The campaign was based on the insight that mothers have more of an effect on their daughters' self-esteem than anyone or anything else, so they targeted mothers to build good feeling in their daughters.

By allowing mothers and daughters to feel that Dove was the beauty product for them, no matter how they looked, Dove reinforced their self-esteem. At the same time, Dove repositioned itself by circumventing the entire beauty category, making them the brand for people who might not feel they look like models (and who does?). On top of achieving great results for people on a personal level, Dove's sales rose by 10% in two consecutive years. Who said doing good wasn't good for business?

STADSMISSION
Garbergs, Stockholm
HOMELESS BANNER

In this innovative campaign by Stadsmission in Stockholm, a small charity for homeless people in the city, people were encouraged to embed homeless banners on their websites to give them shelter. Once they had been given a home, the banners themselves would keep tabs on how long they had been kept there. Over time they slowly changed colour and 'warmed up', also responding with 'heat' when they were clicked. This encouraged interaction from visitors to the sites and led to click-throughs to the Stadsmission site.

After the campaign had been running for just one month there were more than 400 websites giving homes to these banners. This generated 36 million impressions and led to a threefold increase in donations, compared to the same time frame the previous year. An idea like this just begs to be shared and become contagious – the idea is so simple and yet so clever. It proved its worth with the results.

STOCKHOLM PRIDE
Akestam Holst, Stockholm
HOW HETERO ARE YOU?

In order to raise awareness about gay rights and the way people stigmatize gay people, Stockholm Pride launched their How Hetero website, which allows users to submit their Twitter username for analysis. The website then sifts through all of the user's tweets and finds words that could mark them as gay or straight. It then gives a percentage score of how hetero they are.

The score can be embedded onto the user's website, shared via Facebook or via Twitter – enabling the website to spread through social networks. By challenging 'heteronormativity' and the very language that is used by gay or straight people, this website makes users think about these issues in an amusing way and encourages them to investigate their own feelings on homosexuality. This will hopefully result in greater tolerance when people realize they could be less hetero than they thought.

HARIRI FOUNDATION
Leo Burnett, Beirut
KHEDE KASRA

In Lebanon women are treated with less respect than men and gender equality is far from an important issue for most. Domestic violence is widespread and women are even discriminated against by legislation – for example, in any divorce where the children are over nine years old, the mother immediately loses custody. The Hariri Foundation used the very structure of the Arabic language against itself in order to challenge this situation.

In Arabic there are two accents – one is used when addressing men and one when addressing women. By default, all public communications and media channels use the male accent. The Hariri Foundation realized that by putting out communications that spoke directly to women, using the accent for addressing women, they could empower women. A moving, interactive billboard as well as posters were used to spread the message. They proved very effective – the campaign spread across the Lebanese blogosphere and even encouraged the Lebanese government to table discussions about the equality of women in Lebanese society. The highlight of this campaign was when the female Minister of Education for Lebanon appeared in public to support the campaign (the first of its kind in the Arab world) and to encourage women to get involved. Most interestingly, this campaign actually used language as a medium – what could be more contagious than the spoken word and communication itself?

STREETS RUN. POSTCODES OWNED.
N5 WON BY DAVID HELLARD.
NIKEGRID.COM

NIKE
Wieden+Kennedy
and AKQA, London
THE GRID

Nike wanted to engage a new generation of 17–22-year-old runners and, with an innovative use of London's telephone boxes, they turned the streets into a fully interactive game grid. Runners were encouraged to check in at predetermined phone boxes in order to mark their progress as they ran through 40 of London's postcode areas. After registering online, runners just had to dial in their unique code and run from box to box. Each run logged points and players were rewarded extra points for speed, stamina and knowledge of the streets. The more runs you logged in a 24-hour period, the more points you scored. As each postcode was essentially a 'team', whichever postcode logged the most points won the competition. Building from the idea of Nike+, this campaign encouraged running and gamified it like never before. The bragging rights available for winners and the badges they could win incentivized running and competition in a unique, authentic way. The social aspects of the campaign were also groundbreaking, enabling users to interact with Nike and work together to try to win. The results speak for themselves, with over 125 runs logged per hour, 74% of the players within the young target group and 20,000 kilometres run in total.

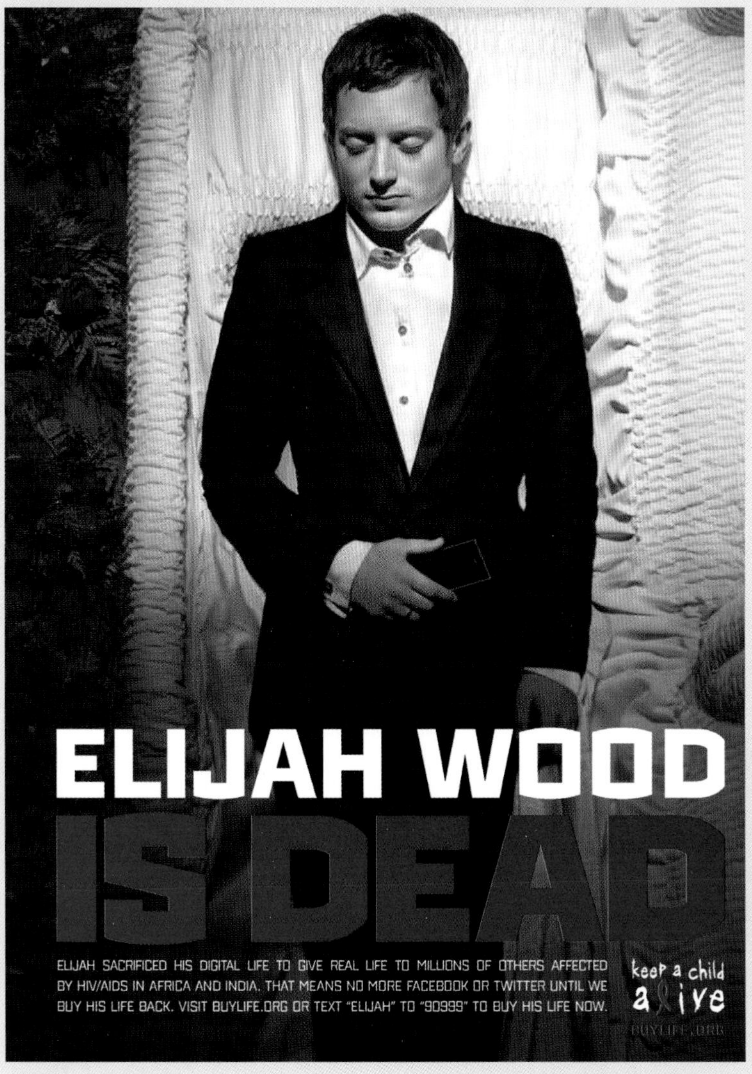

ELIJAH WOOD IS DEAD

ELIJAH SACRIFICED HIS DIGITAL LIFE TO GIVE REAL LIFE TO MILLIONS OF OTHERS AFFECTED BY HIV/AIDS IN AFRICA AND INDIA. THAT MEANS NO MORE FACEBOOK OR TWITTER UNTIL WE BUY HIS LIFE BACK. VISIT BUYLIFE.ORG OR TEXT "ELIJAH" TO "90999" TO BUY HIS LIFE NOW.

keep a child alive

SERENA WILLIAMS IS DEAD

SERENA SACRIFICED HER DIGITAL LIFE TO GIVE REAL LIFE TO MILLIONS OF OTHERS AFFECTED BY HIV/AIDS IN AFRICA AND INDIA. THAT MEANS NO MORE FACEBOOK OR TWITTER UNTIL WE BUY HER LIFE BACK. VISIT BUYLIFE.ORG OR TEXT "SERENA" TO "90999" TO BUY HER LIFE NOW.

keep a child alive
BUYLIFE.ORG

KEEP A CHILD ALIVE
TBWA\Chiat\Day, New York
DIGITAL DEATH

From the bottom of my heart, thank you to all of the fans, friends and artists who joined this cause. I'm incredibly inspired by all of the donations that have been made to help us achieve our goal and so humbled by the outpour of support from everyone.

ALICIA KEYS, KEEP A CHILD ALIVE

In order to raise awareness and, more importantly, funds for AIDS treatment in Africa and India, Keep a Child Alive (a charity started by Alicia Keys and Leigh Blake, a renowned charity worker), in association with world famous celebrities, created the 'Digital Death' campaign. Celebrities as well known as Lady Gaga, Justin Timberlake, Alicia Keys, Usher, Ryan Seacrest, Kim Kardashian and Elijah Wood all died digitally, leaving their Twitter accounts and Facebook pages silent.

The only way to get them back was to 'buy their lives back' by visiting a website and donating money. Once donations had reached $1 million these celebrities would revive their digital lives, sharing with their fans.

The amount was reached in just five days, with fans donating $500,000 and noted pharma billionaire and philanthropist Stewart Rahr matching the amount.

With this inventive use of 'creative blackmail', Keep a Child Alive was able to raise awareness through over 30 million people who followed these celebrities on Twitter. At the same time, other Twitter users were encouraged to die digitally to raise awareness, with over 3,600 people doing so, extending the reach of this campaign even further.

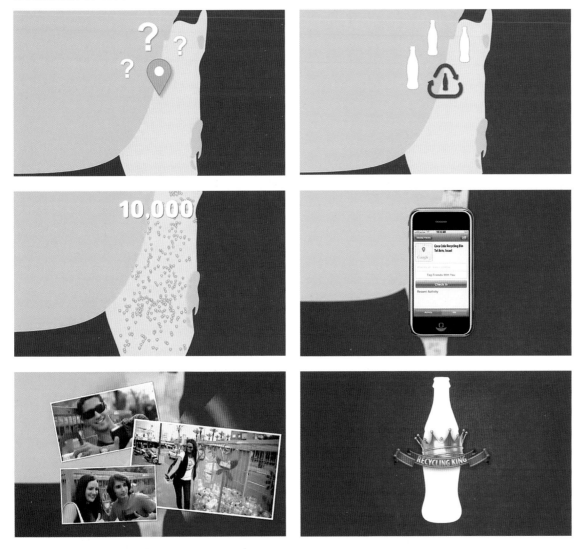

COCA-COLA
Publicis e-dologic, Tel Aviv
RECYCLING KING

In a bid to increase the number of plastic bottles recycled in Israel, Coca-Cola made use of Facebook Places. They uploaded the locations of 10,000 recycling bins across Israel onto Facebook Places and encouraged people to check in and post pictures of themselves throwing away their plastic Coke bottles. Whoever recycled the most bottles would be dubbed the recycling king or queen.

By making use of the way social media works and the 'me too' aspect of it, Coca-Cola was able to get users to encourage other users to recycle. If people see their friends doing responsible things, they will often do the same. While this campaign did good by encouraging people to recycle and made them aware of recycling bins in their vicinity, it also increased sales of Coca-Cola in Israel and reinforced the idea that Coca-Cola is a responsible company. What better results could you ask for?

We constantly look for ways to integrate people's real-life experiences with their online ones in an intuitive and easy way. In this campaign we succeeded in doing that for a good and important cause and that makes us even happier.

PUBLICIS E-DOLOGIC

#SOCIAL PEACE
GATHERING PUBLIC SUPPORT

RIO DE JANEIRO STATE
GOVERNMENT
FSB Comunicações, Rio de Janeiro
SOCIAL PEACE

In November 2010, gangs from the favelas (slums) in Rio de Janeiro began attacking people and torching cars, but the local people felt they had to tackle problems of violence, crime and lack of safety alone. The challenge was to take this feeling of individual hopelessness and turn it into a mass movement that would incorporate everyone within the city, not only aiming to educate people about work being done to tackle crime, but also to unify the people of the city.

Social media were used to humanize the efforts of the police and the government and to keep people abreast of news. It also served to dispel any rumours about actions being taken, allowing the oft-mistrusted police to communicate directly with the citizens of Rio.

The results were very promising. In just four days the @paznorio Twitter account had around 3.5 million followers and information on Orkut, Brazil's most popular social network, reached 1 million people. By opening up and getting naked, the government seemed less faceless and people realized the police are people too. For the first time in ages, public perception of the police and the government in Rio is up, helping to spread good feeling in the city and pave the way for Brazil to excel at hosting the FIFA World Cup in 2014 and the Olympic Games in 2016.

GENEROSITY

8.

GENEROSITY

Why should you give more to get more?

Be unselfish

Generosity is far more than philanthropic giving: it is an attitude. You can choose either to be generous or to be self-serving. As a brand, either you exceed government regulations and play a bigger role in people's lives, or you can continue the typical alpha-male brand behaviour: I'm the best, biggest and fastest. Consumers, however, expect you to give back. A survey carried out by Edelman in 2010 found that 86% of global consumers believe that a business needs to place at least equal weight on society's interests as on the business's interests. You have to be generous in spirit, attitude and in actions: it goes beyond free gifts that come with a magazine subscription. You have to go out of your way and give time, effort or money to make a difference and make people feel special. Generosity is unselfish and the rewards are manifold.

Add value to people's lives

The roles are reversed: for once you're actually giving something where before you were asking people for their time or to buy or donate. You begin the relationship with an act of kindness such as opening a door for a stranger. Small acts, for instance, having free Wi-Fi at McDonald's, can make a big difference – they unexpectedly add value to people's lives. It may be through adding colour, where there was once grey concrete, for instance, as in Dulux's 'Let's Colour' programme, or by spreading smiles and fun as in Volkswagen's 'The Fun Theory'. Through the 'Million' project Samsung and Verizon cleverly tied their generosity to incentives whereby students were rewarded for doing better in school. The rewards varied from extra minutes to wake-up calls from celebrities. Similar initiatives are now under way in other countries.

Generosity can also just be fun. Do you remember the Cadbury's commercial where a gorilla plays the drums to Phil Collins's 'In the Air Tonight'? The ad, which was less of an ad, was all about entertaining people rather than interrupting them with a hard sell. That is in itself very generous. If you haven't seen it, find it on YouTube – it will make you smile.

Get attractive, be generous

In his book *The Generous Man*, Danish scientist Tor Nørretranders claims that, from an evolutionary perspective, the more generous or arduous an action we undertake, such as making art or sharing one's food, the sexier we become. One example he uses from nature is the peacock's plumage that is cumbersome, ostentatious and inefficient, but for the same reasons is very attractive to peahens. Generosity might at first seem contrary to common business sense, but that's what makes it such an

GENEROSITY GONE GARGANTUAN

In 2010, Warren Buffett and the Bill & Melinda Gates Foundation kickstarted the biggest fundraising drive in history, The Giving Pledge. Over 69 billionaires in the US have so far pledged to give at least half of their fortunes away. Meanwhile, the Gates and Buffett are trying to get billionaires in other countries to pledge too.

appealing and convincing brand story. You're making an unselfish gesture, and if you can succeed despite the disadvantages you appear stronger. It's the classic tale about the hero who overcomes obstacles to save the princess. In 2011, Coca-Cola went as far as changing their iconic red cans to white in an effort to raise funds and awareness for polar bears, together with the World Wildlife Fund (WWF). Polar bears have been a cornerstone of Coca-Cola branding since the 1920s, but sacrificing the brand colours of the cans was apparently going too far: consumers confused the new packaging with Diet Coke and Coca-Cola had to rethink the effort. They nevertheless donated $3 million towards the cause.

Invest time and care

If you do a little extra for your customers and are generous towards them then they'll be happier. Word will spread and you will attract more customers. At first you give yourself a competitive disadvantage, inefficiency over efficiency, but this is followed by a positive halo. Be sure to make your customers feel special by going the extra mile in terms of time and care, as Chevrolet did in Columbia by giving taxi drivers an education (and pride) through sponsoring their very own university. Google also sacrificed time and effort when they applied their well-known Street View to 17 International art museums so art lovers

EVER TRIED TO GET A BED HOME ON A BICYCLE?

IKEA Denmark based their generosity on research that showed 20% of their customers rode a bicycle to their stores. As a consequence, they made bicycle trailers available free of charge for customers to take home their purchases, benefiting both the customers and the environment.

could walk around and enjoy the museum's vast collections. Go to Googleartproject.com and you can gaze in awe at Botticelli's *The Birth of Venus* in high resolution at the Uffizi Gallery in Florence.

Be generous in whatever you do and say

It's important that generosity is implemented as a mindset in your business throughout the organization, from how you treat your stakeholders to your product offerings. For example, Nike has taken on the betterment of sustainability practices for the industry as a whole with an initiative called GreenXChange, which is designed to drive and share sustainable solutions and patents between companies. This initiative clearly shows the amazing transformation happening throughout the business world. It used to be the case that some of a company's most valued assets were its patents, and now Nike is giving them away for free and asking others to follow. Another example is Facebook – it is sharing the technology behind its energy-efficient data centre with rival companies. Generosity is no longer just a nice-to-have halo over a brand or a kind gesture, it's an idea taken very seriously in many boardrooms. When you give, you get back or, in the words of sociologist Simon Sinek, 'When givers need help, they can expect to get it. When takers need help, they will be expected to pay for it.'

One example of this is Walmart's healthy food programme in the US. Aimed at giving underprivileged Americans the opportunity to buy healthier food at lower prices, this programme has received the First Lady Michelle Obama's blessing. Some critics claim this is an excuse to enter new markets, but in the end Walmart adds value and gets value back.

Join the trend of Random Acts of Kindness

In most cases companies have embraced generosity in campaigns or as part of an initiative instead of as a brand value. A tendency that is ballooning at the moment is called Random Acts of Kindness, which a brand can join by making a small generous act towards customers or potential customers. Interflora, the flower delivery service, launched a Twitter campaign in the UK through which it gave away flowers to Twitter users it felt needed a little cheering up. One of the florist's supportive tweets read, 'Sorry to hear you're feeling ill – would some surprise flowers make up for the sugar incident?' Similar campaigns have been adopted by everyone from airline KLM to beauty product company Biotherm. For a brand, it's a great way to add some authenticity, nerve and a pumping heart in order to connect with and add a little value to the lives of new or existing customers. With any luck, it will also make people smile.

Add to people's generous story about themselves

We're wired to be generous. Studies show that generous people are happier and have more friends. It's also proven that an altruistic act releases dopamine and oxytocin in the brain, increasing our sense of wellbeing. Giving is actually the greatest gift. For the same reason, people want to show off that they're generous: a practice dubbed 'Conspicuous Compassion'. This is best illustrated by the use of Pink Ribbons pinned to lapels to show support for breast cancer awareness or the wearing of Product (Red) sneakers or clothes. When planning activities, brands should think about how their generosity can be part of their consumers' personal story of generosity, an idea also mentioned in the Connection chapter. When raising funds for the *Rainbow Warrior III* ship, Greenpeace rewarded online donors with a certificate and printed their names on a special wall in the ship's conference room for their

'The Million Project', The New York City
Department of Education, Droga5, New York
(see page 185)

'Pepsi Refresh Project', Pepsi,
TBWA\Chiat\Day, Los Angeles
(see page 188)

online buddies to see. The circle is complete. Generous brands are more attractive, making people more attractive, attracting more people to make a difference.

It's simple: the more you give, the more you get

Human beings have survived as a species because they evolved to cooperate and care for those in need. The same development seems to be traceable in business – favouring those brands with a heart and a true involvement with their customers and the surrounding world. Generosity can be a clear differentiator in a crowded market, as the 'Pepsi Refresh Project' shows. Generosity is a powerful story to tell about a brand and can attract new customers, new suppliers and new partnerships, and can also open the door to new markets, doing good all the while. As the many examples of generous companies show, it is survival of the kindest in today's business world. In fact self-sacrificing is self-serving. At the end of the day, the more you give, the more you get back.

Interview
BRADFORD K. SMITH

Bradford K. Smith is the President of the Foundation Center, which maintains the largest database of grants and grantmakers in the US. Their mission, as stated on their website, is: 'To strengthen the social sector by advancing knowledge about philanthropy in the US and around the world.' I spoke to Bradford about the importance of philanthropy and how it could help us deal with some of the many problems we are facing in the world. Given that in 1980 there were just 22,000 independent foundations in the US and today there are 76,000, it goes without saying that these foundations will have a greater impact on the world than ever before. This also shows us that there is ever-increasing interest in this field.

To begin with we spoke about philanthropy, which Bradford defines as **'The voluntary use of private wealth for public good.'** From there, he described the genesis of the Foundation Center and how it has always been rooted in transparency, dating as far back as 1956. **'In the 1950s the US Congress investigated foundations for alleged support of "un-American activities". A group of visionary leaders came to the conclusion that the best way to combat this kind of distrust and suspicion was to prove that foundations had nothing to hide. In 1956 they created the Foundation Center as a public information service about the work of philanthropy. The founding quotation comes from Russell Cornell Leffingwell, then-Chair of the Carnegie Corporation board, who told his congressional inquirers, "We believe the foundation should have glass pockets." In 2010 we launched a website, www.glasspockets.org, to help foundations meet the growing demands for transparency in a digital age.'**

He continues, telling me where philanthropy fits in on the global scale of doing good. **'Philanthropy is not a replacement for government and never should be. But philanthropy can do what governments cannot** or, sometimes, will not do. Foundations do not sell products on the market, run for office or raise funds, therefore they have a precious independence with which to address unpopular causes, attend to the needs of those who have fallen through the social safety net, and innovate. Foundations often experiment with programmes and solutions that government can then take to scale.'

Philanthropy is not limited to the West, though. Bill and Melinda Gates and Warren Buffett have recently taken their The Giving Pledge initiative to India and China, in recognition of their growing economic power. **'Philanthropy is definitely on the rise in countries like China, India, Brazil, Mexico, Turkey and others. Let's be clear about one thing: big philanthropy has always been about the rich. Andrew Carnegie and John D. Rockefeller, who started the first modern foundations 100 years ago, were not poor. The second largest number of billionaires, 115 to be exact, on the Forbes global list comes from China. Philanthropy is growing in these countries precisely because very large fortunes are being accumulated by wealthy individuals. In this regard, Bill and Melinda Gates and Warren Buffett are leading by example. But we also see growing cultures of philanthropy in many countries where people of varying economic strata are volunteering their time and donating to the causes of their choice.'**

I ask Bradford about philanthropy from the corporate world and it seems that even though there has been improvement, it is still not widespread. **'Corporate philanthropy has expanded together with the overall expansion of the US economy over the last few decades. Many corporations choose to create foundations while others maintain robust corporate giving programmes. Some have both. Still, corporations account for only 5 percent of charitable giving in America.'**

When it comes to sustainable business and what it can offer the world, Bradford is excited, but suitably wary. **'In today's world social change is produced by governments, foundations, non-profits, social entrepreneurs, and businesses, often working together in partnership. Sustainable business is a very encouraging trend in terms of its potential to create a more equal and environmentally sound world. It has the potential to produce positive change on a much larger scale than corporate philanthropy, given the power and resources many businesses command. It is still business, though, and will ultimately be defined and shaped by pressures for profitability and competition, whereas philanthropy will be needed to address the many problems the market cannot resolve.'** At the same time, Bradford reminds businesses of the importance of generosity and giving. **'Today, most businesses realize that trust and image are highly** valuable assets. They take years to build and one crisis or scandal to destroy. Moreover, surveys demonstrate that highly talented professionals entering the job market prefer to work for a socially responsible business than one interested only in making money. Philanthropy, pro-bono volunteer work and corporate giving programmes play a huge role in creating a positive image.'

Throughout his career, Bradford has spent a lot of time working with transparency and looking at how it can affect businesses and foundations. **'Any sector in today's world that has a significant impact on people's lives – government, business, the church, and foundations – is expected to be transparent. Technology is accelerating this trend. Whether you like it or not, people will be logging on and searching for information about your organization and pushing it out to their online networks. The old communications maxim about telling your story rather than letting others tell it for you is more true today than ever.'**

When talk turns to the challenges facing foundations (including private, corporate and public foundations), transparency comes up yet again. **'Demands for greater transparency will certainly grow. In addition, as governments have less money with which to support already weakened social safety nets, there will be more pressure – from the public and governments themselves – to direct how foundations spend their money. This could jeopardize what people call "philanthropic freedom". The best way to defend this freedom is for foundations to be more transparent about all the good they are doing. Philanthropy in America has tended to keep a low profile and let good works speak for themselves. Few even had a communications professional on staff, let alone a department. All that has changed. Today you have to be able to communicate, in as many media as possible, what you are doing.'**

When it comes to brands, it's an issue of communicating well and backing up your claims with real results. **'In general, I think people are quite willing to recognize the important work of social enterprises or even traditional businesses that are socially responsible. But businesses have to be careful to make sure that the PR claims for such work do not surpass the reality. People have to be able to trust the claims you are making for yourself.'**

I ask Bradford who is responsible for making these changes and improving our lot – society, government or brands – and he answers that it's a question of collaboration and working together. **'This is a great question, if not THE question of our time. The idea that government has the responsibility and the means to resolve society's most pressing issues is long gone. And we have been disabused of the** notion that markets alone will magically be capable of doing so. We live in a networked world of social change, and it is different combinations of government, business, non-profits, foundations, talented entrepreneurs, and social movements (both offline and on) that will make inroads in meeting the challenges we face.'

//

Philanthropy, pro-bono volunteer work and corporate giving programmes play a huge role in creating a positive image.

//

COCA-COLA
Ogilvy, Buenos Aires
FRIENDSHIP MACHINE

To encourage people to work together
and take advantage of Friendship Day
in Argentina, Coca-Cola launched
'friendship machines', which gave out
a free bottle of Coke for every bottle
bought. They functioned just like normal
vending machines, but there was one
catch – they were 3.5 metres (12 ft)
high. This meant you had to have
a friend with you, to help you reach
the buttons.

This fun and generous idea
reinforces Coca-Cola as the brand
that sells happiness – it makes people
smile and it makes them feel good
about the brand.

It's all about giving a little bit back. **Eco-conscious BlueMotion technology.**

Das Auto.

VOLKSWAGEN
Ogilvy, Cape Town
DONATED AD SPACE

To make the public aware of their new environmentally friendly, high mileage, low emissions BlueMotion technology in South Africa, Volkswagen donated prime ad space in their print campaign to local NGOs. The unexpected window of an ad within an ad immediately draws the attention of the viewer and in some ways nods to the way we browse the Internet – windows within windows.

All parties win in this case. Volkswagen reinforces the idea that they are a brand that cares and the NGOs to whom they are donating space get valuable exposure. Ad space in magazines in South Africa is expensive, so giving some of it to charities that could never afford it made a lot of sense. Just as BlueMotion technology is about giving back to the environment, Volkswagen proves they are a brand that walks its talk.

It's all about giving a little bit back. **Eco-conscious BlueMotion technology.**

Das Auto.

DULUX
Euro RSCG, London
LET'S COLOUR

To reposition themselves in the paint market, Dulux launched the 'Let's Colour' project, which aims to use colour to make people's lives better. In a global war against grey, drab and bland, they have committed themselves to painting streets, houses, schools and squares. So far, the 'Let's Colour' project has visited South Africa, the Netherlands, Turkey, France, India, the UK and Brazil – spreading colour and happiness wherever it has gone.

Through some beautifully shot time-lapse films, Dulux has shown how their paint can transform the saddest looking places into something exciting and energizing – all through the use of colour. Once again, we see that when a brand partners with an initiative that is very close to (or inseparable from) its product offering, the effects are much more powerful.

This campaign has been very effective – over 250,000 people viewed the film online in the first month of its launch. By donating all this paint, Dulux has executed a visually stunning campaign that is not only generous, but also encourages massive collaboration from people – a great example of goodvertising.

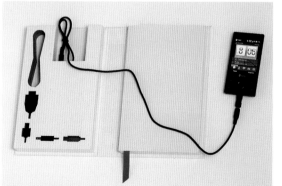

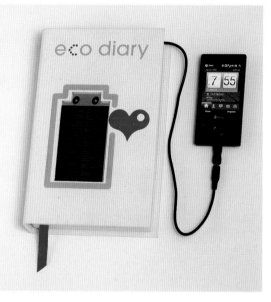

CELL C
Net#work BBDO, Johannesburg
ECO DIARY

The South African mobile phone service provider Cell C direct mailed an eco diary to high-profile Cell C subscribers and all of their staff in South Africa. It featured a booklet full of tips on how to save energy and live a greener lifestyle. Most interestingly, it had a solar charger built into the cover of the booklet, which allowed customers to charge their phones using nothing more than the power of the sun.

The 312 tips on how to live a greener lifestyle were presented as poems, with accompanying illustrations. Some of the tips were as simple as encouraging people to turn off all their lights and electrical appliances at home and to eat dinner by candlelight. Others involved pictograms of how many kilometres your car travels per year and how many trees you would need to plant in order to offset the carbon dioxide emissions.

By doing something that is both fun and simple, Cell C not only showed their customers that they are a brand that cares, but also a brand that is generous. If enough customers followed the tips they could have a positive impact on the environment too.

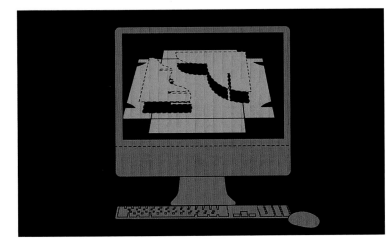

IKEA
Hubble Innovations, Berlin
CLEAN ATTITUDE

What we love about this idea is that it doesn't just tell you how sustainable IKEA is, but proves it directly. And furthermore we didn't have to use any extra material. We could convey IKEA's attitude by using material that is already there – we just let the customer turn it into something useful. That's what makes it truly IKEA – the people had their part as well.

DENNIS MAY, CREATIVE DIRECTOR OF HUBBLE INNOVATIONS

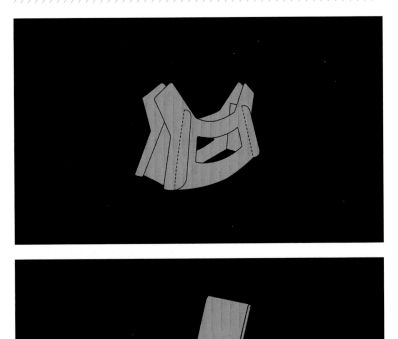

IKEA in Austria cleverly showed how to reuse packaging that would usually be thrown away. What could be more aligned with the values of IKEA? Customers were used to building their own furniture, so doing the same with the packaging made perfect sense. IKEA also ran a competition for people to submit their own ideas for new products to be built from cardboard – the winning ideas were implemented on the packaging.

The campaign was such a success that it soon spread across the design world and was then implemented by IKEA across the globe. Everyone was a winner. IKEA was able to show their green credentials to the world without spending any money on traditional media and consumers got added value from their purchases, feeling that IKEA is not only generous, but concerned about the environment too. On top of that, the world benefits from less waste and less landfill space being used. In a world where we see so much unnecessary packaging, it's a breath of fresh air for packaging to be more than something you throw away.

million

THE NEW YORK CITY DEPARTMENT OF EDUCATION
Droga5, New York
THE MILLION PROJECT

After looking at the public education system from a supply and demand perspective, Droga5, along with renowned Harvard economist Dr Roland G. Fryer, realized that they needed to turn the entire equation on its head. Despite increased spending per pupil, smaller classes and greater education of teachers, the school system was performing no better than it had before. They recognized that the problem might not lie solely with the supply side (the education system), but also with the demand side (the students), so they saw there was a need to motivate students in an innovative way.

In 2007, nearly 3,000 students in the New York City school system were given free phones (donated by Samsung), preloaded with mobile credit (provided by Verizon). According to how students performed in school (this was based on attendance, grades and studying), they were rewarded with mobile credits for calling, texting, internet use and downloads. By linking something students want to classroom activity, they created a real demand for education.

This generous means of incentivizing performance shows a new way of speaking to teens that they understand and, in terms of results, this campaign was undeniably successful. Some 65% of parents who allowed their child to participate said he/she was doing better in school compared to the start of the programme. On top of this, more than 75% of the students involved in the programme said it had impacted their school positively in at least one of the following ways:

- They were working harder at school
- They were 'more competitive in a good way'
- They were interacting more with teachers

More than 75% of parents whose children were in the programme also noted at least one of the following changes in his/her child since the start of the campaign:

- They spent more time doing homework
- They got more excited about certain classes
- They received higher grades and/or better progress reports
- They studied more with friends

This campaign shows that with fresh thinking even the most confounding problems can be solved, with good results for all the players involved. 'The Million' ran a second programme in Oklahoma City during the 2010–11 school year, and hopefully more states are in the pipeline.

BCR
Rogalski Grigoriu, Bucharest
MONEY SCHOOL

In Romania after the financial crisis of 2008, one of the oldest banks in the country, BCR, created the 'Money School' – an online social media-based initiative that aimed to teach people how to save. Through the use of the 'Super Lion', an imaginary currency based on the leu (Romania's standard currency which translates as 'lion'), consumers were encouraged to speak to each other and learn how to handle money properly. Interactive lessons from 'The Headmaster' and examinations tested the knowledge of the students, with a young couple winning the prize for the couple who saved the most.

The results were incredibly positive, exceeding BCR's expectations. 8,711 teams applied to join the programme, 74% more than they were aiming for, and 80% of those who participated in the programme felt they learned how to be more responsible with money (compared with a goal of 30%).

BCR demonstrated real generosity and showed that they cared, giving their customers tangible results they can use for the rest of their lives.

NORTE BEER
Del Campo Nazca Saatchi & Saatchi,
Buenos Aires
THE BEST EXCUSE EVER

Norte is the leading beer in the north-west of Argentina, but they found they were losing ground to premium beers being served in bars. They felt that by giving back to the area from which they come they could improve their standing in the eyes of their consumers.

Built on the insight that women would rather their partners did something other than go to a bar, Norte made going to a bar a good thing. For each bottle of Norte bought, they donated one minute of time to doing good. This gave men a legitimate excuse to go out to bars with their friends – they just had to put their bottle caps in special counters. By the end of the campaign, just over 50,000 minutes of time had been donated by Norte. Their teams did things such as refurbish schools, plant trees and improve public parks. On top of this, research carried out after the campaign found that people saw the personality of the brand as, 'a fun man, who at the same time is a good, sharing and responsible person'.

Girlfriends can be proud of their boyfriends. And the most important part: boyfriends can go to the bar with their friends trouble free.

DEL CAMPO NAZCA SAATCHI & SAATCHI

WHAT DO YOU CARE ABOUT?

pepsi **refresh** project

refresh**everything**.com

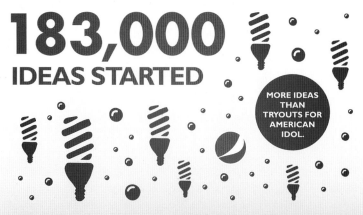

183,000
IDEAS STARTED

MORE IDEAS THAN TRYOUTS FOR AMERICAN IDOL.

47
ORGANIZATIONS STARTED

98
SCHOOLS IMPROVED

HAPPY 2010

refresh**everything**.com

DO GOOD

every *pepsi* refreshes the world

SOLAR-POWERED BILLBOARD

In a bold move that provided tangible results for the surrounding community, South Africa's Nedbank asked, 'What if a bank really did give power to the people?' A billboard was erected with solar panels that generated electricity to power local community buildings and the local school.

This is a classic example of goodvertising, a positive brand message combined with real results that improve people's lives. The positive benefits for advertising like this extend not only to the people receiving the free electricity, but also to Nedbank itself.

By applying a healthy dose of generosity and creativity (the thinking behind this billboard is great) we can see how this billboard won an Outdoor Grand Prix at Cannes in 2007. Nedbank has recently extended this idea by erecting billboards with wind turbines as well as solar panels. Power to the people indeed!

PEPSI
TBWA\Chiat\Day, Los Angeles
PEPSI REFRESH PROJECT

In a radical move in 2010, Pepsi pulled out of advertising at the Super Bowl for the first time in 23 years. Rather than add to the noise of advertising, they decided to take $20 million and do good with it. Known as the 'Pepsi Refresh Project', it provided social grants for great ideas that could make a real difference to people's lives.

At first Pepsi was faced with very harsh criticism. People said the campaign was not in line with Pepsi's product offering and that the amount of money they were throwing at it was dangerous. At the end of the day, though, Pepsi proved them wrong.

Rather than run the campaign as a traditional donation scheme, where consumers could 'collaborate' with Pepsi by voting for a pre-decided charity, Pepsi allowed the crowd to do everything. Users of the site put forward the ideas and the community voted on them. Each month $1,300,000 was given away.

Critics of the campaign were soon to eat their words. The 'Pepsi Refresh Project' became such a hit that in the first three months alone the site garnered over one billion impressions. More votes were cast in the 'Pepsi Refresh Project' than in the last US

presidential election. In order to incentivize voting and push sales, Pepsi has recently released specially marked packs that allow for power voting – these votes are worth more than standard user votes and can help people see a project they believe in come to fruition.

This is more than your average CSR (Corporate Social Responsibility) campaign simply signing off a cheque to charity. This is a solemn commitment from Pepsi to do good and collaborate with their consumers to make the world a better place. By putting the power in the hands of the consumer, Pepsi is

allowing them to feel as if they are involved in the change and that they are helping to make a difference. This forms incredibly strong bonds with consumers, tying them in to the Pepsi brand while leading to real change.

CHEVROLET
Sancho BBDO, Bogota
TAXI DRIVERS' UNIVERSITY

In Bogotá, the capital of Colombia, there are 100,000 taxis, but no recognized taxi drivers' schools as there are in London or New York, for example. Seeing a gap in the market and a way to make people aware of their cars, Chevrolet started the Taxi Drivers' University with special radio shows to back up the learning. The university is free to any taxi driver regardless of what brand of car they drive. By the end of 2011, Chevrolet will have had 4,000 graduates.

This university not only empowers taxi drivers to do their jobs better, but also creates a lifelong relationship between these taxi drivers and Chevrolet. They hope that this relationship will result in more taxi drivers choosing their brand. Generosity itself is reciprocal and this is an investment from Chevrolet in the future. They improve the lives of taxi drivers and might be rewarded with sales in the future.

I registered in Chevrolet's University, motivated by my children, because I want to be more than what I am.

TAXI DRIVER INVOLVED WITH THE PROJECT

VAI-VAI
PACKAGING FOR GOOD

Vai-Vai is a company that sells naturally extracted coconut water with no added preservatives or sugar. They run their company in a cooperative way, reinvesting in the communities that produce their coconut water – this has a positive effect on 8,000 families in the Philippines. On top of this, their coconut water is transported in the most sustainable way, as they eschew carbon-guzzling trucks and opt for trains and boats where possible.

This is not enough for this generous company, though. They have dedicated one panel of their (obviously recyclable) packaging to NGOs and other causes. This dedicated panel changes from month to month and is openly described by the company as 'free advertising'.

By taking such a simple idea, Vai-Vai is not only doing good for the causes they support, but also for their company. Consumers who see this level of generosity from a brand will struggle to feel anything other than positive towards it.

INNOCENT
THE BIG KNIT

In order to harness the power of generosity and allow people to feel they are part of the solution, Innocent started 'The Big Knit' in 2003. People all across the UK were encouraged to knit hats to fit over the tops of Innocent smoothies, and for each bottle sold with a hat on it Innocent donated 25p to Age UK, a charity for the aged. The money made the old feel that they are still valued, with funding for home visits, befriending and a number of winter events.

Around 80% of the hats received by 'The Big Knit' were actually knitted by the people who benefit directly from Age UK, allowing them to be involved and at the same time to get them together at Age UK centres. This creates a self-fuelling circle of good.

At the end of 2011, Innocent hopes to have raised £1 million over the eight years of 'The Big Knit'. With these hats, Innocent has also been able to show consumers in store just how much they care and how generous they are, increasing good feelings about their brand. Even the hats themselves are like a little gift for each customer, showing more generosity.

Together we can reach over 350,000 people this winter who desperately need our help to keep warm and in touch with others.

INNOCENT

MERCEDES-BENZ
Jung Von Matt, Elbe
TRANSPARENT WALLS

Mercedes-Benz wanted to make consumers aware of their PRE-SAFE precrash system, so they projected real-time footage onto walls to show what was going on around the corner. This made tricky intersections in Germany safer, because as people drove up they could effectively see around the corner, as if the walls were transparent.

By making driving safer and helping people to detect dangerous situations before they happened, Mercedes-Benz showcased a vital function of the PRE-SAFE system. It goes without saying that this campaign is also somewhat buzzworthy.

Not only does this execution achieve great synergy with the product being promoted, but it also covers one of the commandments of goodvertising. This campaign dares to ask the 'what if?' question and comes up with a great answer. What if people could see through walls to avoid accidents? What if your car could do that for you? This refusal to work within the boundaries of traditional thought gives us this creative and generous answer, which positions Mercedes-Benz as the safe car brand of choice.

9.

INSIGHT
What's the true motivation?

The 'Truth®' Campaign, American Legacy
Foundation, Crispin Porter + Bogusky and Arnold
Worldwide, Miami (see pages 212–13)

You have a difficult task ahead if you want people to give up or limit something they enjoy: whether it's taking shorter showers, living more healthily or saving energy. If you've tried to quit smoking you'll agree that you have to know a lot about yourself and your behaviour to succeed. For a brand to make you quit, the challenge is even greater. The advertising legend Bill Bernbach gives us a nice perspective on it, 'Nothing is so powerful as an insight into human nature…what compulsions drive a man, what instincts dominate his action… If you know these things about a man you can touch him at the core of his being.'

FREE WILL IS AN ILLUSION

'If you go through all of the research that's been done in psychology recently, you end up with the position that the conscious will is an illusion.'
Malcolm Gladwell

The power of an insight

Here's an example of the insight behind the most successful American anti-smoking campaign to date, dubbed 'Truth®'. In 1998, the agency Crispin Porter + Bogusky (CP+B) was briefed to communicate messages such as, 'Don't smoke, it's only for grownups' or 'It's gross and makes your teeth gross'. CP+B thought it would only make things worse because they were convinced that young people saw smoking as an act of rebellion. So with this insight into youth behaviour, they provided young people with another tool of rebellion, rebellion against the tobacco industry. The same industry that poisoned their mums and dads and was now trying to sell them the same nails for their own coffin. For the youth the message rang true and the campaign is still running over a decade later, proving the longevity of an insightful campaign.

Use insights to create a strong connection

To change people's behaviour or attitude you have to move beyond their intellect and appeal to their feelings and what motivates them. In advertising as well as in any other communication industry, much of the best work is based on a strong insight. Here an insight means an

Opposite 'It's Not Happening Here, but it is
Happening Now', Amnesty International,
Walker, Zurich (see pages 208–209)

197

understanding of your audience's fundamental needs and wants. It's the key to why your audience do what they do or believe what they believe. For youths, smoking wasn't about being cool, it was about rebellion. Insights are a glimpse into your audience's fundamental needs and wants, hopes and dreams, concerns and fears. They are the small secrets they don't necessarily share with others and perhaps are not even aware of themselves. If you use a genuine insight in your campaign then your target audience will feel touched and understood instead of interrupted by an advertising message.

Speak to them as an individual, not as a target group

A lot of marketers confuse what the advertising world calls observations with real insights, but it's very important to differentiate between the two. The difference is that an insight is anchored in your target group's inner needs and wants, whereas an observation is more a social rule, common knowledge or a factual observation. 'Men shouldn't cry' or 'women like shopping' are observations stating the stereotypical notions. These generalizations are likely to make your audience feel you are talking to them as a target group or a crowd rather than as an individual. Observations generally speak to your audience's intellect, and their response might be: I know that. Insights spark a different response: I feel that.

Anti-smoking messages such as 'smoking kills' are based on fear tactics and are trying to reason with their audience, whereas an insight deals with why you smoke on an inner level – as with the 'Truth®' campaign. Sometimes it's necessary to use an insight into a feeling that the target group themselves have tried to suppress – because it was easier for them not to care. In a recent campaign, Amnesty International identified such an insight, 'I really don't care what happens on the other side of the globe.' It's a harsh insight to deal with, but the reality is that we as humans tend to identify with those whose values and lives are most similar to our own. This usually happens to be those who live near us. In response, Amnesty International, together with the advertising agency Walker, launched transparent outdoor executions that made it seem as if human rights abuses were being played out in front of viewers on the street. The campaign line read, 'It's not happening here, but it is happening now.' This campaign really succeeded in bringing abuses happening on the other side of the world into a pedestrian street in Zurich, for instance, and confronted people with a strong insight into their nature – one that exposed their hard-heartedness.

Speak to the control centre of behavioural change

A good insight can be disarming – it touches the unconscious. As discussed in the Compassion chapter, brain science shows that we make decisions in a part of the limbic brain called the amygdala – home to feelings such as trust, loyalty, fear and desire. This part of the brain doesn't have a capacity for language, so when you make decisions in the amygdala those decisions are instinctive rather than rational. You feel and know it's the right thing to do, but you cannot explain why. Many of the decisions we make as consumers are controlled by this instinctive gut feeling rather than rational thinking. This also explains why consumers' actions are more easily influenced by an insightful approach – since you speak directly to the control centre of behavioural change.

Express your insight creatively

Despite the elusive and non-verbal nature of insights, many still rely on traditional research methods such as focus groups to gain them. Research often serves as reassurance for someone who's afraid to make a decision. How can you find answers to something people don't necessarily know themselves and may battle to express? Research should rather be used as a source of inspiration and not as a source of answers. Moreover, it is one thing to gain an insight but you also need to grasp how that insight can be freshly used. The American Humanist Carol Wintermute describes it well: 'Science states meanings; art expresses them.' A Brazilian water conservation campaign managed to bring an insight to life in a clever, creative way. The insight was: youths are tired of don'ts. As a result they went for a 'do' message: pee in the shower and save water. A generic brief about saving water was suddenly turned into a fun and quirky message because of the right insight – but also because of the right strategy. Insights stretch an arm out and say, 'I know how you feel'. As a consumer, you feel spoken to instead of advertised to.

Apply great thinkers, great strategists

If you're able to combine an insight with an inventive strategy to give people a fresh look at themselves, their actions and motives, then that's where the real magic happens. You need great thinkers, great strategists who can match insights with marketing objectives in a relevant and groundbreaking way. Campaigns with a true human insight have a greater impact because they speak to the audience's hearts and to what motivates them. It's up to brands to decode people's irrational behaviour and to use it to create a crisp, compelling message that encourages action or a change of attitude. Then and only then might people do the logical thing and properly look after themselves, others and our precariously balanced planet.

'Pee in the Shower', SOS Mata Atlantica
Charity, F/Nazca Saatchi & Saatchi, São Paulo
(see page 207)

FROM ANALYSIS TO INTUITION

Insight lab? Google employees have
to dedicate 20% of their work time
to creative innovation and their
employment policy aims to hire
a diverse range of people who bring
different skills and personal qualities to
the table.

Interview
KIM PAPWORTH
& TONY DAVIDSON

Sometimes it feels that enough emphasis is not placed on the partnerships that can create great advertising. Kim Papworth and Tony Davidson fall into that category – they've been working together since 1985 and are still together, a quarter of a century later. They themselves have described it as a marriage and I must admit that, sitting talking to them via Skype, there is most definitely an ease between them that can only come from many late nights working together in advertising studios.

Kim and Tony have created and overseen some of the world's most loved advertising campaigns, including Levi's 'Flat Eric', Nike's 'Run London' and Honda's 'The Power of Dreams' campaign, including 'Cog' and 'Grrr'. Partners at Wieden+Kennedy, they were the first people outside of the Portland, Oregon office to have such an honour bestowed upon them. When speaking to them, though, you don't feel intimidated – their understated British humility takes care of that, albeit quietly. They have said themselves that they aren't always sure what they're doing, they just do what feels right.

I started by discussing with Kim how exactly one goes about executing a digital handshake and Tony arrives soon after. I'm glad they could fit me in: they were having a busy day in the office and I could sense the tension. We started off talking about Honda's 'Grrr', the importance of it at the time and, interestingly, their opinion that it would have looked very different if it were done today. With the emergence of new channels of communication, they believe that advertising can and should do more, and should be able to respond accordingly. They also spoke about the importance of finding a story in the history of the brand, and working with a brand whose values are aligned with yours. With a brand such as Honda, who are so dedicated to motion and moving people forwards, building on their enthusiasm is almost 'easy'.

Kim says, 'I think when it's done the right way...you go out with something strong, but you hold back some money because you're going to need [it] once it's hit. You have to react and watch it and do stuff on the move, while it's hot... We've seen it a couple of times recently where suddenly something just goes mental and if it happens when you're on the back foot and you're not ready for it...then you'll miss the moment. You have to go in going: right, if this thing takes off then we've got to be prepared.'

At the same time, though, they caution against getting caught up in trying to satisfy the latest and most hyped media channels. Tony explained, 'You don't need that. You need a great idea that people will talk about.' I asked them whether the attempt to do good advertising then required a different starting point from traditional advertising. 'I think all that's happened is the power has switched

For agencies like Wieden+Kennedy it has always been about the truth, so that hasn't changed – it's not like suddenly we've all had a big meeting and decided, hang on, we need to get more truthful.

more: the consumer has more ability to bring a brand down. Therefore you have to be more open and more honest. It hasn't changed completely – before TV a good idea was still a good idea and people talked about it and they said, have you seen what they've done! Whether it was an artist who broke all the rules or an architect, this hasn't changed. And I think the worry is that we get caught up in all the hype. Many of the same rules still apply: a good film script is still a good film script, only now film can be anywhere – and more interactive if we so choose.'

Kim continues, talking about honesty from brands: **'For agencies like Wieden+Kennedy it has always been about the truth, so that hasn't changed – it's not like suddenly we've all had a big meeting and decided, hang on, we need to get more truthful. It's always been about that, so for us it isn't a problem.'** In the same vein, he goes on to talk about the control a brand has over its perception with consumers. **'A brand had a lot more control over its voice and what was said about it [in the past], whereas now...the brands are a lot more open to criticism, and if they do something bad everyone will know about it really quickly.'** Tony chips in, **'How you react to that situation is part of your brand.'**

I like this idea of brands being seen holistically – they are not just their marketing messages or their products, they are their behaviour, their hiring policies, their waste and discarded materials, their stores and their mistakes. With the multi-armed, two-way media channels we now have at our disposal these are opportunities, not threats. Kim says, **'I think consumers expect more from the brands that they like. They expect them to do interesting things, they expect them to have strong opinions, they expect...that if something is going on...that they are going to be responsible and do something about it.'** When asked about whether this was an opportunity or a threat, Kim said, **'I think it's good. I think it means that good brands have to be better and if you're a big brand that isn't, then you've got to change.'**

Tony continues from where Kim left off, **'If you're good as a person... you don't go around saying, "I'm good, I'm good." You do it – you do good. More and more consumers expect this behaviour of their brands, and when brands do something that could potentially hurt them it will get out and it will hurt, so be very careful what you choose to do. Why did so many companies in the UK suddenly sign up to Fairtrade? Because in their mind, and importantly in their consumers' minds, it was seen to be doing good.'**

When we were speaking about awards and doing good, Tony (who was President of D&AD in 2007) makes the very valid point that doing advertising for the sake of winning awards is not a good thing. It often becomes about 'trophy hunting' for the individual or the agency rather than doing what is right for the brand. Globally, scam ads have become a real problem at award shows. Great advertising campaigns and ideas are ones that truly transform a brand's business and build fans of the brand.

As our time is up, and Kim and Tony stand up and rush off, I am left with a very poignant message from Tony, **'If advertising is to remain relevant and add to people's lives, it has to change. Advertising as we know it will not exist in the future.'**

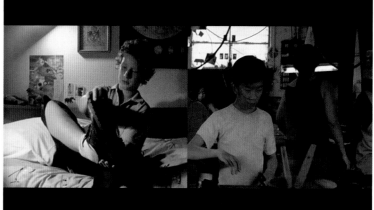

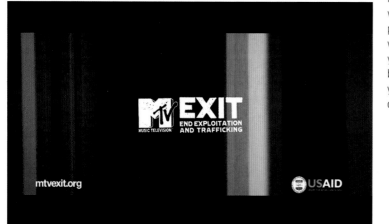

MTV EXIT
Colman Rasic, Sydney
ALL I NEED

MTV EXIT and Radiohead teamed up to create the music video for 'All I Need', which aims to educate people about human trafficking across the world. It shows two parallel stories of a young boy in the West and a young boy working in a sweatshop in Asia and highlights the differences between the two.

This video was shown on all MTV networks across the world, and can be viewed online and downloaded onto phones. As of mid-2011, it had been viewed just over 3.1 million times. If you add the number of times it will have been seen on TV across the world then you start to get an idea of the number of people this video has reached.

As you watch the video you start to feel a real connection with the two boys. The boy working in the sweatshop is someone to whom you can relate. It is so powerful because you can imagine yourself or someone you know in the same situation, simply because of where they were born or their family situation.

BOLTHOUSE FARMS
Crispin Porter + Bogusky, Miami
EAT 'EM LIKE JUNK FOOD

In the first move of its kind, Bolthouse Farms marketed and recategorized carrots as junk food. They would no longer be boring little veggies, but would become vending-machine fare, with packaging and marketing to match. The observation was that carrots are, by nature, the perfect junk food. They're small and sweet, brightly coloured and perfect for snacking.

When the campaign started, carrots in the packaging shown were placed in supermarkets in two cities. Special vending machines were made and installed in local high schools, next to all the other junk food vending machines. Each different style of packaging (chic, extreme and futuristic) was accompanied by a satirical junk food TV ad. Within a month, sales of carrots had spiked by 12%.

This leads us to realize that in order to get people to eat better, maybe all we need to do is make the marketing sexier – a great insight that informed this campaign. It has worked for fast food companies and junk food for ages – perhaps it is time to use their secret weapon against them.

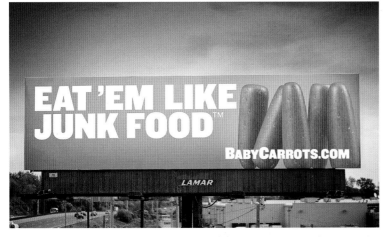

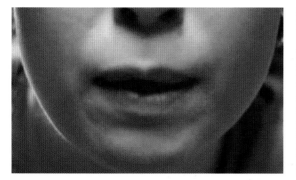

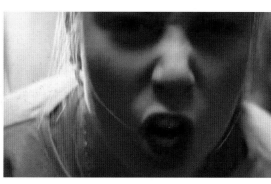

BARNADO'S
BBH, London
WHAT WE HEAR

Barnardo's is a charity that prides itself on reaching out to troubled youths, no matter what their circumstances. A series of interactive films, in which viewers were placed in the position of the charity, made this abundantly clear. For the first time in history, viewers could see interactive full-screen HD films online and be transported into the world of Barnardo's.

The films showed teens screaming and acting in a way that would scare most people, but they were dubbed over with what Barnardo's knew these teens were actually saying. Users could choose to listen to either soundtrack. Many of the people working with Barnardo's have to do this on a daily basis and they want the public to know that they can make a difference.

By giving consumers an insight into the way Barnardo's sees things, the ad shows that not only can the world be a better place if people listen well, but also that Barnardo's is the organization you should go to if you need help dealing with troubled youths. It simplifies what Barnardo's does in a clever way and makes it much easier for viewers to understand and be aware of their work.

When we see
a troubled youth
we see a child
who needs help.

URBAN MINISTRIES OF DURHAM
McKinney, Durham, North Carolina
CHECK-IN FOR THE HOMELESS

The Urban Ministries of Durham (UMD), a non-profit organization in North Carolina, launched a Foursquare initiative to raise awareness of homelessness. By adding places where homeless people would check-in, the idea was that people would become more aware of the choices homeless people have to make. Places such as abandoned warehouses, dumpsters, vacant construction sites and even a tent under an overpass were added. If people checked in to these places then this would raise awareness among their social group.

To drive the message home, the tips section for each location told the user about UMD, their activities and homelessness in the area. This insightful approach was based on an understanding of how people use their mobile devices and how to incorporate that, making this campaign very effective. The unexpected nature of the check-in points created a powerful message that could lead to positive behavioural changes and raise awareness among the target audience.

WHAT IF THIS TEXT GETS BACK TO STEVE? HE'S PRETTY **STRONG AND I DON'T** WANT A PUNCH HOLE WHERE **MY FACE USED TO BE.**

LG
Y&R, New York
GIVE IT A PONDER

We all know how much teens and tweens love to text, but what messages are they sending to each other and what are the consequences of those messages?

LG partnered with renowned American actor James Lipton (and his well-known beard) to encourage young people to 'give it a ponder' before engaging in risky mobile behaviour. Lipton exhorts people to think twice before 'texting a picture of their junk' or spreading rumours. He pulls off his beard, hands it to a teen and, while stroking it thoughtfully, they think about the consequences of their actions. There was even an app that allowed teens to superimpose a beard onto their faces when video chatting, a world first.

In an engaging, memorable and amusing way, LG puts forward a positive, responsible message. This campaign was built on the insight that teens found it easier to think of the consequences for themselves rather than the consequences for others. And it turned out to be very successful: 59% of teens who recalled the campaign thought LG was a socially responsible company. In addition, 62% of teens agreed that LG has 'phones that are good for text messaging' – a higher percentage than any manufacturer, including the all-powerful iPhone.

IF MY BOYFRIEND SEES THIS TEXT HE'LL BE MAD. **LIKE A GRIZZLY BEAR** THAT GETS A SALAD WHEN IT **REALLY ORDERED FRIES.**

THIS RUMOR COULD GET ME IN TROUBLE. **REAL TROUBLE TOO,** NOT SEXY PILLOW FIGHT TROUBLE.

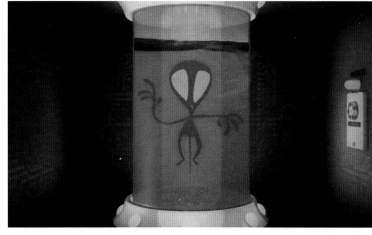

SOS MATA ATLANTICA CHARITY
F/Nazca Saatchi & Saatchi, São Paulo
PEE IN THE SHOWER

The SOS Mata Atlântica charity, which works to protect the Atlantic Rainforest in Brazil, was faced with a dilemma. People were tired of morbid environmental campaigns with negative messages, but SOS needed help. They decided to put a positive spin on things and encouraged people to pee in the shower in order to save water. Backed up by playful TV spots, this campaign and its playfulness soon went viral – spreading like crazy.

The campaign started in Brazil, but the idea was picked up across the globe, with many media outlets running stories based on the idea. It went on to be featured in 66 countries across five continents.

When an idea is so much fun, it demands to be shared. What this campaign proved is that positive messages can yield good results for the environment. In the past, people have used guilt, doom and gloom to get people to change their behaviour, but perhaps being positive is equally, if not more, effective. People would rather share something positive than something that puts a dampener on your day.

AMNESTY INTERNATIONAL
Walker, Zurich
**IT'S NOT HAPPENING HERE,
BUT IT IS HAPPENING NOW**

In this ambitious poster campaign in Switzerland, 200 posters painstakingly re-created their background, so that the poster seemed not to be there at all. Superimposed onto each poster was an image that depicted the global issues with which Amnesty International is currently dealing — including torture, human rights abuses, unfair detention and child soldiers. By making these issues real to people and contextualizing them in the viewer's immediate surroundings, Amnesty International found a very powerful means of furthering their cause. It is easy for people to identify with the issues when they are in their local setting. This insight meant that these problems were no longer on the other side of the world and easy to ignore — they were on people's doorstep.

As a result of these posters, Amnesty International saw a twentyfold increase in visits to their website, proving that great ideas will always encourage action.

SCOPE
Leo Burnett, Melbourne
SEE THE PERSON

This Australian campaign from Scope, a not-for-profit supporting children and adults with disabilities, takes the form of a music video performed and recorded by the band Rudely Interrupted. Of the six members, five live with physical and intellectual disabilities. As the video progresses from darkness into light, the band members are revealed and we notice their disabilities, challenging our original perception.

By getting the audience to enjoy the song before they see the band, this video confronts you with your own prejudices (however strong they may be) and forces you to see people with disabilities in a different way. Rudely Interrupted's single was available on iTunes and the band toured across Australia, with proceeds going to Scope.

The campaign cost $10,000 to create and generated over $1.7 million worth of media coverage. The video had over 100,000 views online and, most importantly, Scope's fundraising grew by 70% as a direct result of the campaign.

When people watch this music video, they experience a perception change. They are forced to listen to the music before they can make any judgments about who's making it. When they discover who's behind the music, they realize how capable people living with a disability really are.

LEO BURNETT

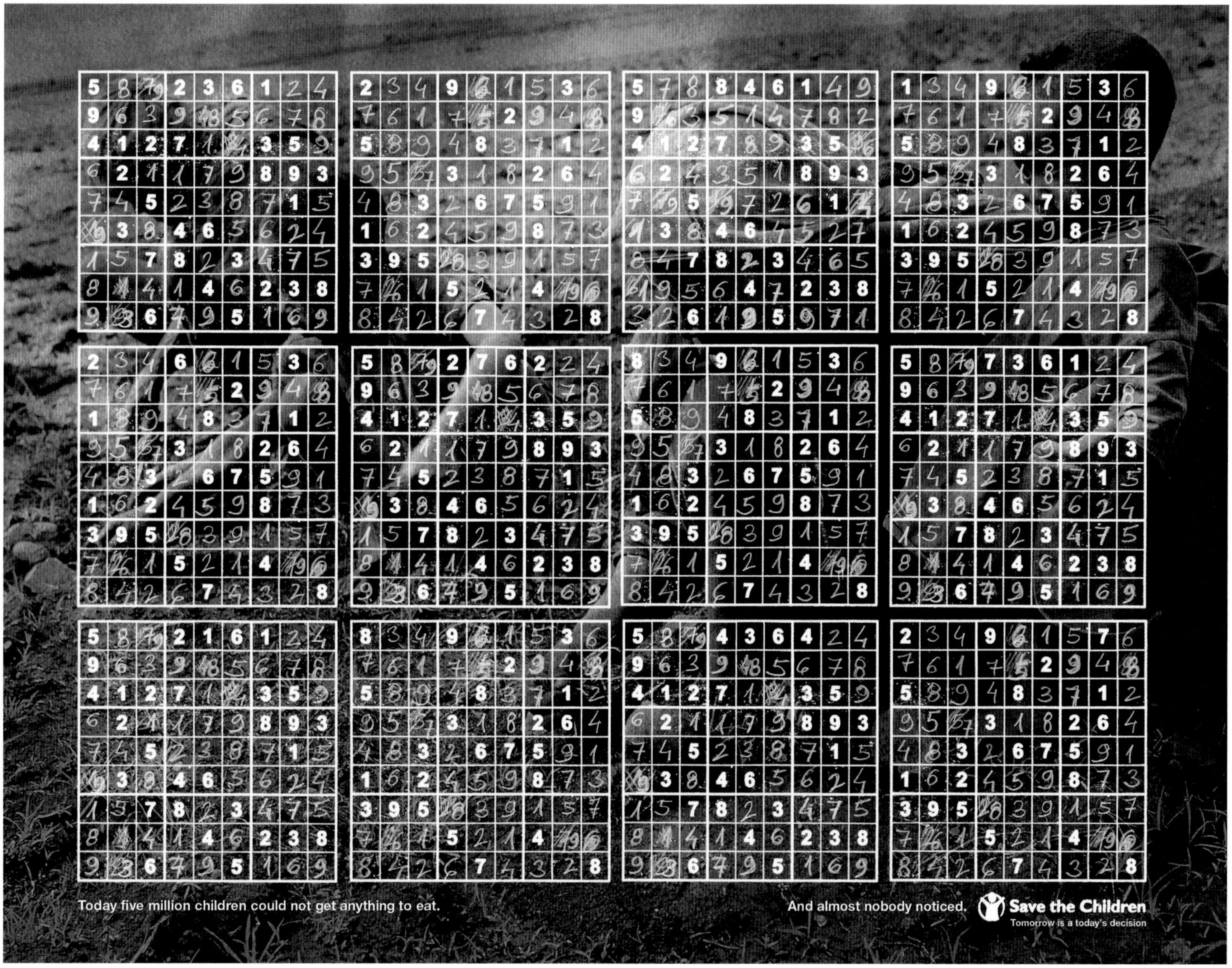

Today five million children could not get anything to eat.

And almost nobody noticed.

Save the Children
Tomorrow is a today's decision

SAVE THE CHILDREN
Shackleton, Madrid
SUDOKU

Many people spend huge amounts of time on idle pursuits such as doing Sudoku puzzles or checking football scores, but perhaps wouldn't spend the same amount of time helping hungry children.

Save the Children created these print ads with a single-minded message that almost guarantees an emotional response from the consumer. It is difficult to justify your addiction to brainteasers or football scores when you realize just how many children are in need.

AMERICAN LEGACY FOUNDATION®
Crispin Porter + Bogusky and Arnold
Worldwide, Miami
THE TRUTH® CAMPAIGN

In one of the most successful and
admired youth anti-smoking campaigns
in the world, we see innovative ways
of encouraging people never to start
smoking in the first place. Based on
the original insight that smoking is itself
an act of rebellion, so that one way
to counteract the need to smoke is to
find something else to rebel against,
the 'Truth®' campaign has gone from
strength to strength.

Instead of bombarding teens with
revolting details and visuals, this
campaign took the teenage need to
rebel and turned it around. By using
any and all relevant media — including
TV, radio, cinema and print advertising;
online elements; grassroots touring and
branded entertainment, the 'Truth®'
campaign always finds ways to stay
relevant to its target audience.

The 'Truth®' campaign has proven
to be one of the most effective
anti-smoking campaigns in history.
Research has shown the campaign kept
approximately 450,000 teens from
starting to smoke in its first four years
of existence (from 2000 to 2004).

*We will stay ahead of them [the tobacco companies]
by being more breakthrough and cutting edge than
they can ever be. We are young. They are old
and tired.*

THE TRUTH® CAMPAIGN

10.

POSITIVITY
What is the positive angle?

A POSITIVE BRAND

There are plenty of reasons not only to make your campaigns more positive, but also your brand. It's about being a positive force for good for people and the planet, and taking on the challenges with a smile. Brands such as Coca-Cola and Google have this positive attitude in their DNA.

'For every tank that is made in the world, 131,000 stuffed animals are made.' This is one of the many feel-good messages in Coca-Cola's heart-warming 'The Choir' commercial. Another uplifting fact is that 'For every corrupt person in the world, there are 8,000 donating blood.' It's no coincidence that Coca-Cola's new happiness platform, of which 'The Choir' is also a part, was launched during the global recession. In challenging times people are craving compassion and a positive outlook, for someone to say that it's going to be all right. This wisdom can also be applied when dealing with the doom and gloom of subjects such as the climate crisis, deadly diseases or palpable poverty. Why shouldn't people need the same injection of hope and optimism? This sentiment is actually valued by LOHAS consumers. They are the largest group of combatants for the health of people and the planet, are optimistic about the future and believe that they as individuals can make a difference and effect positive change. Brands should seek to infuse their communication and very essence with this life-empowering: go-get-'em optimism.

Find your positive attitude, it might be contagious

There is plenty of space out there for brands to take on a positive attitude or an encouraging outlook on life. The US retailer Sears dared to do so by launching their Good News Now website together with Yahoo and ABC News. Don Hamblen, Sears's Chief Marketing Officer, explains the initiative: 'We recognized there was so much negative news out there and people needed a positive break, so we developed a site with heart-warming stories of kindness and good deeds.' An effort like this might actually resonate on a greater scale. A paper from 2011 by A. Gruzd, S. Doiron and P. Mai investigates whether positive Twitter messages are more likely to be retweeted than negative messages. Interestingly, their findings were that positive tweets were three times

Above 'Choir', Coca-Cola,
Santo, Buenos Aires (see page 225)
Opposite 'Check Them', Veritas Spiriti, McCann
Erickson, Skopje (see page 224)

I FEEL...

Wefeelfine.org monitors people's emotions online by tracking the use of 'I feel' and 'I am feeling'. One of the emotions that popped up in my search was, 'I feel so happy, it's the start of another week, it's Monday.' You can even sort the emotions based on location, gender, feelings, weather and other parameters.

more likely to be passed on than negative ones. Just like a smile, positive messages seem to be contagious.

Use the power of the positive

In a 2010 report, scientists from the University of California, Berkeley, found that people actually become more sceptical of the climate crisis when they see doomsday messages. Instead of triggering behavioural change, these negative messages were found to push people into denial and prevent them from doing anything to change their lifestyle or limit their carbon footprint. Ben Stewart, Head of Media at Greenpeace UK, supports this line of thought in an article published in Ethical Consumer: 'Bashing people over the head with the results of the latest doomsday climate research isn't getting anywhere. Instead we've got to talk about what is engaging and positive in terms of the response to climate change which can have many benefits to society: for example, energy security and green jobs.'

Other public campaigns seem to go for a similar positive approach – in the anti-smoking lobby, for instance, where positive encouragement or reinforcement is beginning to replace the 'smoking kills' strategy. Research at the University of Missouri carried out in 2011 found that overly negative scare tactics in anti-smoking campaigns might actually backfire, making the target group avoid the campaign but not the cigarettes. In other bodies of research it was found that negative campaigns have a greater effect in the short term because of a stronger response, but if you're aiming for long-term behavioural change then positive messages seemed to have a better, more encouraging effect.

Use humour (cleverly) to raise awareness

Humour in advertising has been subjected to thorough research, but the research has been less extensive on more serious campaigns related to public awareness. Just because you're dealing with serious issues such as health or poverty, you shouldn't necessarily refrain from using humour. In fact, as in other advertising, a little laugh or smile might actually get you the attention you need. Moreover, a positive angle may serve as a cheerful reminder or a reassuring pat on the shoulder rather than scaring people. For humour to be effective you must know your target group well. This is why campaigns using humour are often built on a strong insight, such as MTV's safe-sex ads, with a campaign line that reads, 'Sex is no accident, always use a condom.' One of the ads shows a girl slipping on a banana peel, accidentally landing on a trolley, which crashes into a toilet, so that the girl lands with her legs spread on a naked man sitting on the toilet. The ad cleverly disarms any potential excuse from its target group of young viewers in an amusing way that makes them think twice about safe sex – and with a glint in the eye. It's a great example of making the target group look at their habits in a new way by having them laugh at themselves.

Add joy to your media choice

Sometimes the choice of media can make a thought-provoking message witty. A testicular cancer awareness campaign from Macedonia called 'Check Them' created the right kind of humour through the choice of media. It's not easy to get men to self-examine, so instead of using scare tactics the campaign added wobblers and stickers showing a hand about to grab a pair of testicles with the message: 'Check them'. The hand wobblers were placed on cinema seats and other places where they would create an eye-catching and fun visual that was hard to ignore.

'Sex is No Accident', MTV,
Grey, Düsseldorf (see page 230)

Make your humour relevant

'Nobody buys from a clown', said the advertising icon David Ogilvy as a warning against uncalled-for humour. As long as your positive or humorous angle resonates with the target group, the seriousness of the message, and your brand then there's no tomfoolery about it. Equally, there may be a risk in not using humour and being perceived as an undertaker or being ignored because of your audience's apathy towards your fearmongering message. One brand that struck the right chord is Axe, with their 'Shower pooling' campaign, which targeted young Canadians (aged between 19 and 24) and encouraged them to save water. The campaign went for a fun and sexy approach, which fits perfectly with the brand's personality. Axe encouraged 'groups of like-minded individuals to share their showers and save a valuable natural resource in the process'. Another brand that has also succeeded in matching its brand with its messaging and cause is MTV. As already mentioned, the 'Sex is no accident' ad is a great example of how a serious subject has been well delivered to MTV's young, entertainment-craving audience.

Which are more powerful – teddies or tanks?

Think twice before adding to the negative voices in the media landscape and instead use your voice as a strong exponent for positive encouragement – it might just be contagious, remember? Ask yourself if the message can be communicated in a more positive – or perhaps even more joyful – way. Maybe you should rethink your choice of media so that you can add positive encouragement when it is most needed: for example, a condom reminder for new-found lovers on their way home from a night out. Faced with the dilemma raised in Coca-Cola's 'The Choir' commercial, you can use either 'tanks' or 'teddies', 'fear' or 'hope' to get your target group to change their attitude or behaviour. There is no right answer for every assignment, but before you choose the typical oh-so-serious black-and-white commercial with a voiceover that sounds like James Earl Jones, ask yourself if there is a positive angle.

Interview
NIALL DUNNE

Niall Dunne is Chief Sustainability Officer (CSO) at British Telecom and was previously Managing Director of Saatchi & Saatchi S (Saatchi and Saatchi's sustainability arm) in London, where he was responsible for Europe, the Middle East and Africa. After starting his career at Accenture, where he helped businesses to optimize their operations and become more profitable, he came to realize that there was more to be done – that businesses, corporations and brands could (and should) be more responsible. I can't help but be enthused by Niall's infectious optimism – something that shines through when he speaks.

Telling his own story, Niall says that it was while he was working for Accenture that he saw the long-term risks for humanity – he knew that there was more to be done. **'It occurred to me, looking at what risks were really material to these businesses in five, ten years' time, that there were much more material risks for humanity... There were things like climate change and water scarcity and population instability, and all these kinds of things made me look at the fact that, fundamentally, the human race is not set up for success! Nobody was looking beyond, to see what kind of systems we will need, not just to mitigate but to navigate some of these much more material risks, and fundamentally transform a lot of the systems that we were living our lives by. And I looked at who was dealing with it currently and there were the non-governmental organizations – so that would be your Greenpeaces and your World Wildlife Funds – all of these. And, yes, they were all doing a noble job and really trying their best, but ultimately they were all looking at business to try to get business to take this much more seriously.'**

Niall knew that working within the business world, using his insights and skills, would enable him to make the biggest difference. **'I saw them [businesses] being much more able to think strategically about what a lot of these problems are and invest for the future... You know people will tell you that it's quite a complex thing – but it's kind of not. The two most complex systems on the planet – that of humanity and that of the environment – are at odds with each other and, kind of, with capitalism and democracy and religious tolerance. All of these things are not cognizant of how these two worlds need to work together.'**

Niall expands on this theory, on what role brands have to play and on how transparency is needed more than ever. At the same time, this offers astute businesses great opportunities to get one up on the competition and do good at the same time. **'You and I evolved as hunter-gatherers for a hundred thousand years, with a really transparent relationship with our environment, where we understood cause and effect. Now, what's happened is that brands have stepped in to be between us and our environment and are actually seeing that causal relationship** that we used to have. So we're coming up against the limitations of that model right now. And one of the key paradigm shifts that needs to happen is to take opaqueness out of the relationship and to put transparency back in, so the relationship with the consumer becomes about price and quality and transparency. But, also, business gets to stand for something.'

As far as Niall is concerned, it's not all doom and gloom. We can rise to this challenge with the help of business. Also, marketing and advertising have to change to meet these challenges, becoming not only more transparent but also more accountable and more honest. **'Business and brands are, to me, the game-changer that we need to utilize in the face of this kind of seismic challenge. Paradoxically, they're kind of the ones that have created the problem as well… Now when you think about what the brand can do as an agent for driving more conscientious consumption, more collaborative consumption, it's an absolutely brilliant platform. Because you know this – a brand is not just a sexy pink and fluffy platform that only three guys know what the hell it's about and nobody else can relate to – it's a language, it's a way in, it's a way of engaging and even now, more so than ever, it's a way of activating and inspiring and moving away from marketing at people to marketing with them… Recent research showed that a consumer is more likely to trust the opinion of a stranger they've met online than the claims of a marketing agency. So the consumer is more networked and more social than ever before and all of these networks are converging around brands and second-guessing everything that they are being told. So power is really back with the consumer and the only way to find a way back in is to engage transparently and start the discussions and use those networks as an asset.'**

When it comes to the climate crisis itself, Niall makes a really good point – the average consumer needs arguments framed in a different way in order to act on them, and the selection of tools marketers have today are more powerful than ever. I think it goes without saying that marketing campaigns around these issues may not be gaining as much traction as they should. **'What the hell is carbon? It's a colourless, odourless, tasteless gas. How are we going to make that potent and personable to people? We're not. So we need to completely reframe the argument – make it about jobs, make it about security of supply or make it about local sourcing or whatever it is, but this is where marketing comes in – because we get this. And now we have a completely different suite of toys to play with – social media, decentralized communications, decentralized thinking and this more networked consumer. I think I've mentioned to you the rise of the SoLoMo consumer, which is the social, local, mobile consumer, who is networked more than ever before and cognizant of the global**

A brand is not just a sexy pink and fluffy platform that only three guys know what the hell it's about and nobody else can relate to — it's a language, it's a way in, it's a way of engaging and even now, more so than ever, it's a way of activating and inspiring…

context, but will make decisions based on who's around me right now, what's around me right now, how is it relevant to my world and feeling good because of that experience?'

Despite all of the world's problems, from the climate crisis to the global population explosion, Niall remains positive. It is tempered, though, with the responsibility we all should take for making the future brighter. **'Being an optimist, I fundamentally believe in the power of humanity, of collective will, of mobilizing the masses to actually effect mass behaviour change… I think it was Clinton who said we can choose not to do anything, but we can no longer choose not to know. I think the job of communications is to make sure that people do know. And if they choose not to do anything at that stage that's fine, but you've got to back the fact that humanity has got as far as we have because we've made more better decisions en masse than we've made bad decisions. So you've got to trust that the system of humanity will get there, but we need to get there faster.'**

With people like Niall spearheading this business revolution, I can only hope that the masses will be mobilized in time, and that the communications industry can help them along the way. It seems to me that the stakes are pretty high.

1500 LITRES OF WATER

300 LITRES OF WATER

AXE
Crispin Porter + Bogusky, Canada
SHOWER POOLING

Axe has always been known for its cheeky ad campaigns featuring scantily clad women and sexy scenarios, so it wasn't much of a surprise when they announced this campaign that encouraged people to shower with their friends for Earth Day. The idea was that sharing a shower with other people could be a great way to save water.

It's difficult to tell how many people really did jump in the shower together, but this campaign spoke to a market segment that is probably more interested in the opposite sex than the environment and framed the argument in such a way that it appealed to them. With the powers of communication and persuasion, it is important to say something in a way that will make the target audience respond positively.

Through this positive tone, Axe has created a campaign that is contagious and easily shared. This campaign doesn't bog consumers down with negative messages — instead it appeals to their sense of fun, which is always a good idea.

RED CROSS
Leo Burnett, Lisbon
THE STORE THAT SELLS HOPE

To shake up their donations category
and inject interest into their cause, the
Red Cross in Portugal opened a store
that sold absolutely nothing – nothing
but hope. In one of Lisbon's busiest
malls, it was fully shop-fitted and
people were encouraged to come in and
buy hope, in the form of a donation to
the Red Cross. As this was done over
the festive season, people were in the
right frame of mind to be charitable
and donate.

Turning hope into a tangible product
makes giving more quantifiable.
Customers are not paying to have a tree
planted 3,000 miles away, but instead
they can engage in the traditional
shopping experience (with all the
feelings of achievement) and do good
at the same time. The idea was
ingenious and as the product sold
was 'hope' it also tapped into people's
dreams, adding a wistfulness and
idealistic feeling that encouraged
people to donate.

The idea proved so powerful that in
the first day of the shop being open it
became one of the top ten shops in the
mall in terms of sales; business hours
even had to be extended in order to
cope with the high levels of demand.
The following year another shop was
opened in Lisbon, while another was
opened in Madrid. This campaign works
so well because they were in the right
place at the right time, with the perfect
product to sell. Everyone feels more
compassionate around Christmas time
and people will always tell their friends
about an idea that is so groundbreaking.

VERITAS SPIRITI
McCann Erickson, Skopje
CHECK THEM

Veritas Spiriti provided a great answer to a difficult question: how do you increase awareness about testicular cancer in a significant way? Rather than use tried-and-tested scare tactics, they decided to use humour – to great effect. In any place where men might find themselves: sports arenas, gyms, barbershops or dressing rooms, they were given a hand. This hand not only induced a ribald chuckle or two, but also encouraged men to check themselves manually for testicular cancer and pointed them to a website. As well as the hands, eggs in supermarkets were stamped with information about testicular cancer.

In Macedonia, the slang word for testicles translates as eggs. This fresh look at a serious problem yielded incredibly positive results. Awareness of testicular cancer in the target audience increased from 1% to 74% and data from the Ministry of Health showed that the number of visits to doctors to check for testicular cancer increased by 11% after the campaign ran. On top of that, online banners for this cause were clicked ten times more than regular banners in Macedonia. This imaginative way of tackling a potentially life-threatening problem proves that when dealing with serious issues you don't always need to be serious.

For every tank being built in the world...

131.000 stuffed dolls are made

COCA-COLA
Santo, Buenos Aires
CHOIR

After looking at the state of the world in 2010 and the way that statistics are often used in a negative context, Coca-Cola in Argentina decided the world needed an injection of positivity. By taking some simple statistics and building on the premise, 'There are reasons to believe in a better world', Coca-Cola produced a heart-warming and uplifting ad campaign. Lines such as 'For every rocket designed by a scientist...1,000,000 moms bake a cake' and 'For every corrupt person...there are 8,000 giving blood' meant that one couldn't help but feel the positive energy in this ad.

The backing track was a children's choir and the ad ended with the statistic that for every weapon bought around the world, 20,000 people share a Coke – making us feel that together we can make the world a better place.

For every corrupt person...

there are 8.000 giving blood.

For every fence someone puts up...

200.000 "Welcome" mats are placed.

While a scientist designs a new weapon...

1.000.000 moms are baking chocolate cakes.

While 1 weapon is sold in the world...

20.000 people share a Coke.

VOLKSWAGEN
DDB, Stockholm
JAZZ CALCULATOR

To raise awareness about Volkswagen's Passat EcoFuel, which emits just 20 grammes of carbon dioxide per kilometre, Volkswagen introduced the 'Jazz Calculator'. It was built on the observation that each human breath contains about 0.05 grams of carbon dioxide. Visitors to the website could choose a route between two Swedish cities and would then be told the length of time a jazz orchestra would have to play to emit the same amount of carbon dioxide.

Visitors were then given a jazz playlist that corresponded to the trip, taking as long as it would take to emit the same carbon dioxide. This was accessible via Spotify and users who did not have an account were given an invitation to join.

By taking a positive spin on a serious issue, Volkswagen made it much easier for consumers to take part in the discussion about carbon emissions. This sense of fun makes it easier for consumers to understand and take on the message about carbon emissions, and also reinforces the idea that Volkswagen is a company with green ambitions.

KIMBERLY-CLARK
JWT+H+F, Zurich
SEE YOU LATER

This print ad was released by Kimberly-Clark to let the public know about their new Hakle Naturals toilet paper, which is made from 100% recycled paper. Simple and powerful, it reads: 'See you later'. This implies that even the ad in your hands could become toilet paper one day. Such a simple, amusing message cannot be ignored.

See you later.

Made from 100% recycled paper.

OK GASOLINE
Uncle Grey, Aarhus
SPONSORS NEEDED

As a gasoline company, OK was faced with the prospect of creating advertising like every other gasoline seller in Denmark – or they could do something different. They were already involved in sports sponsorship, donating money when customers used a loyalty card, so they decided to make this known to the public and use it for their adverts.

A series of ads showed people who were incredibly committed to their sports trying to practise them without the proper equipment. The ads ended with hilarious, unexpected moments, such as the soccer team who have to share a field with javelin throwers, or the trampoline team who have to practise in a vault with a really low ceiling.

By bringing humour to doing good, OK rewarded viewers with the knowledge that every time they bought gasoline at OK they were supporting local sports programmes.

OK sells gasoline. How do you make that interesting? We agreed to focus on another thing than the (boring) product. Why not put some attention to something more likeable like the fact that OK supports local sports?

UNCLE GREY

MTV
Grey, Düsseldorf
SEX IS NO ACCIDENT

In this risqué and humorous campaign, MTV reminds us, sarcastically, that you have no excuse not to use a condom. Showing visually ridiculous scenes in which sex could be described as being an accident, the viewer is reminded that they should always act responsibly.

MTV understands their audience very well and they know that they can handle controversial communications – this campaign shows insight not only into their audience, but also into the fact that many young people will use the excuse 'but it was an accident'.

SALAT OLIVE OIL
Tribu DDB, San José
SHAPE UP YOUR HEART

In a break from traditional olive oil and salad dressing advertising, we see Salat positioning themselves as the condiment to use should you want to protect your heart. By showing people in potentially embarrassing situations where they are about to get a huge fright, Salat makes the product benefit known: olive oil can shape up your heart.

By promoting the good qualities of olive oil through some stunning art direction, these ads take an amusing look at heart disease and heart attacks. Rather than scare consumers away, they invite them in to have a laugh, but remind them that caring for the heart is very important. Why be negative in order to spark responsibility when you can be positive?

YOU HAVE MORE BLOOD THAN YOU NEED. GIVE A BIT.

Santa Casa de São Paulo

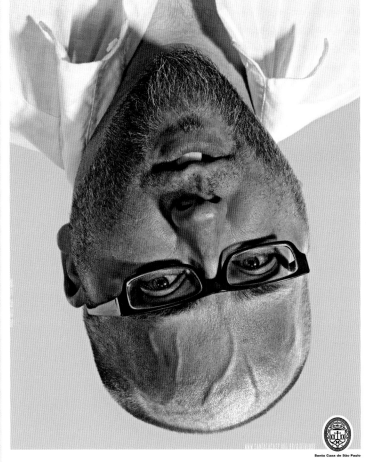

SANTA CASA DE MISERICORDIA DE
SAO PAULO
Y&R, São Paulo
**YOU HAVE MORE BLOOD THAN
YOU NEED**

This series of three print ads for Santa
Casa de Misericórdia de São Paulo
encouraged people to give blood by
taking a positive look at blood donation.
We see three different people hanging
upside down, veins bulging in their
foreheads – we all know that feeling
of blood rushing to our head when we're
upside down.

The images make the viewer laugh,
creating positive associations with
donating blood. This campaign was
positive, simple and actionable.

All Day Full Of Naaka Mukkaaa...

Madras Action Hero

THE TIMES OF INDIA
JWT, Mumbai
A DAY IN THE LIFE OF CHENNAI

Cut to Emotional Rock n Roll

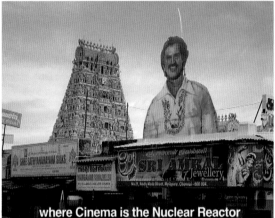

where Cinema is the Nuclear Reactor

To celebrate the 369th anniversary of the establishment of the city of Chennai, the *Times of India* commissioned a film chronicling just what life in Chennai is like. Built on the Tamil phrase 'Naaka Mukka', which translates as 'mother tongue, father nose' and is used to denote the duality of life, this advert aimed to do the same.

In Chennai, many actors leave acting behind and join politics, often jumping from one party to another. This advert tells a story through the use of a cardboard cut-out who starts as an action hero, becomes a politician and then loses it all and becomes a scarecrow. This riot of colour and song shows viewers that if there is any publication that can truly understand and interpret the Indian political, social and cultural landscape it is The *Times of India*.

The advert speaks to people in their own language, using Indian themes, music and traditions. It proved so popular that the soundtrack quickly reached number one on many Indian music channels. Even though it functions as a satire, it is a reinforcement of Indian culture and outlook – creating a feeling of goodness around it to which Indian people can relate.

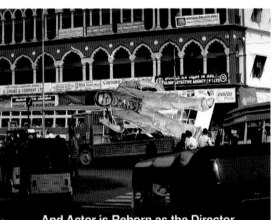

And Actor is Reborn as the Director

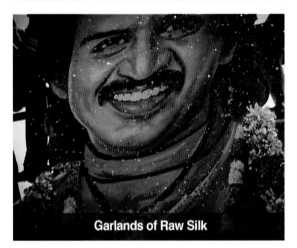

Garlands of Raw Silk

Bubble Bath with Cows Milk

Starting "The Rice Party" with caste mix

MIN A-KASSE
Inkognito Cph, Copenhagen
PROJECT TRUST

The Danish unemployment fund Min A-kasse has fought for the rights of the unemployed and railed against the bureaucratic rules of the government in a number of campaigns in the past. This campaign was a protest against the way the government distrusted the unemployed and sought to control them by various means, including surveillance. They wanted to prove that this distrust was misplaced and launched a global social experiment. At its heart the fund believed that ultimately trust leads to trust and becomes self-perpetuating. What do you believe?

To join the experiment, you had to bet 100 dkk (approximately £12) on a tree of trust and invite your friends to join. Your friends could either take the money or pass the money on to their friends – and so the trust grew from hand to hand like a chain letter of trust. These trust trees soon became a forest of trust and if no one took the 100 dkk after four weeks, you got your money back and trust wins.

This campaign asks the question: can you ultimately trust someone with your money when they are not punished if they take it? The progress was tracked according to a number of parameters such as age group, city, country and gender and has proven very promising. The project is ongoing, but after only two months more than 14,000 people have joined and so far only three have chosen to take the money and choose mistrust.

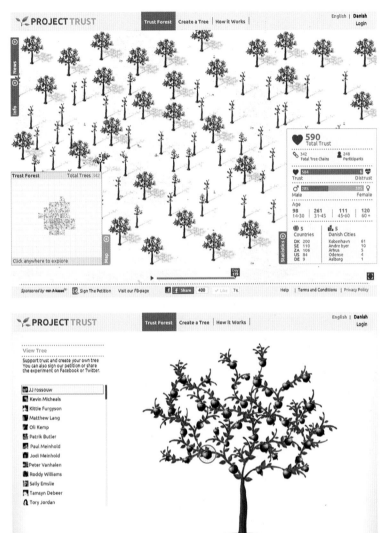

THE TREE OF TRUST

COMMITMENT

COMMITMENT

What is your brand willing to fight for?

For many years doing good was nothing more than a philanthropic gesture: members of the board signing a cheque or an ageing company owner donating money to a cause in which they had a personal interest. Often there were no strategies behind these decisions and the donations were given on an impromptu basis. The long-term effect of these donations was hard to see besides a copper plaque left to erode on a building or a park bench.

Move from promotion to a committed plan

Today more brands are moving from short-term partnerships to long-term corporate citizenships with benefits for everyone. The Body Shop was one of the pioneers in committing to a cause and harvesting the long-term results. Since its inception in 1976, The Body Shop has been known for its fairly produced cosmetics and its strong focus on ethics and environmental protection. Its charismatic, natural frontwoman, Anita Roddick, campaigned to put an end to animal testing, cooperating with the animal rights organization PETA and others. The first campaign was launched in the late 1980s and in 1996 one of their campaigns alone collected over 4 million signatures through their shops in the UK. The Body Shop hasn't spent big bucks on media or advertising – their messages are driven mainly by in-store communication, product labelling, grassroots tactics, word of mouth and through educating and involving the store personnel. Maybe their low-profile media strategy is the secret of their strong activist appeal. In some environmental circles the *comme il faut* has definitely been about doing green, but not saying green.

Stay focused

The Body Shop's long-standing commitment has paid off. As a result, the European Union banned animal testing for finished cosmetics products

in 2004 and for ingredients in 2009. In 2006, The Body Shop was the second biggest cosmetics retailer in the world, with over 2,000 stores in 60 countries and sales of £772 million. The same year L'Oreal acquired The Body Shop for £130 million. Some critics claim that The Body Shop sold out, but there's no question that the success of the world's second largest cosmetics retailer owes much to the firm, value-driven beliefs of Anita Roddick, who brought the issue of animal welfare into the mainstream.

Learn to walk before you run

Not every company is born with an Anita at the wheel. For another quintessential British retailer, Marks and Spencer, getting there was a long journey. At the beginning of the 21st century the company was criticized by NGOs such as Friends of the Earth and Greenpeace for various missteps, including laying off their British workers, leaving pesticide residues on fruit and vegetables, illegally logging trees from rainforests and for using PVC (also known as poison plastic) in their packaging. At the same time, the retailer was facing declining market shares and their profits were at risk. Marks and Spencer chose to incorporate committed sustainable goals gradually across all its business units one at a time and invited NGOs and consumers to the table. The first small steps made sure that they didn't commit to goals on which they couldn't deliver, while still aspiring to responsibility and sustainability.

Share your progress

In 2007, Marks and Spencer's commitments turned into an ambitious campaign called 'Plan A' (with the powerful slogan, 'There is no Plan B') with over 100 goals that covered health, social and environmental issues. This was also seen as a possibility to harvest some of the investments in

NESTLE FORCED TO CHANGE THEIR POLICY

Committing to goals is not always voluntary. Greenpeace's aggressive 'Give us a break' campaign, which aimed to protect the rainforest and the orangutans who call it home, forced Nestlé to change its ways. The world's largest food and drink company committed to a partnership with the Forest Trust to implement responsible sourcing guidelines for its palm oil and went even further, pledging to use only sustainable palm oil by 2015.

Opposite 'A Day in the Life of Chennai', the *Times of India*, JWT, Mumbai (see page 234)

BIG MOTHER IS WATCHING

ClimateCounts.org is a non-profit organization that rates companies' climate commitments on a scale from stuck, starting to striding. ClimateCounts hopes to guide consumers so that they can use their choices and voices, ultimately bringing issues to the companies' attention.

sustainability and differentiate itself in an increasingly competitive market. As Mike Barry, Marks and Spencer's head of CSR, rationalizes, 'We realized we were really on to something. We're never going to beat them on price. But if we can drag them onto a battlefield that's marked out in terms of trust and responsibility, we've got a chance of winning.' Plan A has not only helped push Marks and Spencer ahead in the competitive British retail market and created a strong, value-driven brand, but it's also turned out to be good business. In 2011, Plan A contributed over £70 million to the company's bottom line, up from £50 million the previous year. Their sustainable investment has long since been paid off. Marks and Spencer has demonstrated that being outspoken yields results, as the market notices and values your genuine committed efforts. It's the same point I made in the introduction – the vast majority of consumers want and actually expect you to make a difference in their lives.

Commit to purpose

Marks and Spencer has taken the steps from profit to purpose by following the mantra: get naked, get together and get out there. To summarize, initially they were criticized for their practices, but they *got naked* and decided, with resolve, to find solutions and *got together* with stakeholders from suppliers, NGOs and customers. They have not only put forward tangible, committed goals, but also a bold vision to be the world's most sustainable retailer by 2015. They definitely got there with Plan A and have kept stakeholders up to date with their commitments with great success. This is perhaps best symbolized by the fact that in the lobby of their headquarters they have digital tickers that don't show financial performance, but instead their performance on their commitments – from the number of hangers recycled to how carbon neutral they are.

Bring your commitments to life

The Body Shop and Marks and Spencer are successful because their values are at the core of everything they do. If you make your values come to life every day in everything you do then your organization will become committed at heart. Be clear about your goals and, if you're working together with NGOs or other partners, make sure those goals are aligned. And don't be afraid to get out there. Being a responsible brand is no longer a choice – it's a necessity. Companies all over the world are putting tangible goals forward – playing their part in spinning the Wheel of Good and leveraging sustainability to the mass market, which can be seen in the scope of programmes such as GE's Ecomagination and Healthymagination, Nike's Better World, Unilever's Sustainable Living Plan and Procter & Gamble's Future Friendly. New examples are being added to this list every day. Ninety per cent of companies on the Fortune 500 have implemented a corporate social responsibility strategy or something similar (with varying motives). Here is an example: one of the goals Unilever aims to fulfil is to double its sales while halving the environmental impact of its products over the next ten years. Moreover, Unilever is also limiting salt, saturated fats, sugar and calories in their food, while adding more than half a million small farmers in developing countries to their supply chain. Unilever's biggest competitor, Procter & Gamble, is also upping its environmental and social efforts – goals it hopes to attain by 2020 include powering its plants with 100% renewable electricity, using 100% renewable or recycled materials in its products and packaging, sending zero waste to landfill and maximizing the conservation of resources. For Unilever and Procter & Gamble the competition is no longer only measured in profits, but equally in world-bettering initiatives, meanwhile raising their voices to sing along to the mantra: everything you can do, I can do greener.

Make it tangible, be accountable

Being committed is as much about making it tangible, so that consumers can see that your efforts are not just a shortsighted marketing stunt or a splash of green lacquer. When you commit to a goal and you show the effort you are making then you are showing that you care, and when you first make a promise to your consumers that you are going to improve they will reward you for delivering or punish you if your commitments end up being empty communication.

360-degree commitment

These efforts are not something that should be left in a marketing or CSR (corporate social responsibility) department – you need top-down commitment, because it's about changing the core business for the better. You have to make your efforts sustainable so they can continue to be good for your business. If your campaigning for good isn't linked to profits then your efforts risk being cut off in times of crisis or when the shareholders are scrutinizing your business decisions. For NGOs this counts as well. Too often programmes are dependent on money and never trigger the business entrepreneurship that creates real growth. The initiatives that make a long-term difference are linked to tangible business objectives like those of GE's Ecomagination and Healthymagination, which are deeply rooted in the company's mission to reach a sustainable business goal that delivers $17 billion in profit. People don't mind a company making a substantial profit if it's a good (and sustainable) business – anything other than that is keeping your initiative on a costly life-support system that will eventually be shut down.

Brands need to undergo a definitive shift in mindset from self-interest to shared interests: a brand should begin the dialogue with what interests the consumer instead of pushing self-centred sales messages. People with shared values will often find common ground; this also counts in the relationship between brands and consumers. There are many 'common grounds' to be found in the responsible arena, from the concerned mother who wants to give her children a product she trusts to the busy business executive who wants easy-green products. Look for these shared interests where you as a brand and consumers both have a stake. This may allow you as a brand not only to forge a stronger relationship with consumers, but also to solve important issues for which you both have an interest in finding solutions – together.

Consumers are hungry for leaders to help them navigate and understand a world of uncertainty and risks. A commitment is an agreement: a relationship of trust between you and your customers and other stakeholders, which can be a strong relationship if your commitment translates to real care and tangible outcomes such as Marks and Spencer's 'Plan A'. The Body Shop's continuous struggle for an end to animal testing shows it does make a difference. The company did more than leave its name on a copper plaque, they wrote a chapter in the history books and forever changed the cruel practices of the cosmetics industry – and made a fortune doing so. Consumers want you to do your part: what are you willing to fight for?

FAT LOSSES

A billboard for the 'Campaign for Real Beauty' showing a natural woman asked viewers to use their mobile phone and vote 'fat' or 'fit'. The results were posted in real time on the billboard and over time tipped over to the less flattering 'fat'. Prejudice prevailed.

Interview
AUDREY GAUGHRAN

Audrey Gaughran has been in the vanguard of the battle for corporate accountability for quite some time. She is currently Amnesty International's Director of Global Thematic Issues and was previously Amnesty International's Head of Business and Human Rights for three years. I was lucky enough to be in contact with her and she shared some really powerful thoughts on how businesses can take more responsibility and what governments need to do to ensure that they are held accountable. One of the most interesting points to come out of this was the huge opportunity that is now open for brands wanting to do the right thing and improve their image at the same time.

Audrey's work with Amnesty International has, among other things, focused on legislation, the regulation of the flow of information and globalization. Each of these issues poses its own problems when it comes to corporate accountability and human rights issues, but Amnesty International has done a lot of research into how we can address them.

Audrey began by saying, **'Companies frequently have significantly more political and economic power than the individuals and communities whose lives they affect: they also have far greater legal protection. Yet companies argue – often strongly – against any advances in law that would help protect the rights and interests of affected communities. When it comes to their own corporate and economic interests, they promote and use the law, but when it comes to community interests they promote voluntary approaches and "CSR".'**

In outlining the legal issues that have contributed to this fight, Audrey continues, **'Over the past 20 years we have also seen the expansion of national and international law to protect global economic interests, through a range of international agreements on investment, trade and intellectual property rights… Deregulation, the need to attract foreign investment, and provisions in trade and investment agreements have all squeezed the protection the law can provide people affected by corporate operations – particularly in developing countries.'** She continues to say that not long ago many of these problems were not even raised in the public consciousness. **'It has only been comparatively recently that the impact of corporations on human rights has been on the global agenda… Media reports and campaigns on issues such as child labour, toxic waste and corporate collusion with repressive governments provoked public anger. NGOs and unions connected people buying Gap and Nike with people making Gap and Nike clothing.'**

What this tells us is that there is no better time to change your business practices for the better than yesterday, or preferably two weeks ago. As brands are becoming increasingly accountable for their actions (and they should be), it is the brands that step up and take responsibility that will have the competitive advantage.

From there, Audrey outlines the results of such efforts, **'This exposure led to a range of civil society responses – consumer activism, fair trade, and public name-and-shame campaigns. It also gave birth to a range of business responses, which spanned the spectrum from socially responsible investment and business engagement in ethical trading, to corporate public relations initiatives and greenwashing. As these various ad-hoc responses gathered pace – some successful, some unsuccessful – a clear fault line emerged between voluntary approaches, characterized by corporate social responsibility (CSR), on the one hand, and demands for law and accountability of companies on the other. This fault line reflects important underlying power dynamics. Voluntary approaches rely largely on business as the key actor, effectively keeping the power with them; mandatory approaches rely on states, and – where they are effective – give individuals and communities the possibility to demand action and change.'** At the same time, I can't help but think of the internet and the power it has in opening up corporate doors. It's up to companies whether they see this as an opportunity or a threat. The thing is, nobody is perfect, but opening up and being honest about your intentions and your goals to improve is better than a closed door or over-promises.

Unfortunately, Amnesty International has found that serious abuses appear more prevalent in developing countries, where legislation is often more lax than it is in the developed world. The larger issue at play here is that laws and regulations are often not enforced and the relative power of major multinationals is greater in a poor country. As we see more

Human rights abuses cannot be 'offset'.

products being produced by developing economies and consumed by mature economies, this will only become more of a problem in the future. But, as Audrey says, through a combination of legislation and companies being more open about their information there is a way forward. Again, we see the importance of transparency when trying to do the right thing or the 'good' thing.

When it comes to regulating the flow of information, **'Cases investigated by Amnesty International underscore the huge imbalance in power that is directly related to who has the information. Corporate control over information that is vital to the protection and defence of human rights has been a feature of every case we have looked at. In all cases that we reviewed, the affected individuals and communities faced huge challenges in accessing information necessary to protect their rights.'**

Added to this is the problem that companies who withhold information can easily be seen as untrustworthy, **'The failure to provide people with information not only undermines the company's ability to respect rights (if people don't know what's happening, they can't tell you how it will affect them), and communities' own ability to act to protect their rights, it breeds a climate of suspicion and distrust between communities and companies, which can be very hard to reverse.'** Once again, honesty, openness and transparency are vitally important in having a strong brand in which people can really believe.

Audrey tells me that when it comes to legislation a large problem facing Amnesty International is globalization. As companies have moved different parts of their operations to different countries, it becomes increasingly difficult to hold them accountable because of the differing laws in each country. Also, globalization poses a challenge for companies

to keep an eye on their entire value chain from extraction and production all the way through to the end-user. It is up to companies to ensure their practices and suppliers all across the globe are sticking to the rules. On top of this, companies are putting legal pressure on the system in the other direction. **'While companies can exert substantial direct influence over legal and regulatory frameworks, pro-business changes to the law have also frequently been encouraged by international financial institutions (IFIs) in the context of foreign investment. While IFIs reinforce corporate and economic power, no international institutions of corresponding power to the IFIs exist to require protection of rights and the environment… Another dimension of the state–corporate relationship, and the risk this relationship poses to human rights, is the level of complicity that can exist between states and companies, which fundamentally undermines human rights protection. Government has an obligation to regulate business, but frequently works in partnership with business and is highly dependent on business for political support.'** If government and business can take these partnerships and use them to provide real value and create sustainable solutions to societal problems, we could see some real movement in this field. Transparency is once again the key.

Where companies are trying to undertake CSR campaigns, Audrey and Amnesty International have the following advice: **'CSR is not well defined. It covers a very wide range of corporate activities – from philanthropic projects to general statements of principle on a wide range of social issues, to participation in voluntary initiatives… Within CSR there is a tendency for companies to focus on – and publicize – the good things they are doing and ignore negative impacts of their business operations.'** More companies are beginning to own up to their mistakes and it seems that just owning up to a problem is enough to get consumers on your side. There is no longer a need to be dishonest – if a brand is honest and forthcoming about its mistakes and outlines how it hopes to change, then consumers are generally very happy to be involved.

If your company is not good from the ground up, CSR campaigns can come off as insincere. At the same time, you have to make doing good a core part of your business. Audrey issues a stern warning: **'Too many NGO campaigns are still seen by companies as public relations problems – to be resolved with PR and marketing solutions, rather than systematic action… Human rights abuses cannot be "offset".'**

Just to clarify

The words 'sustainability', 'responsibility' and 'green' are used interchangeably. It's important for me to emphasize that this book is not only about environmental issues, but just as much about how you can make a difference for people, their health and society in general.

Moreover, I've intentionally focused on mainly business-to-consumer brands, but the responsible revolution is equally forceful for business-to-business brands as environmental and societal impacts are measured throughout the whole supply chain. This means that the suppliers you choose are just as important as what you do yourself. I have not focused on the many positive internal aspects of turning your brand from profit to purpose, as many of these aspects have been covered in detail in other literature, but don't let that hold you back from making a difference in these areas. Change needs to happen everywhere – and often starts within the organization.

Most people aren't rich white guys

This book mainly represents reality seen through the eyes of the minority instead of the majority of consumers. I am referring, of course, to the billions of people in the developing world. In *The Corporation*, the documentary classic from 2004, Michael Moore delivers the message clearly in his usual provocative style: 'The fact that most of these companies are run by white men, rich white men, means that they are out of touch with what the majority of the world is.'

We're a global village and even though the purchasing power of the developed countries is still biggest (as long as it lasts), the vast majority of people live in the developing world. We all have to grow together and the developing world is a potentially gigantic market for good. The aspirations to live more responsibly are already there, with many developing countries having equally large LOHAS (Lifestyles of Health and Sustainability) segments as the developed world. They seek a better world and scream for solutions – and brands can deliver these answers. If brands fail to do so, though, their aspirations might follow the fatal footsteps of the developed world and lead to over-consumption and its myriad unwanted consequences.

RESOURCES

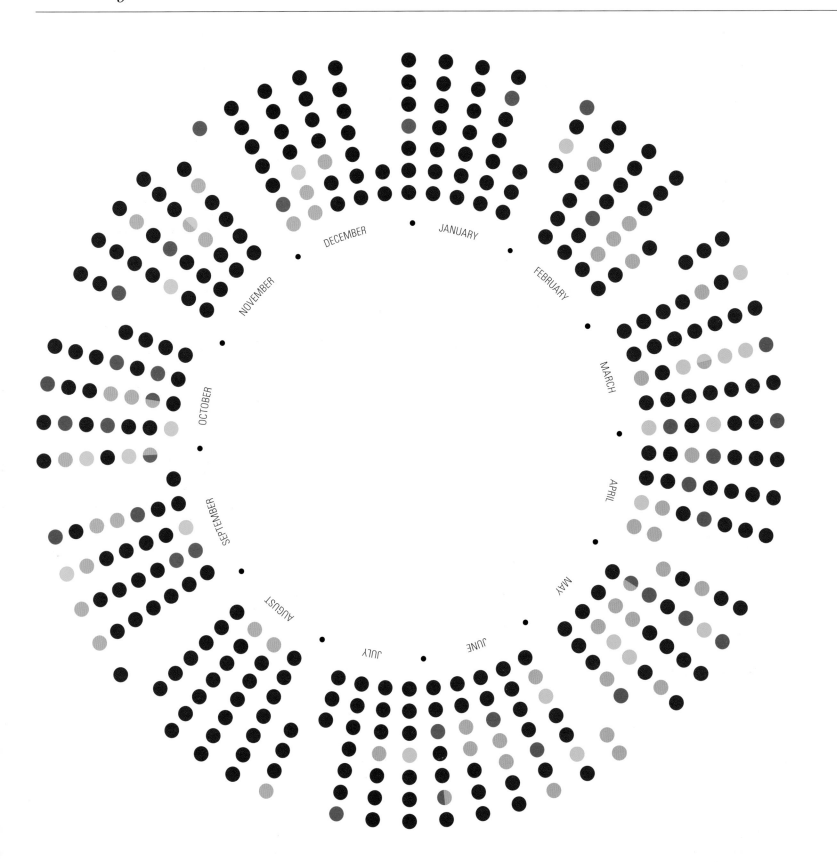

● DAYS FOR US

FEBRUARY
9 WWF National Sweater Day
   (Canada)
20 World Day of Social Justice
21 International Mother Language Day
22 World Thinking Day
28 National Science Day (India)
MARCH
8 International Women's Day
18 BBC Red Nose Day
   (United Kingdom)
21 International Day for the Elimination
   of Racial Discrimination
APRIL
10 TOMS One Day Without Shoes
23 World Book and Copyright Day
29 International Dance Day
30 No Phone Zone Day (USA)
MAY
1 International Labour Day
3 World Press Freedom Day
7 World AIDS Orphans Day
14 World Fair Trade Day
15 International Day of Families
21 World Anti-Terrorism Day
   World Day for Cultural Diversity
25 The Royal Society for the
   Blind Odd Socks Day (Australia)
30 Cell C Take a Girl to Work Day
   (South Africa)
JUNE
1 International Children's Day
2 World Naturist Day
4 The United Nations International
   Day of Innocent Children Victims
   of Aggression
16 The International Day of the
   African Child
20 World Refugee Day
21 World Music Day
26 International Day against Drug
   Abuse and Illicit Trafficking
27 World Diabetes Day
JULY
6 United Nations International Day
   of Cooperatives
18 Mandela Day
AUGUST
4 International Friendship Day
12 International Youth Day
19 World Humanitarian Day
SEPTEMBER
8 International Literacy Day
15 International Day of Democracy
21 International Day of Peace
26 World Maritime Day
27 World Tourism Day

OCTOBER
1 International Day of Older Persons
5 World Teachers' Day
15 World Rural Women's Day
16 UN World Food Day
17 International Day for the
   Eradication of Poverty
24 United Nations Day
NOVEMBER
16 International Day for Tolerance
20 Africa Industrialization Day
   Universal Children's Day
21 World Television Day
29 Adbusters Buy Nothing Day
DECEMBER
2 International Day for the Abolition
   of Slavery
9 International Anti Corruption Day
10 Human Rights Day
18 International Migrants Day

● DAYS FOR OUR BODIES

JANUARY
4 World Braille Day
27 World Leprosy Day
FEBRUARY
4 World Cancer Day
14 Congenital Heart Defect
   Awareness Day
MARCH
24 World Tuberculosis Day
APRIL
2 World Autism Awareness Day
7 World Health Day
11 World Parkinson's Day
17 World Haemophilia Day
25 World Malaria Day
MAY
7 World Asthma Day
8 World Red Cross Day and
   Red Crescent Day
10 World Lupus Day
12 International Nurses Day
   International Chronic Fatigue
   Syndrome Awareness Day
31 World No Tobacco Day
JUNE
14 World Blood Donor Day
19 World Sickle Cell Day
JULY
3 Wonderbra National Cleavage Day
   (South Africa)
6 World Zoonosis Day
28 World Hepatitis Day
SEPTEMBER
9 Foetal Alcohol Syndrome
   Awareness Day
10 WHO Suicide Prevention Day

15 World Lymphoma Awareness Day
21 Alzheimer's Day
25 Ataxia Awareness Day
29 World Heart Day
OCTOBER
1 World Vegetarian Day
10 UN World Mental Health Day
   World Sight Day
12 World Hospice and Palliative Care Day
15 World Handwashing Day
   World White Safety Cane Day
20 International Osteoporosis Day
22 International Stuttering
   Awareness Day
24 World Polio Day
NOVEMBER
1 World Vegan Day
14 World Diabetes Day
DECEMBER
1 World AIDS Day
3 International Day of Disabled Persons

● DAYS FOR THE PLANET

FEBRUARY
2 World Wetlands Day
MARCH
10 Bottled Water Free Day
20 World Sparrow Day
21 World Forestry Day
22 World Water Day
23 World Meteorological Day
APRIL
1 Fossil Fools Day
10 Arbor Day (USA)
22 Earth Day
MAY
11 World Migratory Bird Day
22 International Day for Biodiversity
23 World Turtle Day
JUNE
5 World Environment Day
8 World Ocean Day
JULY
11 World Population Day
SEPTEMBER
16 World Ozone Day
22 World Car Free Day
OCTOBER
2 World Farm Animal Day
4 World Animal Welfare Day
7 World Habitat Day
NOVEMBER
6 International Day for Preventing
   the Exploitation of the Environment
   in War and Armed Conflict
21 World Fisheries Day
DECEMBER
11 International Mountain Day

Every day people, brands and organizations fight for causes they are passionate about.

To focus on the great efforts they are making and the needy causes they are helping, many have chosen to dedicate a day or a month of the year to increase awareness of their causes.

This is a list of both internationally and nationally recognized days. Some were introduced and are supported by bodies such as the United Nations and others are days created by brands. Most days are honoured by special drives, initiatives and functions that culminate on the day of dedication to raise funds, support and, most importantly, raise awareness of the cause.

However, these days can be used for more than just raising awareness around worthy causes – they can also be used to coincide with, or act as the pinnacle of, campaigns surrounding a similar topic, cause or message by advertising and branding professionals. Garnier, for example, launched the World's First Newspaper on 100% recycled newsprint on World Environment Day in partnership with the *Times of India*, with the intention of encouraging the Indian youth to become actively involved in environmental work.

So what are you waiting for? Plan your campaign to coincide with existing designated days or claim one of the many days not yet designated and create your own!

Labels for Good

Consumers are increasingly looking for products that reflect their values, whether these products are healthier, greener or more responsible. Consumers are not only more likely to choose a certified product, but are also willing to pay a premium price for it. There are many different labels worldwide operating on international, national and local levels. And these labels come from a variety of sources – governments, NGOs, brands or the industries from which these labels originate. As you can see from this list, labels take time to create and creating a simple label that is easily understandable is vitally important. A label must tell its story without any extra explanation – this is paramount for quick adoption by consumers. Unfortunately, there are not many labels that live up to these standards. The good news is that labels are a great tool to make the market, your brand and your advertising more transparent.

Animal Welfare Approved (AWA)
The Animal Welfare Approved label is a standard for farm animal welfare. A farm with an AWA label must be a family farm that raises its animals in a pasture or range and it may not produce dual livestock. Farms are also not charged any fees to participate. The AWA label is internationally recognized and scientists, veterinarians, researchers and farmers from around the world have developed its standards.

B Corporations
B Corporations are a new type of corporation that use their power to address environmental and social problems. What sets B Corporations apart from traditional responsible businesses is that they must meet stringent and transparent environmental and social performance standards. The legal structure of B Corporations expands their level of corporate accountability. This certification enables consumers to align themselves with corporations that are in tune with their values and see exactly what the corporation is doing.

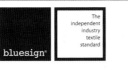

Bluesign
bluesign® is an independent standard that covers textile products that are responsible and sustainable. This standard is seen as a way to ensure textile products are in compliance with new standards without compromising on functionality, design or quality.

Blue Flag
The Blue Flag is awarded to beaches and marinas in 46 countries worldwide. Awarded beaches must meet stringent standards ranging from water quality, information and services, to environmental management and safety. The Blue Flag programme is run by the Foundation for Environmental Education (FEE), a non-government and non-profit organization that aims to promote sustainable development through education about the environment.

CarbonNeutral® Certification
This label is given to businesses that have offset their entire carbon footprint. This is achieved by offsetting their Scope 1 and 2 carbon emissions (Scope 1 covers greenhouse gas emissions directly related to the operations of the business and Scope 2 covers greenhouse gas emissions related to the electricity usage of the business).

The carbon footprint of a business is calculated by the organization and offset by carbon retirement. By offsetting their carbon footprint, businesses can mitigate the greenhouse gases they cannot eliminate through reduced consumption and energy efficiency strategies.

Certified Humane
This label certifies humanely treated animals raised for lamb, poultry, dairy and beef products. This programme forbids growth hormones and animals are raised on a diet without antibiotics, although antibiotics are permitted to treat sick animals. Animals have access to clean and sufficient water and food, and a safe, healthy living environment. Farmers must also meet environmental standards to obtain this certification.

The Climate Registry
The Climate Registry is a non-profit organization that aims to highlight and reward companies that are voluntarily choosing to record and reduce their carbon emissions. It sets transparent and consistent standards that are used to verify, calculate and report greenhouse gas emissions in a single, searchable register.

Cradle to Cradle CertifiedCM Programme
This Cradle to Cradle CertifiedCM programme allows companies to show their efforts in eco-intelligent design. To be eligible for this third-party sustainability label, products are evaluated for: use of materials that are safe for humans and the environment across their lifecycles; design for material reuse, such as recycling

or composting; renewable energy use; water stewardship and social responsibility. There are four levels that can be achieved: basic, silver, gold and platinum. This label applies to products and materials in all categories.

Dolphin Safe
The Earth Island Institute owns this label and monitors tuna companies around the world to ensure that tuna are caught responsibly, without harming dolphins or the marine ecosystem. This label is generally found on tuna cans.

EU Ecolabel
The EU Ecolabel 'flower' is a scheme aimed at helping European consumers distinguish products that are environmentally friendly. It does not include food and medicine.

Fairtrade
Fairtrade International is a non-profit, multi-stakeholder organization that aims to reduce poverty by forming a relationship between producers, businesses and consumers. Products that carry the FAIRTRADE mark have been certified to comply with international Fairtrade Standards which include social, environmental and economic criteria.

Forest Stewardship Council® (FSC)
The Forest Stewardship Council® is an international non-profit organization that promotes the

environmental, socially beneficial and economically viable management of the world's forests.

The Gold Standard Foundation

The Gold Standard label indicates carbon offset projects of the highest quality. It is a vitally important tool for NGOs to develop global carbon markets. Projects with the Gold Standard label use renewable energy and technologies that are energy efficient and are screened for real environmental benefits. Local sustainable development is also encouraged.

Green Seal

Green Seal is an independent non-profit organization founded in 1989. It is awarded to products and services that have to meet stringent, science-based environmental standards that are both credible and transparent. By looking at a product's entire lifecycle, Green Seal ensure tangible reductions in the entire environmental impact.

Heart Foundation Approved

The Heart Foundation Tick is a helpful guide for selecting healthier foods. Foods displaying the Tick logo must meet the strict nutrition standards set by the Heart Foundation. The Heart Foundation developed the Tick as a quick and easy guide for Australian shoppers to identify healthier foods without having to compare ingredient labels.

Marine Stewardship Council (MSC)

The Marine Stewardship Council is an independent non-profit organization that has an eco-label and fishery certification programme. The MSC fisheries standard has three principles that every fishery must meet: the level of fishing activity must be sustainable for the fish population, fishing operations must maintain the ecosystem and the fishery has to meet local, national and international laws.

Planet Positive

Planet Positive is a non-profit organization and a UK-based charity. It is an internationally recognized label for businesses, products, events and people who take positive action by giving their time or donating money to community projects.

Rainforest Alliance Certified™

The Rainforest Alliance Certified™ label is internationally recognized and managed by the Sustainable Agricultural Network. The label guarantees consumers that the identified ingredients in a product have been grown on farms that have met a specific set of criteria, which balance ecological, economic and social factors.

Recycled Content

This is a generic symbol used to show that a product has been recycled or to indicate that a product can be recycled. The Federal Trade Commission in the US, which manages this label, states,

'A recycled content claim may be made only for materials that have been recovered or otherwise diverted from the solid waste stream, either during the manufacturing process (pre-consumer), or after consumer use (post-consumer).'

SMaRT Certified

The Sustainable Materials Rating Technology (SMaRT) label is applicable to 80% of the world's products for building, fabric, apparel, textile and flooring, using environmental, social and economic criteria. The label is managed by the Institute for Market Transformation to Sustainability, an independent standards developer accredited by the American National Standards Institute.

TerraCycle

TerraCycle is a private recycling company that runs a national waste collection programme in ten countries. Non-recyclable waste is collected and made into new products and materials. The TerraCycle logo informs consumers that the product or package can be collected and sent to TerraCycle. Consumers can sign up to have waste collected and then earn incentives, which are paid to a charity or school of their choice.

WaterSense

The United States Environmental Protection Agency (EPA) manages the WaterSense label. The label recognizes products that are 20% more water-efficient than similar products on the market.

WindMade

WindMade is a consumer label that identifies products and companies that use wind energy. It is designed to increase corporate investment in wind power by educating consumers about companies that use wind energy and increasing demand from consumers for more products that are made with wind. To qualify for the label, members must undergo a certification process that verifies where they source their energy.

WWF

The WWF is a global conservation organization and its logo is recognized internationally. The logo is used by companies that are committed to protecting nature and the environment. The label can be used in the following instances: if a product supports WWF's work by being sustainably designed, an organization enters into a partnership with WWF or promotes a product that meets sustainable goals, a business or organization has supported WWF through donations, or a company's product generates income for WWF through licence royalties.

Awards for Good

It goes without saying that in the advertising world awards and recognition are important. Awards honour creative excellence and innovation, but more importantly they inspire agencies, creatives and brands to go further. As I have said again and again, I feel that creativity has a vitally important role to play in helping us out of our current situation. There has never been a greater need for big ideas and the big hearts that go with them. I hope that more awards shows (both at a national and an international level) will take on the challenge to create awards for good – awards that celebrate the efforts of brands as well as NGOs and governments.

ACT Responsible

ACT Responsible is a non-profit initiative launched by the employees of AdForum. Through the ACT Responsible website key players in the advertising industry are brought together, with a common interest in responsibility and doing good. On the website itself and through its travelling exhibitions, ACT not only showcases great responsible work from brands and NGOs, but also inspires creatives and agencies to do more work in the field. By showing the power of creativity to do good and addressing today's issues through their Ad of the Week on their website, ACT Responsible encourages agencies to do more work for good.
act-responsible.org

BestACT

The Golden Drums are an East European advertising awards show. Their BestACT award is given to an idea that makes people change the way they think, feel and behave. In short, an inspiring idea that uses creativity to move people and transform their lives for the better.
goldendrum.com

Cannes Lions
Grand Prix for Good

Given out for the first time in 2010, the Grand Prix for Good is awarded at the Cannes Lions International Festival of Creativity, recognizing outstanding creative campaigns that do good.

Historically, Cannes has not awarded Grand Prix awards to NGO work because of fear of emotional influence on the judges, but this award allows NGOs to get the recognition they deserve. Other award categories for good at Cannes include: Public Health & Safety, Public Awareness Messages and Fundraising and Appeals.
canneslions.com

Core77

The Core77 awards celebrate design and designers from across the globe. They started in 2011 and, while relatively new, they recognize some of the more social aspects of the design world.
core77designawards.com

D&AD
White Pencil

D&AD launched the White Pencil in 2011; the first one was to be awarded in 2012. Each year, D&AD will partner with a worthy cause or charity and set a brief for the creative community to meet. The best answer to the brief, which encourages action to make the world a better place, wins the award.
dandad.org

EACA Care

The EACA Care award recognizes social marketing initiatives as part of their commitment to corporate social responsibility. These awards aim to highlight the power of advertising to do good and reward those who do so. Subjects covered include public health, environment, sustainable consumption and public safety, to name a few. Entries will be included in the online gallery at ACT Responsible and are eligible for inclusion in ACT's World Tour exhibition.
careawards.eu

EthicMark®

The EthicMark® award recognizes socially responsible advertising, marketing, initiatives and PR campaigns by individuals, businesses and non-profit organizations. The EthicMark® award concentrates on work that is not only for a good cause, but also good for business.
worldbusiness.org

Golden Peacock

The Golden Peacock awards are awarded globally for business excellence. Some of their categories include awards for Climate Security, Sustainability, Innovation, Corporate Social Responsibility and Eco-Innovation. The public sector, private companies, government organizations and NGOs can enter these awards.
goldenpeacockawards.com

GoodWorks Effie

As with the standard Effies, these awards are given to communications programmes that have proven to be effective in addressing a social issue or expanding an existing programme that benefits people and the planet. As long as measurable results exist, any communication that aims to give back in some way is eligible, whether it's a full campaign or a unique effort.
effie.org

International Advertising Association Socially Responsible Communications

The IAA Socially Responsible Communications (SRC) award is an international award in association with ACT Responsible that recognizes environmental and socially responsible advertising. The competition is open to advertising, design and marketing that focuses on sustainable development, social responsibility and social issues.
iaaglobal.org

International Green

The International Green awards recognize creative strategies and ideas that lead to more sustainable outcomes. Covering over 20 categories, the International Green awards are fast becoming a yardstick for sustainability and biodiversity.
greenawards.com

One Show Green Pencil

The One Show Green Pencil award is given to the piece of work in the show that demonstrates the most creative environmentally conscious advertising.
oneclub.org

Guides for Good

With the plethora of choices we have, it can be difficult to make the right choice when it comes to food, healthcare, shopping or any number of activities. These guides should help you on your way to making better decisions.

andyou.jnj.com

The &you guide by Johnson & Johnson is designed for both individuals and organizations. The widget takes volunteer and job opportunities, ways to donate, events and news and puts them in all one place.

brandkarma.com

Brandkarma helps people make better brand choices and influences brand behaviour for good.

cdproject.net

The Carbon Disclosure Project (CDP) aims to make carbon emission data available on a global scale. To date, more than 3,000 organizations in over 60 countries have disclosed their greenhouse gas emissions, water management and climate change plans through the CDP. This information is made available so that reduction targets can be set. It also means that organizations can improve their performance, using the information from the CDP as a benchmark. As climate change is a global problem, the CDP aims to develop standardized carbon reporting, so that some parity can be found in the field.

climatecounts.org

ClimateCounts helps fight climate change by making it easy for consumers to see which companies are taking meaningful climate action.

dosomething.org

This website uses the power of online to get teens to do good things offline.

ecofashionworld.com

Eco Fashion World is a resource of sustainable designer brands and online fashion stores that are responsible and sustainable. Users can search by brand, store, category, eco criteria or country.

ecotourismlogue.com

Ecotourismlogue helps you to make decisions about responsible and sustainable travel. Information is given on where to stay, how to travel and what you can do to travel in a greener way.

fastfood.com

Fastfood.com and its accompanying mobile app provide comprehensive information on more than 360 American fast food restaurants. The guide offers users information on each menu item at the featured restaurants, including caloric value, detailed fats breakdown, and cholesterol and sodium levels, among other things.

findyourfootprint.com

This app from P&G helps you to work out your own carbon footprint.

foodzy.com

This website makes healthy eating a fun game.

gaiaguide.org

GAiA Guide is a resource guide for ecology and sustainability. It provides information on how to live more greenly and also features upcoming ecology events.

givmo.com

Givmo is a website that allows users to offload their unwanted goods rather than throwing them away. For every item that is given, Givmo donates $1 to charity.

goodguide.com

GoodGuide allows users to find safe, healthy, green and ethical products based on scientific ratings. The mobile app also consists of a clever barcode scanner that makes it easy to get the backstories of products.

greenerchoices.org

The Greener Choices guide from ConsumerReports gives information and tips on how to live in a greener way, from shopping to recycling. It also has a section where you can search eco labels, allowing users to educate themselves about the labels out there – which ones to trust and which ones to be sceptical of.

greenguide.co.uk

The Green Guide was first published in the UK in 1994, making it the longest-standing guide of its kind in the country. It features over 15,000 entries, from green education to green weddings, and highlights products, services and businesses that are ethical, natural, organic and traded fairly.

greenmap.org

Green Map engages communities worldwide in mapping green living, nature and cultural resources – making it easier to enjoy your city responsibly.

greenyour.com

Green Your offers five areas of your life where you can be green: your home, your office, your body, your lifestyle and your transportation. Each section is broken up into further subsets, offering great detail on how to improve what you can.

guidestar.org

GuideStar gathers and publicizes information about non-profit organizations.

iucnredlist.org

The Red List provides the most objective, scientifically based information on the current status of globally threatened biodiversity, from plants to animals.

justgiving.com

JustGiving uses the power of the internet to enable people to raise far more for charities than they normally could – easily and cost effectively.

maps.google.com/biking

This innovative move from Google Maps allows users to find bike routes in their city of choice. Routes are designed to aid bikers – they avoid steep hills and heavily congested areas. This guide also shows users where to find dedicated bike trails, roads with bike lanes and roads that are considered good for biking. Also look out for Google's walking and public transit guides on Google Maps.

montereybayaquarium. org/cr/seafoodwatch

The Monterey Bay Aquarium has produced Seafood Watch, a sustainable seafood guide. It provides people with information on which seafood species are sustainable and safe to eat in restaurants or to buy in supermarkets or fishmongers. The mobile app alone has been downloaded over 240,000 times.

networkforgood.org

Network for Good makes it as easy to donate and volunteer online as it is to shop online. They also make it simple and affordable for non-profits of any size to recruit donors and volunteers via the internet.

planetfriendly.net/living

Planet Friendly's Sustainable Living Guide is a directory of sustainable products and services, employment opportunities, education and organizations. It also offers tips and how-to guides to living more sustainably.

recycle.co.uk

This UK website is a recycling marketplace that allows users to share and swap items that they no longer need or use. This reduces waste going to landfill sites and saves people money.

scorecard.goodguide.com

Another initiative from GoodGuide, this website shares information about pollution problems and toxic chemicals. Users can find out about the pollution problems in their community and learn who is responsible.

sourcemap.org

Sourcemap makes supply chains transparent.

sustainableguide.com

Sustainable Guide is a resource for all sustainable living topics, from solar energy to permaculture. It also offers a green business directory and green products to purchase.

sustainlane.com

SustainLane is, in its own words, a 'people-powered sustainability guide'. Users can sign up for a free account and discuss sustainability with others, as well as write reviews of local businesses. SustainLane also provides a blogging platform for interested parties and runs the SustainLane US City Rankings, which surveys the most populous US cities in terms of their sustainability practices.

thecarrot.com

TheCarrot is a life-tracking tool that covers a variety of topics. You can use it to set goals that can help you achieve healthy nutrition, lose weight, manage diabetes or hypertension, stop smoking and get fit.

uk.oneworld.net/guides

This OneWorld guide features information on developing countries and features a vast number of topics ranging from HIV and AIDS to how to volunteer in developing countries.

virtualwater.eu

Virtual Water shows how much fresh water is used to produce selected products. It aims to make people think twice about what they consume.

volunteermatch.org

VolunteerMatch strengthens communities by making it easier for good people and good causes to connect. It offers a variety of online services to support a community of non-profits, volunteers and business leaders committed to civic engagement.

yiuco.com

Yiuco allows users to buy, sell and exchange products that come exclusively from recycling, reusing or remanufacturing. It also serves to promote upcycling, recycling and reuse.

Picture Credits

2 Agency: Metaphoria; Creatives: Bernice Lizamore, Andrew Donaldson; Source: Natural Marketing Institute's LOHAS Consumer Trends Database®
7 Agency: Wieden+Kennedy, London
8 left Agency: Ogilvy, Johannesburg
8 right Agency: CAA; Advertiser: Chipotle
10 Advertiser: Innocent
12 Agency: Lowe Brindfors, Stockholm; Advertiser: Save the Children (Rädda Barnen); Art Directors: Pelle Lundquist, Emmeli Österdahl; Copy: Stefan Pagreus, Aron Levander; Account Supervisors: Johan Öhlin, Malin Sävstam, Anna Laestadius; Account Managers: Anna Tanser Wolin, Kristin Enersen; Planner: Mehrnaz Forslund; Digital Director: Mårten Forslund; Technical Producer: Tobias Löfgren; Typographer: Ola Lanteli; Photographer: Jon Hertov; Production Company: B-Reel; Director: Johan Perjus; Sound: Redpipe
13 Agency: Ogilvy Earth Creative, @ivanisawesome
18 Agency: Crispin Porter + Bogusky, Boulder
20 Agency: DraftFCB, Buenos Aires
24 Agency: Crispin Porter + Bogusky, Boulder
25 Agency: DDB, Paris
26–27 Agency: CAA; Advertiser: Chipotle
28 Agency: DraftFCB, Buenos Aires
29 Agency: Droga5, New York
30 Agency: Havas Media, Miami; Photographer: Antonio Yusiff
31 Agency: McCann Erickson, Singapore
32 Agency: Muhtayzik Hoffer, San Francisco
33 Advertiser: Nike
36–37 Agency: BBH, London
39 left Agency: Bassat Ogilvy & Mather, Barcelona
39 right Agency: Clemenger BBDO, Melbourne
42–43 Agency: TBWA, Paris
44 Agency: Leo Burnett, London; Advertiser: Department for Transport; Creative Team: Paul Jordan, Angus MacAdam; Planner: Becky Barry; Director: Chris Palmer
45 Agency: Ogilvy & Mather, Düsseldorf
46 Agency: Contract Advertising, New Delhi
47 Agency: Publicis, London
48 Agency: SapientNitro
49 Agency: Jason Zada

50–51 Agency: Lowe Brindfors, Stockholm; Advertiser: Save the Children (Rädda Barnen); Art Directors: Pelle Lundquist, Emmeli Österdahl; Copy: Stefan Pagreus, Aron Levander; Account Supervisors: Johan Öhlin, Malin Sävstam, Anna Laestadius; Account Managers: Anna Tanser Wolin, Kristin Enersen; Planner: Mehrnaz Forslund; Digital Director: Mårten Forslund; Technical Producer: Tobias Löfgren; Typographer: Ola Lanteli; Photographer: Jon Hertov; Production Company: B-Reel; Director: Johan Perjus; Sound: Redpipe
52 Agency: FoxP2, Cape Town
53 Agency: Happiness Brussels, Brussels
54 Agency: Wieden+Kennedy, Portland; Advertiser: Nike; Digital Agency: Deeplocal
55 Agency: BBH, London
56 Agency: Saatchi & Saatchi, London; Art Director: Rob Porteous; Copywriter: Dave Askwith
57 Agency: DDB, London
58 Agency: Bassat Ogilvy, Barcelona
59 Agency: Lowe Bull, Cape Town; Advertiser: Flora; Production House: Urban Brew; Patient and Brand Ambassador for 2008/2009: Wally Katzke
60–61 Agency: Clemenger BBDO, Wellington with the assistance of Kit Cosmetics (sister brand to Mecca Cosmetica); Advertiser: NZ Transport Agency
61 Agency: Clemenger BBDO, Melbourne; Advertiser: Guide Dogs Australia
64–65 Agency: TBWA, London
66 left Agency: Marcel, Paris
66 right Agency: JWT, Singapore; Executive Creative Directors: Ali Shabaz, Tay Guan Hin; Art Director: Christiano Choo; Copywriter: Pradeep D'Souza
70 Agency: TBWA, Berlin
71 Agency: Babel, São Paulo
72 Agency: Ogilvy & Mather, Frankfurt
73 Agency: Duval Guillaume, Brussels
74 Agency: TBWA, London
75 Agency: Leo Burnett, Sydney; Advertiser: WWF Earth Hour
76 Agency: Marcel, Paris
77 Agency: AlmapBBDO, São Paulo; Creative Director: Luiz Sanches; Art Directors: Renato Fernandez, Vinicius Sousa, Daniel Manzi; Copywriter: Fabio Ozório; Photographers: Daishi Pais, Mariana Valverde; Graphic Producer: José Roberto Bezerra; Account

Executive: Marina Fernandes; Media: Paulo Camossa, Jr., Laerte Brandão; Approval: Dagmar Garroux, Célia Fernandes
78 Agency: DDB, Paris
79 Advertiser: Ben & Jerry's
80 Agency: Droga5, New York
81 Agency: DDB, Paris
82 Agency: Ogilvy, Kolkata
83 Agency: Kempertrautmann, Hamburg
84 Agency: Big Spaceship, New York; Advertiser: General Electric
85 Agency: DDB, Berlin (Omnicom Group)
86 Agency: MetropolitanRepublic, Johannesburg
87 Agency: Leo Burnett, Chicago; Worldwide Chief Creative Officer: Mark Tutssel; Chief Creative Officer: John Condon; EVP/Group Head: John Montgomery; Creatives: Vince Cook, Gary Fox-Robertson, Brian Shembeda, Avery Gross; Senior Producer: Laurie Gustafson; VP Content Architect: Denis Giroux
88 Agency: Fuseproject, France
89 Agency: DDB West, San Francisco
90 Agency: Grey, Hong Kong
91 Agency: JWT, Singapore; Executive Creative Directors: Ali Shabaz, Tay Guan Hin; Art Director: Christiano Choo; Copywriter: Pradeep D'Souza
94 Agency: BBDO West, San Francisco
97 Advertiser: DriveNow by BMW and SIXT; Agency: Millhaus, Munich; Project Manager: Christian Pottkämper; Photographer: David Ulric
100 Agency: AKQA, London
101 Agency: AgenciaClick Isobar, Rio de Janeiro
102 Agency: Ester, Stockholm
103 Agency: Leo Burnett, Sydney
104 Agency: BBDO West, San Francisco
105 Agency: Wieden + Kennedy, Portland; Photographer: Melodie McDaniel
106 Agency: Lodestar UM, Mumbai; CEO: Shashi Sinha; COO: Nandini Dias; General Manager: Sujata Pawar; Media Controller: Rajeshwari Narayanan; Business Head Brand Experience: Dhruv Jha; Account Executive: Nikita Khambe; Associate VP: Meghna Godkhindi
107 Agency: DDB, Berlin
108 Agency: Prime and United Minds, Stockholm; Advertiser: Electrolux
112 Agency: Wieden+Kennedy, London
113 Agency: Wieden+Kennedy, London
115 Agency: DDB, Stockholm
118 Agency: JWT, Madrid

119 Agency: Goodby, Silverstein & Partners, San Francisco
120 Agency: DDB, Stockholm
121 Agency: TBWA\Hunt\Lascaris, Johannesburg
122 Agency: Leo Burnett, Sydney
123 Agency: Wieden+Kennedy, London
124–25 Agency: Wieden+Kennedy, London
126–27 Agency: Wieden+Kennedy, London
128 Agency: Wieden+Kennedy, Portland
129 Agency: Saatchi & Saatchi, New York
132 Agency: Drill, Tokyo; Advertiser: NTT DOCOMO, Inc.; Creative Director: Morihiro Marano; Copywriter: Noriko Yamada; Art Director: Jun Nishida; Sound Design: Kenijiro Matsuo (Invisible Designs Lab. Company, Ltd); Director: Seiichi Hishikawa (Drawing and Manual); Cinematographer: Eitaro Yamamoto (Sahdow-dan); Producers: Toshifumi Oiso, Hideyuki Chihara (Engine PLUS); Agency Producer: Ayako Yoshinoyu (Dentsu Inc.); Editor: Hitoshi Kimura
133 Agency: TBWA\Chiat\Day, Los Angeles; Chief Creative Officer: Rob Schwartz; Photographer: Steve Boyle
134 left Agency: Publicis, Brussels; Advertiser: Reporters Sans Frontière/Reporters Zonder Grenzen; Creative Directors: Paul Servaes, Alain Janssens; Art Director: Daniel Vandenbroucke; Copy: Kwint de Meyer; Digital Account Director: Nadia Dafir; Account Managers: Michael Ogor, Nathalie Tavernier; Agency Producer: Dominique Ruys; Strategy: Tom Theys, Vincent D'Halluin; Web Design: Denis Evlard by www.reed.be; Sound Studio: Think 'n Talk; Translation: Fabrice Storti, Richard Weiss
134 right Agency: Nordpol+, Hamburg
135 Advertiser: ColaLife; Photographer: Simon Berry
138–39 Agency: Prime PR and DDB, Stockholm
140 Agency: Mortierbrigade, Brussels; Advertiser: Studio Brussel; Contacts: Peter Claes, Jan Van Biesen; Creative Directors: Jens Mortier, Joost Berends, Philippe Deceuster; Creative Team: Dieter Vanhoof, Joeri Vandenbroek, Tim Driesen; Strategy: Stephanie Zimmerman; Producer: Patricia Van De Kerckhove
141 Agency: Dentsu Razorfish, Tokyo
142 Agency: Beacon Communications, Tokyo

143 Agency: Cake Group, London; Photographer: Andy Fallon

144 Agency: Crispin Porter + Bogusky, Boulder

145 Agency: Nordpol+, Hamburg

146 Agency: TBWA\Chiat\Day, Los Angeles; Chief Creative Officer: Rob Schwartz; Photographer: Steve Boyle

147 Agency: Jung Von Matt, Hamburg

148–49 Agency: Ogilvy, Johannesburg

150 Agency: DDB, Shanghai; Advertiser: The China Environmental Protection Foundation; Chief Creative Officer and ECD: Michael Dee; Creative Director: Jody Xiong; Art Director: Jody Xiong; Copywriter: Jason Jin; Illustrator: Jody Xiong; Designer: Jody Xiong; Typographers: Jody Xiong, Jerry Cao; Agency Producer: George Ooi; Production House Producer: Gemini Wong; Print Production Director: James Chen; Photographer: Kenno Zhao; Director: Qiu Bo

151 Agency: Publicis, Brussels; Advertiser: Reporters Without Borders/ Reporters Zonder Grenzen; Creative Directors: Paul Servaes, Alain Janssens; Art Director: Daniel Vandenbroucke; Copy: Kwint de Meyer; Digital Account Director: Nadia Dafir; Account Managers: Michael Ogor, Nathalie Tavernier; Agency Producer: Dominique Ruys; Strategy: Tom Theys, Vincent D'Halluin; Web Design: Denis Evlard by www.reed.be; Sound Studio: Think 'n Talk; Translation: Fabrice Storti, Richard Weiss

152 Agency: Drill, Tokyo; Advertiser: NTT DOCOMO, Inc.; Creative Director: Morihiro Marano; Copywriter: Noriko Yamada; Art Director: Jun Nishida; Sound Design: Kenijiro Matsuo (Invisible Designs Lab. Company, Ltd); Director: Seiichi Hishikawa (Drawing and Manual); Cinematographer: Eitaro Yamamoto (Sahdow-dan); Producers: Toshifumi Oiso, Hideyuki Chihara (Engine PLUS); Agency Producer: Ayako Yoshinoyu (Dentsu Inc.); Editor: Hitoshi Kimura

153 Agency: Saatchi & Saatchi, Stockholm

156 Agency: TBWA\Chiat\Day, New York; Creatives: Mark Figliulo, Lisa Topol, Jonathon Marshall, Eric Stevens, Josh DiMarcantonio, Ani Munoz, Isabella Castano; Production: Josh Morse, Howie Howell, Katherine d'Addario, Rayana Lucier, Chris Reardon, Michael Bester, Peter Kuang, Chris Kief; Account Management: Nikki Maizel, Keiko Kurokawa, Greg Masiakos; Photography:

Markus Klinko & Indrani, G. K. Rei; Talent: Alicia Keys, Bronson Pelletier, The Buried Life Cast, Daphne Guinness, David LaChapelle, Elijah Wood, Jaden Smith, Willow Smith, Janelle Monae, Jay Sean, Jennifer Hudson, Katie Holmes, Khloe Kardashian, Kim Kardashian, Kimberly Cole, Pink, Ryan Seacrest, Serena Williams, Swizz Beatz, Usher

158 left Agency: Wieden + Kennedy and AKQA, London

158 right Agency: StrawberryFrog, New York

162 Agency: StrawberryFrog, New York

163 Agency: Abbott Mead Vickers BBDO, London; Advertiser: The Metropolitan Police

164 Agency: Ogilvy, Toronto; Photographer: Gabor Jurina; Directors: Yael Staav, Tim Piper; Model: Stephanie Betts

165 Agency: Garbergs, Stockholm

166 Agency: Akestam Holst, Stockholm

167 Agency: Leo Burnett, Beirut

168 Agency: Wieden + Kennedy and AKQA, London

169 Agency: TBWA\Chiat\Day, New York; Creatives: Mark Figliulo, Lisa Topol, Jonathon Marshall, Eric Stevens, Josh DiMarcantonio, Ani Munoz, Isabella Castano; Production: Josh Morse, Howie Howell, Katherine d'Addario, Rayana Lucier, Chris Reardon, Michael Bester, Peter Kuang, Chris Kief; Account Management: Nikki Maizel, Keiko Kurokawa, Greg Masiakos; Photography: Markus Klinko & Indrani, G. K. Rei; Talent: Alicia Keys, Bronson Pelletier, The Buried Life Cast, Daphne Guinness, David LaChapelle, Elijah Wood, Jaden Smith, Willow Smith, Janelle Monae, Jay Sean, Jennifer Hudson, Katie Holmes, Khloe Kardashian, Kim Kardashian, Kimberly Cole, Pink, Ryan Seacrest, Serena Williams, Swizz Beatz, Usher

170 Agency: Publicis e-dologic, Tel Aviv

171 Agency: FSB Comunicações, Rio de Janeiro

174 Agency: Euro RSCG, London

177 left Agency: Droga5, New York; Advertiser: New York City Department of Education,

177 right Agency: TBWA\Chiat\Day, Los Angeles

180 Agency: Ogilvy, Buenos Aires; Executive Creative Director: Gastón Bigio; Head of Art: Jonathan Gurvit; Creative Directors: Javier Mentasti, Ignacio Ferioli, Maximiliano Maddalena; Copywriter: Nicolás Vara; Art Director:

Ignacio Flotta; Producer: Marcelo Ramos (Central de Producers); Agency Producers: Esteban García Ciraldi, Jose Cardelli (Ogilvy Action Yunes); Planning: Julieta Rey; Account Team: Karina Aiello (Ogilvy Action Yunes), Guadalupe Acuña, Natalia Noya; Post-Production: La Sociedad Post

181 Agency: Ogilvy, Cape Town; Art Director: Prabashan Pather; Copywriter: Sanjiv Mistry; Account Director: Jason Yankelowitz; Account Manager: Lauran Baker

182 Agency: Euro RSCG, London

183 Agency: Net#work BBDO, Johannesburg

184 Agency: Hubble Innovations, Berlin; Chief Communications Officer: Amir Kassaei; Creative Director: Dennis May; Art Director: Gabriel Mattar; Copy: Ricardo Wolf

185 Agency: Droga5, New York

186 Agency: Rogalski Grigoriu PR, Bucharest

187 Agency: Del Campo Nazca Saatchi & Saachi, Buenos Aires; Advertiser: Norte Beer; Title: The Best Ever Excuse; Executive Creative Directors: Maxi Itzkoff, Mariano Serkin; Creative Director: Fernando Militerno; Account Team: Jaime Vidal, Patricia Abelenda; Agency Producers: Adrian Aspani, Camilo Rojas, Lucas Delenikas; Advertiser's Supervisors: Ricardo Fernandez, Eduardo Palacios, Lucas Adur

188 Agency: TBWA\Chiat\Day, Los Angeles

189 Agency: Net#Work BBDO, Johannesburg

190 Agency: Sancho BBDO, Bogota

191 Advertiser: Vai-Vai

192 Advertiser: Innocent

193 Agency: Jung Von Matt, Elbe

196 Agency: Walker Werbeagentur, Zurich

197 Agency: Crispin Porter + Bogusky and Arnold Worldwide, Miami

199 Agency: F/Nazca Saatchi & Saatchi, São Paulo

202 Agency: Colman Rasic, Sydney

203 Agency: Crispin Porter + Bogusky, Miami

204 Agency: BBH, London; Talent: Tara Hodge

205 Agency: McKinney, Durham, North Carolina

206 Agency: Y&R, New York

207 Agency: F/Nazca Saatchi & Saatchi, São Paulo

208–209 Agency: Walker, Zurich

210 Agency: Leo Burnett, Melbourne; Advertiser: Scope; Director: Tov Belling; Production House: The Pound; Music: Rudely Interrupted

211 Agency: Shackleton, Madrid; Creative Director: Juan Nonzioli; Art Director: Pablo González De La Pena; Copywriters: Juan Nonzioli, César Sastre; Producer: Itaxaro Vicuna; Art Director: Marta Guitérrez; Art Executive: Zaida Vázquez; Advertiser: Save the Children; Advertiser Supervisor: Alison Gallagher

212–13 Agency: Crispin Porter + Bogusky and Arnold Worldwide, Miami

216 Agency: Crispin Porter + Bogusky, Canada

217 Agency: Santo, Buenos Aires

219 Agency: Grey, Düsseldorf

222 Agency: Crispin Porter + Bogusky, Canada

223 Agency: Leo Burnett, Lisbon; Creative Director: Renato Lopes

224 Agency: McCann Erickson, Skopje; Advertiser: Veritas Spiriti; Creative Director: Ivica Spasovski; Art Director: Vladimir Manev; Photography: Tomislav Maric; Director: Ilija Karov; DOP: Alesandar Krstevski; Post Production: Aleksandar Spasoski, Vertigo; Managing Director: Vladimir Dimovski; Project Manager: Biljana Petrova; Chairman: Srdjan Saper

225 Agency: Santo, Buenos Aires

226 Agency: DDB, Stockholm

227 Agency: JWT+H+F, Zurich

228–29 Agency: Uncle Grey, Aarhus

230 Agency: Grey, Düsseldorf

231 Agency: Tribu DDB, San José; Advertiser: DIPO SA, Aceite Salat; Illustration Partner: Morpho Studio; Creative Directors: Pablo Chaves, Javier Mora, Paula Guevara; Art Directors: Joaquín Brenes, Frank Fernandez; Copywriters: Frank Fernandez, Paula Guevara, Esteban Jiménez

232–33 Agency: Y&R, São Paulo; Advertiser: Santa Casa de Misericórdia de São Paulo; Campaign: Blood Donation; Creative Directors: Rui Branquinho, Flávio Casarotti, Sergio Fonseca; Copywriter: Lucas Casão; Art Director: Guilherme Rácz; Photographer: Brandon Voges, Bruton Stroube Studios

234 Agency: JWT, Mumbai; Writer and Executive Creative Director: Senthil Kumar

235 Agency: Inkognito Cph, Copenhagen

246 Creative: Shaun McCormack

Further Reading

Brains on Fire: Igniting Powerful, Sustainable, Word of Mouth Movements
Robbin Phillips, Greg Cordell, Geno Church, Spike Jones
John Wiley & Sons, Hoboken, NJ, 2010

Brand Spirit: How Cause Related Marketing Builds Brands
Hamish Pringle, Marjorie Thompson
Wiley, Chichester, UK and New York, 2001

Branded! How the Certification Revolution is Transforming Global Corporations
Michael E. Conroy
New Society Publishers, Gabriola, BC, 2007

The Business of Changing the World: Twenty Great Leaders on Strategic Corporate Philanthropy
Marc Benioff, Carlye Adler
McGraw-Hill, New York, 2007

Cause Related Marketing: Who Cares Wins
Sue Adkins
Butterworth-Heinemann, Oxford and Boston, 1999

Cradle to Cradle: Remaking the Way We Make Things
Michael Braungart, William McDonough
North Point Press, New York, 2002

Do Good: How Designers Can Change the World
David B. Berman
New Riders, Berkeley, 2009

Ecological Intelligence: The Hidden Impacts of What We Buy
Daniel Goleman
Broadway Books, New York, 2010

The Great Disruption: Why the Climate Crisis will Bring on the End of Shopping and the Birth of a New World
Paul Gilding
Bloomsbury Press, New York, 2011

The Green Marketing Manifesto
John Grant
John Wiley & Sons, Chichester, UK and Hoboken, NJ, 2007

Information is Beautiful
David McCandless
HarperCollins, London, 2009

Just Good Business: The Strategic Guide to Aligning Corporate Responsibility and Brand
Kellie A. McElhaney
Berrett-Koehler Publishers, San Francisco, 2008

Naked Conversations: How Blogs are Changing the Way Businesses Talk with Customers
Robert Scoble, Shel Israel
John Wiley & Sons, Hoboken, NJ, 2006

Nudge: Improving Decisions about Health, Wealth, and Happiness
Richard H. Thaler, Cass R. Sunstein
Penguin Books, New York, 2009

The Oxford Handbook of Corporate Social Responsibility
Edited by Andrew Crane, Abagail McWilliams, Dirk Matten, Jeremy Moon, Donald Siegel
Oxford University Press, Oxford and New York, 2009

Pour Your Heart into It: How Starbucks Built a Company One Cup at a Time
Howard Schultz, Dori Jones Yang
Hyperion, New York, 1997

The Responsibility Revolution: How the Next Generation of Businesses Will Win
Jeffrey Hollender, Bill Breen
Jossey-Bass, San Francisco, 2010

Social Innovation, Inc.: 5 Strategies for Driving Business Growth through Social Change
Jason Saul
Jossey-Bass, San Francisco, 2011

Social Marketing: Influencing Behaviors for Good
Philip Kotler, Nancy R. Lee
Sage Publications, Los Angeles, 2008

Sustainable Value: How the World's Leading Companies are Doing Well by Doing Good
Christopher Laszlo
Stanford Business Books, Stanford, 2008

We First: How Brands and Consumers Use Social Media to Build a Better World
Simon Mainwaring
Palgrave Macmillan, New York, 2011

What's Mine is Yours: The Rise of Collaborative Consumption
Rachel Botsman, Roo Rogers
Harper Business, New York, 2010

WorldChanging: A User's Guide for the 21st Century
Edited by Alex Steffen, with Carissa Bluestone, introduction by Bill McKibben
Abrams, New York, 2011

Acknowledgments

I couldn't have done this alone

This book couldn't have been realized without the help of many wonderful and inspiring individuals. First of all, a big thanks to my parents for raising me with love and a democratic and socially engaged mind. I also owe a big thanks and lots of love to my girlfriend Rebecca: you've been very patient in the creation of this baby of a book.

I particularly want to thank Paul White, who's been an indefatigable, invaluable and instrumental part of writing, researching and discussing the book. I also owe a huge thanks to the rest of my team, whose huge efforts and late evenings have taken this book further than I ever could have done alone. Thanks to Saba Nejat, Tamlyn McPherson, Cris Robertson and Tara Smith. Also, thank you Bernita Lewin for keeping your cool even when at one point the assignment seemed never-ending. I also really want to thank Andrew Sanigar, Hannah Consterdine and Ilona de Nemethy Sanigar and all the others at Thames & Hudson for believing in my book.

A very special thanks go to all the interviewees, who have taken time in their busy calendars to share their views on the challenges ahead: Connie Hedegaard, Alex Bogusky, Andreas Dahlquist, Morten Albaek, Hannah Jones, Mike Schalit, David Droga, Rob Schwartz, Bradford K. Smith, Kim Papworth and Tony Davidson, Niall Dunne and Audrey Gaughran. Your views and thoughts have inspired me to believe there is a sustainable way forward.

I couldn't have done it without the contributions and input of all these people either: Paul and Jono plus all the others at Leftfield, Gwynne Rogers, Martin Gjerløff, the guys at FoxP2, the sweet couple at PixelProjects, all the like-minded at Robert/Boisen & Like-minded, Andrew Donaldson and Bernice Lizamore, Simon Bauer, Ivan Colic, Shaun McCormack, Melissa Baird, Porky, Kristian Merenda, Kristian Ruby, Sophie Hamon and Cannes Lions, Julia Emmerich, Mary Remuzzi, Jason Zada, Dyana Daulby, Isobel Barnes, Kronk, Ulrik Ahlefeldt, the guys from Ironflag, Jeremy Miller, Meagan Phillips, Ivica Spasovski, Julia Albu, Daniel Mikkelsen, Tobias Lau, Viv Gordon, Joakim Lundstöm, Sandra Lehnst and Luerzers Archive. I hope I haven't forgotten anyone, but if I have then you have my thanks and apologies in advance.

List of Advertisers